FOUR MOUNTAINS

ENCOUNTERING GOD IN THE BIBLE FROM EDEN TO ZION

FOUR MOUNTAINS

ENCOUNTERING GOD IN THE BIBLE FROM EDEN TO ZION

MICHAEL NIEBAUER

Four Mountains: Encountering God in the Bible from Eden to Zion

Lexham Press, 1313 Commercial St., Bellingham, WA 98225
LexhamPress.com

Print ISBN 9781683597629
Digital ISBN 9781683597636
Library of Congress Control Number 2024946841

Lexham Editorial: Todd Hains, Rachel Joy Welcher, Paul Robinson, Katrina Smith
Cover Design: Gabriel Eason
Typesetting: Mandi Newell

25 26 27 28 29 30 / US / 12 11 10 9 8 7 6 5 4 3 2

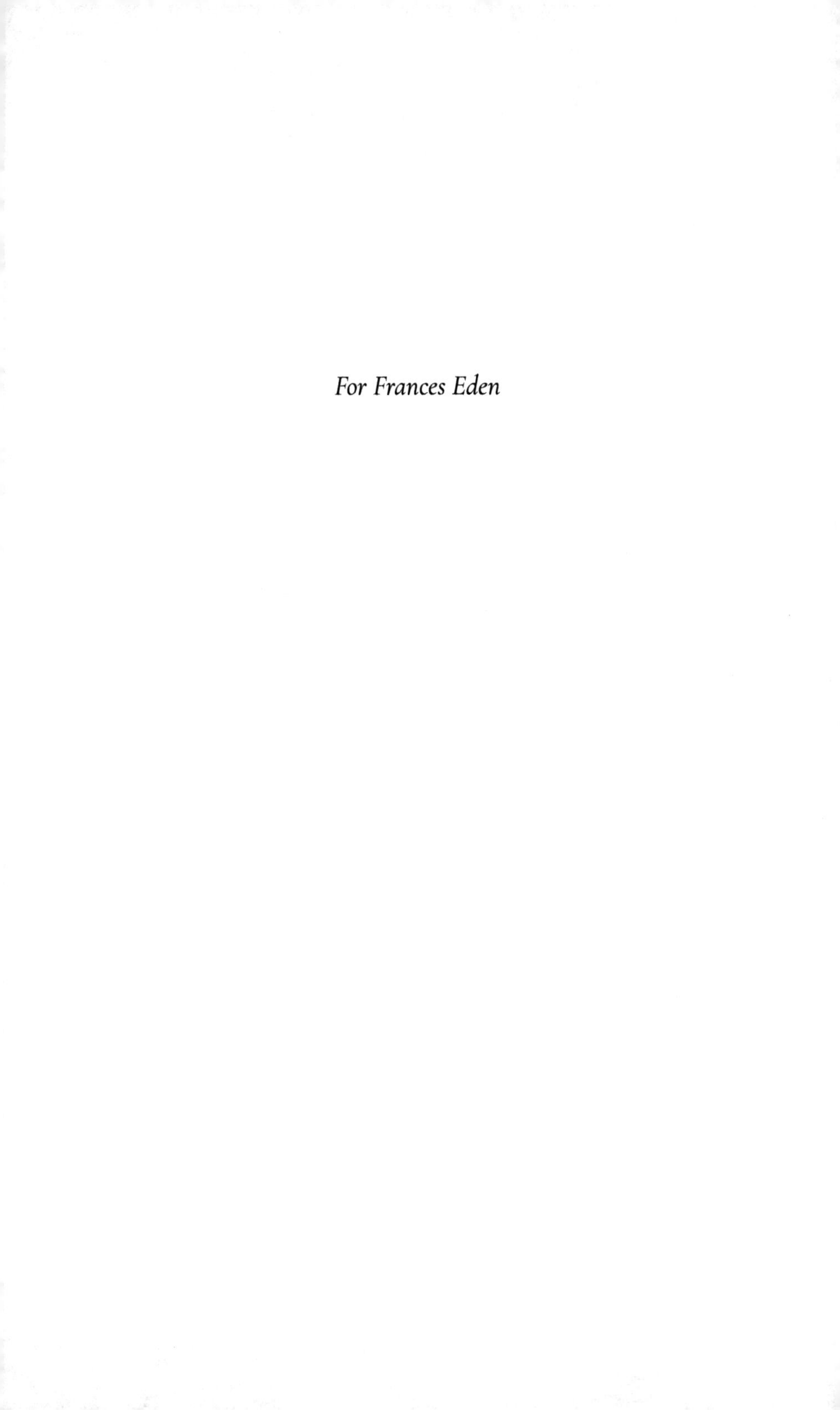

For Frances Eden

TABLE OF

CONTENTS

LIST OF FIGURES

Your symbols, Lord, are everywhere.

—Ephrem the Syrian

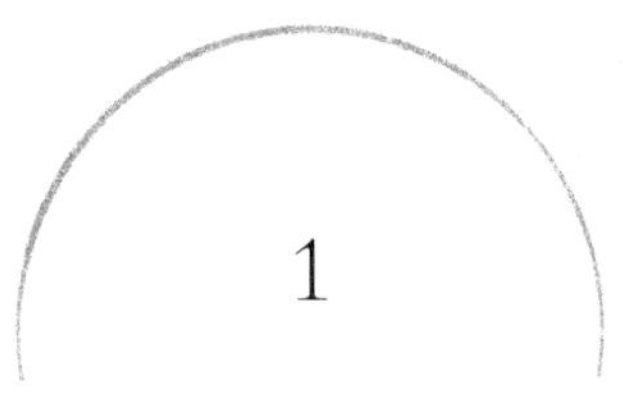

STORY AND SYMBOL

I still remember the first time I ever picked up a Bible. I was twelve years old and had wandered into a seldom used room in our home. On a dusty shelf, I found a large white Bible embossed in gold, opened randomly to 1 Corinthians, and began reading about "boasting in the Lord." Knowing nothing about the context of this letter, I quickly turned to a random page in Leviticus, only to discover a strange depiction of an ancient, sacrificial ritual. Two questions emerged that day that would continue to perplex me throughout my Christian life. The first concerned the connection between these two books of the Bible: What does a passage about animal sacrifices have in common with a letter exhorting a church to stop boasting? The only threads linking these passages together seemed to be the thin strings glued to the book binding. The second question concerned the significance of these passages: How does one encounter the living God in a passage about animal sacrifice?

What I discovered on that Pennsylvania afternoon thirty years ago remains true today: the Bible cannot be read like any other book. While it contains the same kinds of words on the same kinds of pages as novels and biographies, it cannot be read in the same way. Christians claim that the Bible is a story—a story with a beginning, middle, and end, with specific characters and themes, and a distinctive narrative arch. But what the reader is confronted with is a hodgepodge of stories, poetry, and letters written by a number of different authors over hundreds, if not thousands, of years. How can one clear narrative be discerned out of this collection of writings? Furthermore, Christians claim that the Bible enables a direct and immediate encounter with God through Jesus Christ on every page. Yet it is often hard to see how this is possible, particularly when one reads the Old Testament: How can old stories about war, ancient proverbs about farming, and apocalyptic visions help us connect directly to the Son of God? We can refer to these questions as the *horizontal* and *vertical* challenges of reading the Bible.

This book stitches together these disparate pages of the Bible by focusing on the image of the mountain. Specifically, it tells the story of the Bible through the encounters between God and humanity on Mount Eden, Mount Sinai, Mount Tabor, and Mount Zion. Focusing on these mountain stories and the symbols associated with them will allow us to engage in horizontal and vertical readings of the entire Bible.

A RETURN TO SYMBOL

Throughout the centuries it has been the responsibility of pastors to help Christians overcome these horizontal and vertical challenges in order to encounter God on each of the Bible's pages. In recent years, there has been a welcome rediscovery of the horizontal reading of scripture through an emphasis on narrative:

the Bible is a single story about creation, fall, redemption, and restoration. This has provided an extraordinarily helpful way for Christians to see how the books of the Bible fit together.[1] However, there are limits to this narrative approach, as it can deemphasize those books of the Bible that seem less important to this central story. The poetry of the psalms, the vivid accounts of worship in Leviticus, and the chaotic visions of the prophets just do not seem to be as important as other books that push the story along. Furthermore, a focus only on this horizontal, linear reading of the Bible can tend to make the Old Testament seem, well, *old.* It becomes simply the history of all that had to happen before Jesus was born. Now that Jesus has arrived, those stories are no longer important. The Old Testament becomes the prequel of a movie: interesting for diehard fans, but not essential to the main event.

Fortunately, there are other ways of reading the Bible that have helped readers stitch together the connective tissue of the Bible both horizontally *and* vertically. One way, preferred by many ancient Christians, is to focus on *symbols*. The Bible is filled with words that describe specific objects like trees, water, and swords. When we read these words, a symbol of these objects enters into our minds. For instance, when I read the word sword, I picture in my mind a sharpened piece of steel attached to a wooden hilt. An ancient method of reading Scripture is to look for places where these symbols are used throughout the Bible in order to discern how they help us better understand the biblical story, with the ultimate goal of discovering how they point to Jesus. Symbols, in a sense, are the binding agents of the Bible—they bind the individual books of the Bible together, they bind those books to Jesus, and finally, they bind Jesus to the reader.

This approach was predominant amongst early Christian theologians such as Marcarius and Gregory of Nyssa, and aspects of this approach can be found throughout Christian art and theology, from the poems of John Donne to the sermons of the African American preacher C. L. Franklin. But the most prominent champion of reading the Bible for symbolism was Ephrem the Syrian, a fourth century theologian and poet. His most famous work is a collection of poems called *Hymns on Paradise*, which chronicle Adam and Eve's life on Mount Eden, and how our eternal goal of life on Mount Zion serves as a return to our original Edenic paradise.

These authors offer us a way of understanding how these various symbols allow us to read the Bible both horizontally and vertically. First, they string together, horizontally, the various books of the Bible so we can see how one collection of books tells a single story. The entire story of the Bible points to our universal need for relationship with God through faith in Jesus Christ. Once we come to faith in Jesus, these same symbols allow us to read the Bible vertically: they serve as constant reminders of Jesus and allow us to have a more immediate encounter with God on every page of the Bible. Because this approach was second nature for ancient authors, their commentaries on the Bible often float seamlessly between the horizontal and the vertical.

AN EXAMPLE: THE TREE OF LIFE

What did this method of reading look like in practice? One example is found in Genesis 2, where we read about the tree of life. This description immediately brings to mind images of a bark-encrusted, wood trunk and silky, soft, green leaves. Later, at the end of the Bible, the tree of life makes another appearance next to Jesus on Mount Zion in Revelation 22. Ancient readers would draw the obvious conclusion that these trees somehow horizontally connect the story of Eden in Genesis with the story of Zion in Revelation. But ancient readers went further than this by reading these passages vertically, with the assumption of faith in Jesus. They noticed how Jesus stands next to the tree of life in Revelation and drew a connection between the person of Jesus and the tree. The main similarity was wood: trees are composed of wood, and Jesus died on a wooden cross. Therefore, the symbol of the tree, and other references to trees and wood in the Bible, began to be associated with Jesus's death on the cross.

For instance, Abraham's worship of God at the tree of Mamre was also seen as an instance of the worship of Jesus underneath the wooden cross, and the wood thrown into the water by Moses to purify it became a sign of the cross which purifies our hearts. The tree of life, as well as other passages related to wood in the Bible, are now capable of pointing vertically to Jesus, allowing us to participate more fully in his saving power. Furthermore, these passages can now be associated with *our* personal relationship with God. You can walk outside and, upon seeing a large tree, be instantly reminded of the tree of life and of Jesus's death on a wooden cross. This captivation of our imagination enables a seemingly mundane walk in the park to become a reminder of the gift of life and the saving power of the cross. An encounter with Jesus is no longer limited to the few minutes we spend reading the Bible each day but is now available whenever we feel the coarse wood grain on our fingertips, or rest under the cool shade of a maple tree.

THE MOUNTAIN

While the Bible can be read through a whole host of images similar to the tree of life, there is one key symbol that strings together nearly the entire Bible: *mountains*. Mountains are locations in the Bible where human beings encounter God. At key moments throughout the Bible, God calls individuals up to a mountain top so that they might encounter his glory and hear his words.

In what follows, I will discuss the story of the Bible through the individual accounts of four mountains: Eden, Sinai, Tabor, and Zion.[2] Each story culminates with an encounter between God and humanity on the peak of a mountain. All four stories share other symbols as well, such as trees, water, garments, and glory. Together, the accounts of these four mountains tell a dramatic and dynamic story of the creation and redemption of the world and God's relationship with human beings:

The story of *Mount Eden* concerns the creation of the world, which culminates with the creation of Adam and Eve. This story chronicles humankind's fall away from God into sin and brokenness which leads to a fall off of Mount Eden. Mount Eden introduces the reader to many of the key symbols (mountains, rivers, trees, garments) that will reoccur throughout the rest of the Bible.

The story of *Mount Sinai* is the story of how God begins the process of rescuing his creation by forming a people, the Israelites, who are capable of having a limited relationship with him. The culmination of this story comes when the Israelites journey through the wilderness and arrive at Mount Sinai. It ends with the prophets revealing what has been accomplished by God through this journey, but also what needs to be completed by Jesus.

The story of *Mount Tabor* is the story of how God finally and definitively addresses the problem of sin by becoming a human being. It is primarily the story of Jesus, and one of its culminating points is the revelation of Jesus in his divine glory on Mount Tabor.

The story of *Mount Zion* is the story of how God finishes his rescue mission by sending his Spirit into the hearts of the followers of Jesus, allowing them to participate in spreading the good news of Jesus's victory of sin and death throughout the world. It culminates in the return of Jesus, a final judgment on sin, and the descent of heaven to earth on top of Mount Zion. The Mount Zion pictured at the end of the book of Revelation serves as both a return to Mount Eden and a fulfillment of the hopes of Mount Eden.

While this book will give the linear, horizontal progression of the biblical story through an account of these four mountains, there will be moments that examine how these various symbols also orient the reader vertically: pointing to faith in Jesus and a life lived in relationship with the God of the universe. As we will discover, the Bible invites us to see our own relationship with God as existing on a kind of spiritual mountain, where we walk alongside Adam, Moses, and Peter in ascending to partake in God's glory.

MELODY AND HARMONY

One of the ways we can understand how the mountains and symbols of the Bible stitch the story of redemption together both horizontally and vertically is to think of them as musical notes, capable of providing both melody and harmony. Melody is a series of single notes played over time to make a song. For instance, one can play fourteen notes over half a minute to create the song "Twinkle, Twinkle, Little Star." Each note is essential to forming a coherent melody. Harmony, however, takes these same notes and stacks them on top of one another to create a single sound, called a chord.

We can play the symbols over linear time to get the melody, the story of the Bible. The main melody is provided by the mountains: Mount Eden is the starting note of a melodic line that stretches through Sinai and Tabor and ends with the last note, Mount Zion. From there, more melodic lines are discovered by tracing each symbol through the whole story of the Bible. We can tell the story of the Bible through water, or through trees, or through fire. Each time we make these horizontal, melodic connections through different passages of the Bible, we discover a new song, with a beautiful and catchy melody that gets inside our heads and never leaves.

In addition, we can take these same symbols and stack them on top of each other to create a single harmonious chord. When we see particular symbols repeated in the Bible, we are invited to read them in tandem with each other. In so doing we discover that each passage of the Bible that involves a symbol can enrich our reading of another passage that has that same symbol. For instance, we learn more about Jesus's crucifixion when we see the wood of the cross as the same wood that was stained with blood at the Passover. The Passover now becomes a story about the cross, and vice versa.

We are even invited to interweave our own experiences at church, in prayer, and in nature into these harmonious chords. The symbols in the Bible can be seen in our daily lives, creating further opportunities for connections and ways of understanding spiritual concepts. We are invited to let the Bible interpret our experiences in the world, allowing for a fuller and richer life with God in the present. For instance, our experience at church drinking the cup of communion wine can become an opportunity for us to experience the celebration of Abraham and Melchizedek (chapter 6), the death of Christ on the cross (chapter 13), and our future heavenly feast with Jesus on Mount Zion (chapter 17). This enables a fuller and richer vertical encounter with God the Father, Son, and Holy Spirit. As we will discover, the reason we can do this is because the Bible is from God, and God exists outside of time. When we enter into the Bible, we are entering into the life of God, and this enables us to make the past and future of the Bible our present, to read ourselves into its stories and see our life through its pages.

This book is intended to help you read the Bible horizontally and vertically, melodically and harmonically. As the melody progresses through Eden, Sinai, Tabor, and Zion, the various symbols encountered in each chapter will help you draw connections between books of the Bible. These same symbols will invite us to stack the stories of the Bible on top of each other, seeing how each passage enriches the other. Many of the quotes that open each chapter are examples of this kind of harmonious reading of the Bible.

THE ADVANTAGES OF THIS APPROACH

By focusing on the significance of mountains throughout the Bible, I will present an alternative to approaches that focus solely on narrative, but my hope is to complement the incredible work done by authors who have taken different narrative approaches.

The Bible is the richest book ever written and, as such, invites multiple avenues of explaining its central contents. A focus on mountains and other related symbols, however, highlights aspects of the Bible that are missing from other accounts.

In fact, it highlights many parts of the Bible that are often ignored by modern readers. When we pick up the Bible, it is easy for us to jump to the most important and easiest-to-read passages, skipping the hardest and (seemingly) dullest parts. This often means privileging New Testament books such as the Gospels and the letters of Paul over the Old Testament. Because mountains are prevalent images throughout the Bible, an approach that centers upon them highlights many passages, including the ones that can get overlooked. Books such as Exodus, Leviticus, Hebrews, and Revelation become richer when understood through the symbolism of the mountain. Even odd stories of animal sacrifices and apocalyptic visions are rendered intelligible and vibrant when seen against the backdrop of life with God on his mountain.

This approach also invites a fresh reading of the Bible. Viewing Scripture through mountain symbology restores non-linear, vertical readings of key passages. The Old Testament is not dead history, but a living text that invites us to see ourselves as bound up in its stories, and as persons sharing in the joys and struggles of Adam, Eve, and Moses. Every page becomes an opportunity to see Jesus and examine our own relationship with him. Each page, story, and symbol is an opportunity to be raised up into the very life of God, to understand more fully God the Father, the Son and Holy Spirit. We do not have to wait until we get to the New Testament to hear about Jesus, baptism, or communion. When we read the Bible vertically, we discover that God wants to teach us about himself, his Son, and our life with him, from the very beginning of the Bible. Reading the Bible this way has reminded me that there are unending riches in its pages, an inexhaustible fountain of life from which we can drink whenever we are thirsty.

And lastly, this approach gives a more vivid account of what life with God encompasses in the present and in our eternal future. Often, we can read the Bible with a focus solely upon the question of how we gain access to God, rather than on what happens after we do. It can lead us to focus almost exclusively on the question of salvation: how am I saved from sin and how can I enter into a relationship with God? Though these questions are of the utmost importance, our fixation with them can lead us to think that the Bible has very little to tell us concerning the events of our lives *after* we believe. The goal of life becomes getting *to* heaven, while our conception of life *in* heaven is virtually non-existent.

While the Bible does tell us how we can be saved from sin and enter into eternal life with God, it also tells us what we are saved *for*. The vivid portrayals of the mountains are meant to show us what life with God is like, both now and in eternity. As we will discover in the ensuing chapters, mountains represent our home with God; the place where we work, worship, and experience peace with him and his creation.

HOW TO READ THIS BOOK

This book is for anyone who wants a fuller grasp of the biblical story, whether they are new to Christianity or have been a Christian their entire life. Those new to Christianity will discover that the mountains in the Bible reveal a straightforward story that is dramatic and compelling. Older Christians will discover a new way of reading the Bible, one that draws together some of the more forgotten books of scripture and sees the connections between the Bible and Christian worship. My hope is that all readers might learn to cultivate an eye towards the way God uses symbols to weave together a beautiful, biblical tapestry. But above all, I hope everyone who reads this book will grow in their love for and knowledge of God the Father, Son, and Holy Spirit.

In order to help readers encounter the Bible horizontally, I have based each ensuing chapter on a series of passages from the Bible that will take the reader from its beginning in Genesis to its conclusion in Revelation. It is suggested that one reads the corresponding biblical selections before reading each chapter. Those relatively unfamiliar with the Bible may want to read the biblical selections two or three times.

In order to help readers encounter the Bible vertically, I have included below descriptions of the key symbols that are used throughout Scripture. This compendium of symbols is akin to a legend on a map: when one sees a symbol on a map, they turn to the legend to understand the meaning and significance of that symbol. As one encounters these symbols in scripture and in the pages of this book, they can turn back to this map legend, which will enable the reader to understand how these symbols stitch the Bible together and point us upward to a relationship with God through Jesus Christ.

Ultimately, this book seeks to draw all of its readers into the exciting drama of the Bible and to see themselves as caught up within its story. In essence, we are each invited to climb the mountain alongside its protagonists and the forbearers of our faith.

A Guide to the Symbols of the Bible

Symbol	Meaning
Mountain	Home with God, relationship with God, paradise, God's presence
Water	Death, life, chaos, separation, baptism, river of life
Tree/Wood	Tree of life, the cross, tree of knowledge of good and evil
Fire	Holy Spirit, purification, holiness, judgment
Glory/Sun	God's presence, God's glory
Garments/Clothing	Covered in God's glory, being close to God
Bread and Wine	Manna, Communion, the body and blood of Christ, wedding celebration
Sword/Spear	Prevents humanity from entering Eden, prevents full access to God
Cloud/Curtain/Veil	The presence and hiddenness of God, prevents access to God's full presence
Oil	Anointing, product of tree of life, healing
Blood/Lamb	Sacrifice, Jesus's death, lifeblood, innocence
Altar	Place of sacrifice, table of worship, Communion table, wedding feast table
Wind	Holy Spirit, breath of God
Stone	Foundation of Eden/Zion, stones of the temple, living stones of the church, Christ the cornerstone
Serpent	Evil, sin, Satan, death
Trumpet	God's voice, holy teaching, judgment, resurrection

PART 1:

THE STORY OF MOUNT EDEN

Do you see the excellent distinction and the wonderful craftsmanship, surpassing all comment, happening by a single word and command?

—John Chrysostom

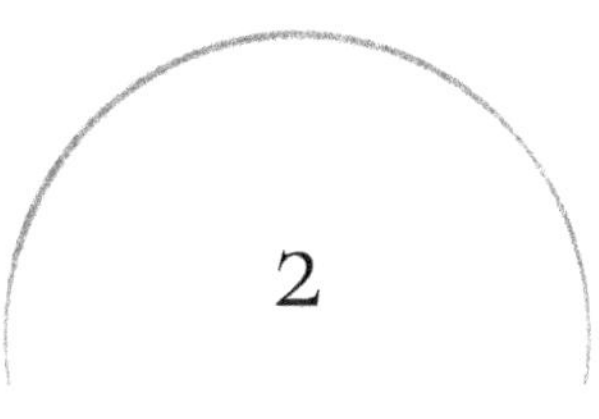

2

GOD CREATES

On Genesis 1–2:3 and Psalm 104:1–24

Every breath we take is a reminder that we were created by God. The words formed with our breath remind us of the word of God spoken by the Father when he created the sun, moon, earth, and sky. The oxygen that pumps through our lungs reminds us of the divine wind of the Holy Spirit, which moved over the abyss at the beginning of creation.

I remember the precise moment I fell in love with jazz music. I was listening to *Blue Train* by John Coltrane in my bedroom at age 15, when Lee Morgan's trumpet solo began in the middle of the track, and reverberated within my heart and soul in ways that I can barely describe in words. Before that moment, jazz music sounded to me like a random clash of noises and notes, the auditory equivalent of gibberish. But in the middle of that trumpet solo, those harsh noises suddenly transformed into sweet melodies. I began to recognize how the sounds of the piano, bass, and drums fit like puzzle pieces together to provide harmony and rhythm to undergird the beautiful melody. In that moment by the stereo in my bedroom, I crossed the Rubicon from liking to *loving* music, and there was no turning back. One of the natural outflows of this newly acquired love was that I picked up an instrument and learned to create music myself.

We create out of love and out of our loves. When we fall in love with someone or something, it often energizes us to create. If you fall in love with paintings, you might pick up a brush. If you fall in love with architecture, you might pick up a slide rule. If you fall in love with a person, you might write them love letters. The Bible says something similar when it talks about God creating the world. It tells us that God created the world, not by accident or out of necessity, but out of love. As such, we can use the metaphor of the artist and their artwork to guide our understanding of Genesis 1.[1] The purpose of the first chapter of the Bible is to tell us the identity of the artist (God), how he goes about creating the world (through order and abundance), and finally, the purpose of this creation (delight).

WHO CREATES? GOD THE FATHER, SON, AND HOLY SPIRIT

We can learn more about a work of art or music if we get to know the person who made it. In an art appreciation course, one might read the biographies of Van Gogh and Da Vinci to better understand their paintings. A painting does not simply fall out of the sky, but is created by a person, and as such, reflects something about them. Their art bears a stamp, a kind of reflection of their personality. So, when we learn something about an artist and the way they painted, we can better understand their artwork. My appreciation of the jazz album *Blue Train* led me to learn everything I could about John Coltrane and the making of that album. I even researched the specific location where it was made and the engineers who recorded it!

At some point in our lives, most of us have wondered where the world came from and who created it. Fortunately for us, the Bible begins by giving us some answers to these deep human questions. The opening lines of Genesis reveal the identity of the creator of all things: God the Father, the Son and Holy Spirit. He is one God in three persons, what Christians call the Trinity. We can see the Trinity in the wind and words in Genesis 1. In the Bible, the symbol of *wind* is often associated with the Holy Spirit and the breath of God. Also, the words of God are often associated with Jesus, who is both the Son of God and the Word of God (see John 1:1). In Genesis 1:2 we see that a divine wind is hovering over the waters, which is the presence of the Holy Spirit. Then, in the next sentence, God speaks these words: "Let there be light." These words are a sign of the presence of the Son of God. We learn from these first few sentences in the Bible that the creator of the world is one God, but is also three: God is Father, Son, and Holy Spirit. God the Father speaks the Word (the Son), and the wind of the Spirit moves to create light, land, sea, plants, and animals.

An analogy that can help us picture what is happening in creation is to think of what happens when we give a command to a pet. When I tell a dog to sit, three things happen. I first think of the command in my mind, I then exhale wind out of my lungs, and with my tongue form the word "sit." As a result, the dog sits down in response. The thinking, breathing, and speaking are all intertwined actions of one being: myself. Similarly, at creation, we can picture God the Father commanding, God the Spirit as the wind and breath, and God the Son as the words: "Let there be light." The result of this command is light coming into existence. All these actions are simultaneously the work of one God.

This first chapter of Genesis continues to reveal more about the identity of God by telling us how He goes about creating. One thing you will notice in Genesis 1 is that there is no struggle or hardship involved in creation. Unlike other ancient creation stories, the world was not created through epic fights between rival gods. Nor was the world created by some arduous manipulation of matter, like the construction of a modern-day skyscraper. Also, God does not create the world out of loneliness or need or boredom. Instead, God effortlessly created all things seen and unseen, and after each day of creation, delighted in his work by declaring it good. What this tells us is that the world was created by God out of love, like a musician creates a song out of their love of music, or a painter creates a portrait out of their love for art.

God created the world out of love because God is love. Within God there is a dynamic and active love between the Father, Son, and Holy Spirit—the Father loves the Son, the Son loves the Father, and the Holy Spirit is the bond of love between the Father and the Son. And it is this abundant Trinitarian love that "pours out and creates the goodness in things."[2]

HOW DOES GOD CREATE? ORDER AND ABUNDANCE

The artist crafts and shapes their work of love by bringing form and order out of chaos. The painter does not randomly slosh paint on canvas, nor does the pianist smash keys at random. Instead, they turn paint and notes into coherent forms: the glob of blue paint becomes a cerulean skyline and a brown smudge is shaped into an oak tree. These finished works of art all have a certain order and intelligibility to them that can be discovered and appreciated by an audience. For instance, as I delved deep into my love of music, I discovered that beneath the surface of *Blue Train* was an elaborate architecture of chord progressions and rhythmic precision.

God crafted the world by bringing form and order out of the matter he created. He began by creating, controlling, and taming the primordial waters. Water was akin to God's paint, which he controlled and formed to begin creation.[3] He then continued onward—heaven is separated from earth, water from land, and fish from fowl. As the days of creation progressed, God's works became more complex and intricate, from inorganic to organic, from inert to energetic. There is an order and progression to creation that invites our minds to discover, just as I sought to learn about the depth and complexity of jazz music. In fact, many of the first modern scientists were inspired by a Christian view of creation to uncover the logic of creation. In so doing they discovered that this divinely created order extends even to gravitational constants and molecular structures. Isaac Newton, for instance, praised God for the beautiful and intelligible order of his universe, declaring that "it is the perfection of God's works that they are all done with the greatest simplicity. He is the God of order and not of confusion."[4]

While God created in an orderly fashion, this does not mean that the world is ordinary. If creation was only orderly and efficient, it would look more like an automotive plant than an ecosystem. Works of art are more than just structured pigments and notes; they also exude an abundant beauty that exceeds their form. This is why the greatest works of art are the objects of infinite praise and discussion: thousands of people continue to appreciate the *Mona Lisa* and Beethoven's Fifth Symphony centuries after their creation. God's creation invites our awe and wonder in a similar way. The more time we spend in God's creation, the more we discover how many different plants, animals, colors, and sounds exist. When I was young, I thought there was only one kind of orange, a navel orange. But as I grew older, I discovered that there were hundreds of varieties of oranges in many different sizes and shapes. Similarly, one of the first times I walked through a botanical garden, I discovered that God created more than one color of tulip. In fact, He created *thousands* of unique tulip colors and patterns. The varieties of fruits and various colors of flowers do not *need* to exist in the world. Humanity could survive without tangerines and azure petals. But God is an artist who gives out of joy and abundance, providing us more than what we need and giving us a beautiful world that surpasses anything else we could imagine.

We can see the abundance of creation in Genesis 1 through its repeated mention of seeds. Each plant that God makes produces an abundance of seeds, more than what is needed to repopulate the earth. God in a sense overproduces, making a world that generates more than what is necessary for its survival. God showers his creation, just as a grandmother showers her grandchildren with extravagant and unnecessary gifts. When we give out of love, we give abundantly. And since the world was created out of God's Trinitarian love, it exudes beauty and opulence. Our response to this beauty should be to shout God's praise, like the Psalmist: "O Lord, how manifold are your works!" (Psalm 104:24).

GOD'S MASTERPIECE: THE CREATION OF HUMAN BEINGS

Artists are identified by their masterpieces. When I think of Michelangelo, I instantly picture my time in Rome, staring at the Sistine Chapel. When I hear the name Beethoven, I instantly hum the Fifth Symphony. While Genesis 1 proceeds by showing an orderly progression of increasingly complex organisms, it culminates in God's masterpiece: the formation of humankind. In many ways, the creation of humankind is in line with the logical progression of creation, as human beings share many of the same characteristics as other mammals. But God does something special with human beings. While on the first five days of creation God creates through a simple command, on the sixth day he takes a little more time. Like many great artists, God spends more time and devotion on his masterpiece. Specifically, the Father, Son, and Holy Spirit take time to deliberate. There is a kind of Trinitarian conversation that occurs, with God declaring: "Let us make humankind in *our* image, according to *our* likeness" (Genesis 1:26, NRSV, emphasis mine). Gregory of Nyssa sees this act of deliberation as a sign of the special value God grants to human beings: "See how worthy you are! Your origins are not in an imperative. Instead, God deliberated about the best way to bring to life a creation worthy of honor."[5]

It is the *likeness* to God and the *image* of God that makes human beings God's masterpiece. To be created in the *likeness* of God means that human beings are given certain abilities that reflect the abilities of God, most notably the freedom to be creative. Just as God creates the world freely out of love like a great artist, human beings are the only species capable of freely creating works of art out of love. Human beings, however, are given the capacity to do a multitude of creative things such as art and music, but also an assortment of hobbies, sports, and other ventures. Furthermore, humans are given the freedom to choose how to order these loves. In middle school, for instance, I chose playing football over playing basketball, and chose the jazz band over the orchestra.

But the most important freedom we are granted as people created in the likeness of God is the freedom to love others and form relationships. We get to choose to be friends with other people and can choose to spend our time developing closer friendships with some people as opposed to others. Many of us are given the opportunity to marry someone we love, and we are given the freedom to remain single. Our relational freedom culminates in our ability to choose to love God. Human beings are not God's pets, whom he trains to do special tricks on command. Instead, human beings are given the ability to have friendship with God on a personal level. They can choose to love God and use their freedom to cultivate friendship with God in unique ways.

This ability to choose to love someone, and for someone to choose to love us back, is what makes friendships so special. I might love some material object like my stereo or my car, but this love pales in comparison to the love experienced in my marriage. Our relationship with God is the highest of our loves because it is predicated on this freedom. God did not create us out of some need or necessity, but out of love. And he invites us to choose to love him back out of love. But this ability to choose comes with great risks, because it opens up the possibility that human beings will choose *not* to love God or others. We all know that choosing a best friend is riskier than choosing a car, because a best friend can decide to reject our love. When God created human beings, he did not create robots. He created individuals who could choose to love him, and in so doing risked the possibility that they might choose to reject his love.

In addition to being created in the likeness of God, human beings are also created in the *image* of God, which means that they uniquely reflect the glory of God. In the Bible, God's glory is related to his goodness and beauty. Since God is intrinsically and perfectly beautiful, to encounter God is to be overwhelmed by his goodness, perfection, and beauty. God, we can say, radiates goodness and beauty, and we call this radiation *glory*. This radiating glory is shown throughout the Bible through the symbols of the *sun* and *light*.

To be created in the image of God means that human beings have a close intimacy with God, so much so that some of God's glory is reflected through us. Human beings can reflect God's glory just as a mirror brilliantly reflects the sun's radiance. This speaks to the intrinsic beauty and worth of every individual human being. While we are given some of the creative freedom of God, we know that many people never get the opportunity to fully express this creativity. However, each and every person, whether they are still in their mother's womb or forever confined to a hospital bed, still bears the image of God. When we recognize this capacity to reflect God's glory in ourselves and in others, our primary response should be to reflect back to God shouts of praise and worship, which is the ultimate goal of humankind.

THE GOAL OF CREATION: SABBATH WORSHIP

Most artists create with a goal in mind. A symphony is meant to be performed in a grand concert hall, a painting is meant to be viewed in an art gallery. If we are God's masterpiece, what is God's ultimate goal for us? The creation story in Genesis 1 does not conclude with the creation of human beings, but instead culminates in a seventh day, the Sabbath. The pinnacle of creation is not the formation of human beings, but the introduction of Sabbath rest. In understanding the significance of this day, we will in turn understand the ultimate goal of human beings.

On this seventh day we read that God rested. Why does God rest? Surely it is not because God is exhausted or tired, since he is inexhaustible. Instead, God rests in order to delight in what he has accomplished and set an example for human beings who *do* grow weary. The final step an artist takes is to stand back and admire their handiwork. When I lived in Chicago, I played music in several bands, and one of the greatest experiences occurred when we finished recording a song in the studio. It was a moment to stand back and enjoy the great music that me and my friends created together. Likewise, on the seventh day the Father, Son, and Holy Spirit take a step back to admire and delight in all they have created.

We saw in the first few lines of Genesis that God creates out of love and not out of need. We are not created to fill some emptiness in God. God is not waiting for human beings to perform some grand deed before he is proud of what he has created. Instead, God simply delights in his creation before it acts or accomplishes anything on its own. This should bring the followers of God immense peace in this age of anxiety and stress. So much of our anxiety is driven by our desire to achieve, to succeed, and to make a difference in the world. This drive can cause us to believe that our self-worth is tied up with our achievements. We can think that our failures somehow diminish our worth, or even make us disappointments in God's eyes. It is in these moments that we must remember that God does not need our labors or our achievements, but simply delights in us as an artist delights in their masterpiece. His delight in us *precedes* any work we do and even precedes our very existence! As such, our labors in this world are supposed to proceed from an acknowledgement of his love, not an effort to earn it.

The creation story ends with God blessing the seventh day and making it holy by setting it apart from the other days of the week. Since human beings are made in God's image, they are invited to respond by resting and delighting in God every seven days. As God rests to delight in his creation, creation rests to delight in God. This kind of active delighting is what we call worship, which Christians practice each Sunday at church.

The goal of the Christian life is to enter into Sabbath rest, delighting in God and worshiping him. This should profoundly impact how we think of the idea of Sabbath. Many of us think of Sundays, for example, as a kind of relaxing personal day that is supposed to refresh us for the real work of life that takes place during the week. It is our free time to use to engage in whatever strikes our fancy. But in the Bible, God calls us to take this one day a week as a Sabbath day, a day meant not for passive relaxation but active worship of God. This delightful, peaceful, and active worship is the ultimate goal of human beings, and this is why we are invited to spend a day each week devoted to it.

We are created to reflect God's glory and worship him in pure and utter delight. This has been the reason why God's people, from ancient Israelites to modern Christians, have devoted an entire day to refraining from work and gathering together to worship God. As we will discover, the tabernacle, and then the church, is supposed to be a unique and special place where human beings ascend to the top of the mountain to actively delight in God in praise and worship. Sabbath worship is what human beings were created for. Worship in church is meant to be the starting point of each week. Personal devotion to God is meant to be a staple of each day. And the culmination of human life will be the opportunity to eternally worship God on the heavenly Mount Zion. While we oftentimes think of heaven as a place free of hardship, where we will be reunited with our departed loved ones, the main event in heaven will be worship. The Sabbath is meant to give us a glimpse of this ultimate heavenly prize and to train us for that which we will be doing in eternity: worshiping the infinite, ineffable, beautiful God on Mount Zion.

When we fail to prioritize the Sabbath and fail to make time to go to church to worship God, it might not be because we are too busy with other activities in life. It might be because we do not truly believe that the worship of God is the most important thing in life. Whatever personal or practical obstacles that prevent us from entering into Sabbath rest must be overcome, for if one does not learn how to delight in Sabbath worship, then one will find heaven to be quite a disappointing affair.

A GLIMPSE OF PARADISE

Human beings are God's masterpiece, formed in his likeness and image. We are objects of God's infinite delight and are created to respond by constantly delighting in God. Humanity has as its goal an eternal and never-ending Sabbath rest, and God gives us one day a week as an opportunity to experience a foretaste of our eternal life in paradise. What is life like in this eternal paradise, and what does this active relationship with God look like in detail? The Bible continues by describing in detail the location of paradise and our once and future life in it by chronicling the life of Adam and Eve upon Mount Eden.

Both men and women,
are clothed in raiment of light;
the garments provided to cover their nakedness
are swallowed up in glory.

—*Ephrem the Syrian*

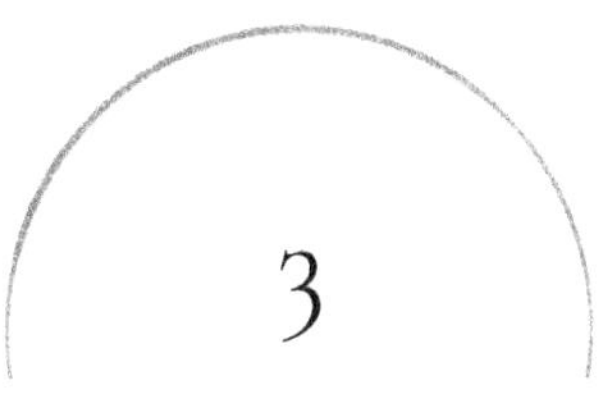

3

MOUNT EDEN

On Genesis 2:4–25 and Psalm 139:1–17

Our souls long for Eden. Every dip in a cool stream foreshadows a plunge into its rivers of life. Each time we recline on the trunk of a shady tree foretells our eternal rest under the tree of life. Each moment of warmth with a close friend inclines our hearts to yearn for that eternal intimacy with God which can only be had on his mountain.

THE MAIN STORYLINE

Genesis 2 gives us the crucial details for understanding the storyline of Bible and introduces us to a host of symbols that sparks in every soul a desire to return to our heavenly home. In this way it is like the opening pages of other books. The opening pages of a novel often introduce the reader to all the essentials for understanding the story: the setting, the main characters, and the story's essential themes. For instance, within the first few pages of *Jane Eyre* one is introduced to its setting (Northern England in the 1880s), its main character (Jane), and its major themes (class status, perseverance, and morality).

Similarly, the Bible introduces the setting, main characters, and major themes in just the first two chapters of Genesis. What is fascinating about Genesis 2 is that it is both the beginning of the story of Mount Eden and at the same time a microcosm of the *entire* biblical story. It presents to us a picture of humanity's life with God, with Adam and Eve serving as representatives for humanity as a whole. Thus, when we read Genesis 2, we are called to see ourselves in the persons of Adam and Eve. The story of Mount Eden is not just an ancient account of God and the first human beings; it is also the story of *our* life with God. We are called to see ourselves living with God on his mountain, to picture ourselves walking with God in the garden and ascending and descending the slopes of Eden.

This chapter will unpack Genesis 2 by describing its setting and main characters, and end by highlighting the major themes that emerge within this account, which are home, harmony, work, and worship. Along the way, Genesis 2 also introduces a number of key symbols (*water, trees*, and *garments*) that will continue to appear throughout the Bible. Many of the melodic lines of the biblical story begin with these symbols, and each of them invites us in turn to make biblical harmony, seeing Jesus at work in Eden and seeing our own lives within the story.

THE SETTING: MOUNTAIN, WATER, AND TREES

Like many stories, the setting of Genesis 2 is a home. We all long for a home. Home is one of the principal markers of our identity. "Where are you from?" is a common question we ask of new acquaintances. For those who are far away from home, this question can evoke a bittersweet longing. The diaries of soldiers during the Second World War are littered with talk of returning home to familiar comforts. Refugees often miss the native foods from their homeland and wish they could share a meal with the friends and family they have had to leave behind. Our conception of home is always tied to physical things and physical locations, and often includes specific elements such as houses, neighbors, food, and climate.

Genesis 2 begins by describing Adam and Eve's home, Mount Eden, the physical location where they dwell with God and one another. As we will discover, mountains will serve throughout the Bible as similar meeting points between God and humankind, as well as provide an enduring symbol of our home with God. Figure 1 that follows gives us a helpful rendering of Mount Eden and the various images that are located on Eden.

A common misconception about Eden is that it was a flat piece of garden land. However, the Bible depicts Eden as a bountiful and beautiful mountain that Adam and Eve traversed daily with God. The careful reader will notice descriptions in Genesis 2 that indicate Eden's topography, most notably in the description of rivers. The river of life flows *down* from the top of Eden and into the four rivers at the bottom, which form the boundary of Mount Eden.

As we discovered in Genesis 1, *water* is both a sign of life and a sign of chaos and death, and we see in Genesis 2 a continuation of these signs in its depiction of Mount Eden: the river running through the garden of Eden is the river of life (Genesis 2:10) and alerts us to the fact that Eden is a place overflowing with vitality. While the river running through Eden is a sign of life, the rivers at the bottom of Eden are a sign of chaos, as they represent the boundary marker that separates home from wilderness. On Eden there is vitality through the river of life, but beyond the borders of the rivers of chaos is the unfinished wilderness, a place still in need of the fullness of God's glory.

The Garden of Eden resides on the top and middle portions of Mount Eden and is the place where Adam is called to have close intimacy with God. While residing on Mount Eden, Adam and Eve are called by God to enter the garden and walk with him. Think of visiting a botanical garden with a dear friend. In experiencing such a beautiful place, teeming with life, you grow closer as you walk, talk, and explore together. Adam and Eve had this type of intimacy with the God of the universe within the Garden of Eden.

Gardens overflow with an abundance of plant life, and the most prominent gardens feature beautiful and exotic *trees*. Trees are essential to human existence: they produce oxygen necessary for breathing, shade on hot days, food for the hungry, and wood for the bitter cold. They are magnificent signs of the splendor of God's creation, towering above all living things. The plant life of the Garden of Eden similarly culminates in a series of trees that produce fruit to nourish Adam and Eve both physically and spiritually. The two most prominent of these are the tree of life and the tree of the knowledge of good and evil. These trees demarcate the middle and top of Mount Eden. The tree of the knowledge sits at the midway point of the mountain and serves as a kind of gateway to the summit of Eden. At the very top of Eden is the tree of life, which symbolizes a full relational maturity between Adam, Eve, and God.[1]

Figure 1: Mount Eden—Genesis 2

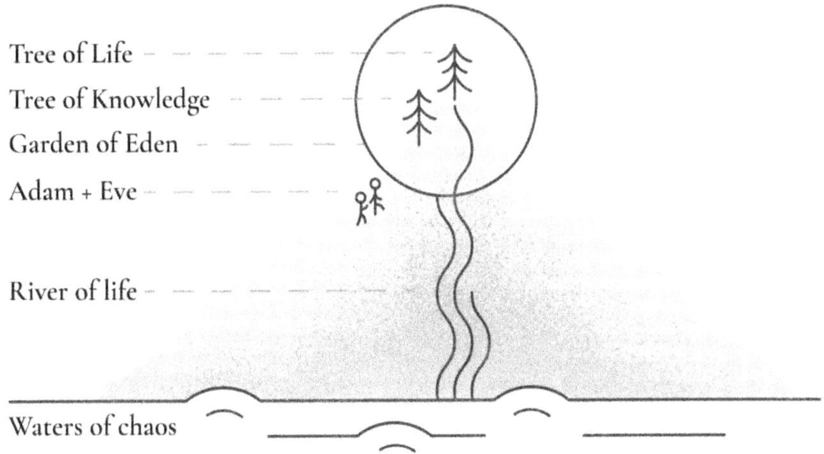

THE CHARACTERS: ADAM AND EVE

While Genesis 2 presents us with vivid images of Mount Eden, it provides us little background information about its two main characters, Adam and Eve. However, the description of the trees on Eden gives us a clue into their lives, as these trees represent stages of developmental growth. As Adam and Eve grew closer to God, they would be able to ascend further and further up Eden, and in turn, eat from more and more trees. What this tells us about Adam and Eve is that, although they were without sin, they were still not fully mature. One of the earliest Christian writers, Irenaeus of Lyon, speaks of Adam of Eve as children, sinless but still in need of growth into full maturity.[2]

The future of a child is one marked by continued growth and maturity, and from time immemorial, cultures have set aside certain ceremonies and rituals to celebrate significant stages of growth. Two of the most prominent of these stages are the transition from childhood to adulthood, and the transition from singleness to marriage. The two major trees in the garden of Eden were meant to signify these two major milestones of maturity.

First, there is the transition from childhood into adulthood. As a child grows, they increase in their capacity for knowledge, and they are able to perform more complex tasks. A child can understand basic math, while an adult can understand complex algebra. A child can ride a tricycle, while an adult can operate an automobile. While such progress happens slowly over time, it is also demarcated by specific events. For instance, Americans celebrate sweet sixteen parties, when a child is deemed mature enough to drive a car. I can remember vividly the first student in my class to get his driver's license. We all piled into his van, cranked loud music, and cruised downtown unsupervised by our parents. It was our first taste of the freedom of adulthood. The keys to his car served as both a reward for maturity and as a gateway to new freedoms and experiences.

Life on Mount Eden for Adam and Eve involved a similar growth from childhood to adulthood. Maturation meant increasing their capacity for knowledge of God and each other, and an increased capacity to handle more complex tasks. The major milestone—the cultural celebration that was meant to mark their transition from childhood to adulthood—was their consumption of the fruit of the tree of knowledge. This fruit was the "solid food" of wisdom for the mature (Hebrews 5:14), meant to be consumed when God deemed Adam and Eve capable of handling a fuller knowledge of his complex creation. Ephrem the Syrian calls this tree a curtain, blocking off the higher part of Mount Eden. Thus, when Adam and Eve were ready, they could eat of this tree and have access to the higher parts of Eden and the tree of life. Eating of this tree "would have been good if partaken of at the proper time."[3]

This explains the perplexing commandment that God gives to Adam and Eve: the prohibition against eating of the fruit of this tree. God gives this command, not as some sort of arbitrary rule meant to deny Adam and Eve, but rather to protect Adam and Eve from receiving knowledge that they cannot handle. God, in a sense, says to Adam and Eve, "wait until you're older," just as we might forbid a 5-year-old from driving a car. Giving a child the keys to a car would grant them power that they are incapable of maturely possessing, and the results of such an action could only mean harm for the child and others. Similarly, God commands Adam and Eve to refrain from eating of the tree of knowledge in order to keep them from harming themselves and each other.

Another major mark of maturity as one grows from childhood to adulthood is the establishment of intimate, committed relationships. When I was little, my friendships were often predicated on trivial things. My friends were those who wanted to play baseball with me outside, and Nintendo with me inside. As I grew older, I became capable of having deeper friendships grounded on mutual love, understanding, and trust. These were relationships where I could be honest and vulnerable without fear of abandonment. A special type of intimate relationship available to adults is the commitment of marriage. The wedding day is perhaps the most pervasive cultural celebration in human civilization. Here, husband and wife commit to cultivating a deep and intimate relationship with each other and commit to nourish this bond throughout their lives together.

As Adam and Eve continued to mature, they would scale Mount Eden and eventually reach the summit, where they would eat from the tree of life. This act of eating from the tree would serve as a kind of wedding day for Adam and Eve, with God. Their ascent up the mountain would be like an ascent up to the altar, and the fullness of fellowship experienced at the top would have been like a rich celebratory wedding reception. A wedding is a celebration where husband and wife choose to enter a lasting, committed, and intimate relationship. It is both a sign of maturity and the beginning of a new life with another. The tree of life was meant to celebrate the moment in which Adam and Eve would have full, mature intimacy with God, entering into an everlasting commitment with the creator of the universe. For us, each tall tree emerging out of the earth is a reminder of this heavenly hope of Eden. We all should yearn to reach the base of this tree, at the top of the mountain, and to run up to the altar to be united with God forever.

THE ACTIONS OF ADAM AND EVE ON MOUNT EDEN: ASCENT AND DESCENT

Genesis 2 presents a detailed account of the setting of Mount Eden and a description of Adam and Eve as children, with the capacity to grow into mature adulthood. It then continues to show how Adam and Eve grow through engaging in various activities on the mountain. We can describe the life of Adam and Eve as one of descent and ascent: Adam and Eve reside on the middle part of the mountain, ascending to be close to God and descending to participate in God's work.

How do Adam and Eve ascend the mountain? This is done primarily through obedience and worship. First, Adam and Eve learn to trust and obey God. God gives a simple command to Adam: eat of the various trees, but do not eat of the of the tree of the knowledge of good and evil (Genesis 2:17). While obedience can sometimes be thought of as a begrudging acceptance of orders, the obedience seen on Mount Eden is more like the delightful obedience of a child. There is a kind of delight that a child has when they first learn a command from their parents. The parent says "turn the page," or "give me a kiss," and their child responds with the ensuing action and a smile on their face. The acceptance of a command becomes in the receptive child an opportunity to acquire new vocabulary and the adulation of their parents. God asks Adam and Eve to follow him with a similar delight. As they receive these commands, they acquire new knowledge and, in turn, delight further in their heavenly Father.

In addition, Adam and Eve are called up the mountain into the garden to worship God. Genesis 2:15 states that Adam was to enter the garden in order to work and keep it. While these words *work* and *keep* imply the cultivation of land, they are also terms used throughout the Old Testament for going to temple to worship God.[4] We still use the phrase "keeping the Sabbath" as shorthand for worshiping God in a Jewish synagogue or a Christian church. When Adam and Eve entered the garden, they were entering into a church service where they were called to honor and worship God.

What does it mean to worship? We can think of worship as the wonder of God. We all long for experiences that transcend the everyday, or that fill us with a sense of awe. We might think here of viewing the Grand Canyon, or attending a concert or football game, or perhaps visiting the Sistine Chapel. Such experiences evoke in us a response of awe, whether a serene wonder at nature's beauty, or a loud cheer at a sporting event. Such reactions are owed to our natural desire to praise in the sight of the extraordinary and point us to our ultimate goal: to stand fully in the presence of the almighty God and to worship him. The term worship is used throughout the Bible to denote the proper human response in the presence of the glory of God.

The garden of Eden is meant to be the specific location in which this worship occurs. In this way it is a kind of tabernacle, or church, where Adam and Eve experience a closeness to God in worship, thus growing in their love and knowledge of him. In essence, Adam and Eve ascend the mountain to go to church, encountering God's presence and responding in worship. As we will discover, in places of worship today, the architecture is meant to reflect this primordial pattern of worship displayed on Mount Eden. Each Sunday is an opportunity for us to scale the mountain of God as we enter his church.

While Adam and Eve ascend to worship God, they are also given the mission to descend the mountain to expand the borders of Eden. We see this mission in God's command to Adam to cultivate the plant and animal life on Eden. Adam is given work to do on the mountain, specifically naming animals and tilling the land. He is a farmer and a zoologist. This might strike some of us as odd: how can a perfect and sinless life still involve work? Many of us don't conceive of eternal life with God as encompassing work—in fact, we hope that heaven involves the absence of work! However, work was intended to be a joyful labor in God's presence. There is joy in interacting with the physical world, of cultivating it and caring for it. This kind of work is praiseworthy and not toilsome.[5] To imagine such interactions stripped of hardship is to imagine what working on the mountain of God is meant to be like. Gardening in Eden is a joyful task that yields plentiful crops rather than an arduous battle with shriveled weeds. In addition, Adam's work as a zoologist is free of hardship: he is able to care for animals while living in perfect harmony with them, nurturing lions without fear of attack, and tending bees without fear of being stung.

To work is to be fruitful, and good work multiplies rather than harms God's creation. We all have a desire to bring something new into the world that honors God and blesses others. Work is meant to be creative and expansive, and just as God creates and expands the world, human beings are called to cultivate his creation and expand it. As Adam and Eve continued to work, plant and animal life grew and multiplied requiring an expansion of Eden in order to contain this new life. The labors of Adam and Eve were meant to bring about an expansion of the borders of Eden, with the eventual goal that Eden would expand to cover all of the earth.

THE RELATIONSHIPS BETWEEN ADAM AND EVE: CREATED IN HARMONY

While Adam and Eve were called to grow closer to God, they were also called to grow closer together, and with the rest of creation. Life on Mount Eden was not lived in isolation. A relationship with God on his mountain brings with it a relationship with the rest of God's creation. Adam was able to draw near to every animal and whisper each one its name. In so doing, he developed a close relationship with bears and tigers, as if they were golden retrievers. While this friendship with animals is remarkable, it pales in comparison to the intimacy afforded by human relationships. We see this clearly in the account of the creation of Eve: while Adam was a friend to animals, he was still lonely. Something was missing. God created Eve so that Adam might live in relational harmony with one who was like him, "bone of my bones and flesh of my flesh" (Genesis 2:23). Human beings are created not only to have a close relationship with God, but also close personal relationships with each other.

It is easy for us to miss the necessity of our relationships. Our contemporary society tends to think of human beings as isolated individuals who create meaning and purpose in their lives through the choices they make. Our identity and purpose begin as a blank slate, a *tabula rasa*, that we fill through the various relational, vocational, and artistic choices we make. To live in such a way, however, is to invite insecurity and anxiety, since such choices may not turn out the way we had hoped. Relationships can end abruptly, our career paths can be thwarted, and misfortune can befall us at any moment.

What the story of Mount Eden teaches us is the opposite. We are not created as isolated individuals, but as intrinsically relational, dependent beings. We are created *for* community—with God and with others. The fact that we are dependent people in need of others is not a sign of weakness or a mark of sin, but part of how we were created by design. On Mount Eden, Adam was without sin, yet he still depended on God for life and Eve for companionship. To grow, Adam had to move *toward*, not away, from others. Similarly for us, our growth as human beings should not lead to independence and isolation, but rather a strengthening of the relational bonds between ourselves, God, and others.

THE RELATIONSHIP OF ADAM AND EVE TO GOD: GARMENTS OF GLORY

I live one mile away from Penn State University, a school that consistently ranks as one of the best in the country in regard to student life and school spirit. Students love being at Penn State and love being associated with the university. As I walk from my house to campus, one of the first things I see is the appearance of numerous people wearing Penn State apparel. Once I step on the grounds of the university, it seems as if *everyone* is wearing something blue and white and has a Penn State logo on their shirt or jacket. When people are on Penn State's campus, they want to be surrounded by the glory of Penn State, even down to the clothing that they put on.

Often our clothing indicates something about our relationships. It indicates the kinds of people we associate with at work, the communities we love, and the things that we value. We know that a person wearing workout gear enjoys exercise, and that a person in a suit and tie is probably going to work in an office. In Genesis 2 the Bible tells us more about the relationship between Adam and Eve and their relationship with God by telling us about their clothing, or more accurately their *lack* of clothing! The creation story of Adam and Eve ends by stating that Adam and Eve "were both naked and were not ashamed" (Genesis 2:25).

Why were Adam and Eve naked and not ashamed? First, since Adam and Eve were without sin, they possessed a kind of child-like innocence. Innocent children are not bothered by their own nakedness. Hence their nakedness was meant to underscore the fact that Adam and Eve were both innocent of sin and children in the process of growing into full maturity in their walk with God.

But there is a deeper meaning behind the assertion that Adam and Eve were naked and felt no shame. They were not ashamed because God's glory was their clothing. As we saw in the last chapter, human beings were created to be in God's presence, to reflect his glory, and to participate in Sabbath worship. As human beings draw close to God in worship, they become surrounded by his glory, reflecting it much like a mirror reflects the brightness of the sun.

To be in God's presence is to be immersed in his glory much like being immersed in the sun's rays. If you look at a friend who is standing in front of the sun, you will notice their shape and outline, yet you will be unable to clearly see many of their features. The radiance of the sun is too powerful, and it envelops much of their physical features. They are, in a sense, clothed in the rays of the sun. On Mount Eden, Adam and Eve were surrounded by God's glory so much that it became a kind of clothing for them. When Eve looked at Adam, she saw him enveloped in God's glory, and hence could not see the details of his body: "It was because of the glory in which they were wrapped that they were not ashamed."[6]

In the Bible, this wrapping is described as a robe or *garment* of glory.[7] When one steps on the mountain of God, they are surrounded by God's glory and wear it on their body. It is a key symbol in the Bible that returns on Tabor and Zion and is a description of what life on God's mountain is like—close intimacy in which the glory of God is revealed and reflected. The simple act of getting dressed in the morning is a reminder that we will one day be covered with God's glory in and through Jesus Christ.

THEMES: HOME, HARMONY, WORK, AND WORSHIP

We can now take a step back and summarize the key themes that emerge from this story. And, as this story of Adam and Eve is meant to be a microcosm of our own life with God, we can then see how this story of Eden impacts our own relationship with God in the present. The four key themes related to our life with God that emerge from Genesis 2 are *home*, *harmony*, *work*, and *worship*.

First, Genesis 2 tells us that the mountain of God is our *home*. Genesis 2 tells us that life with God takes place in a home, Mount Eden. Life with God is not some sort of ethereal place in the clouds, where our disembodied spirit swirls. It takes place on a piece of land, a physical location. It involves interactions with dirt, plants, and animals.

Second, Genesis 2 tells us that our life with God involves *harmony* with him and others. While Genesis 1:1–2:3 gives us an image of peace as Sabbath rest with God, Genesis 2:4–25 expands on this notion of peace to show that such relational harmony occurs not only between individuals and God, but also between human beings and the rest of God's creation. We are created as dependent beings, designed for deep, meaningful, and growing relationships with God and others.

Third, our life with God involves *work*. Life on Mount Eden is not static, but dynamic. Not only are Adam and Eve growing, they are also given the gift of helping God's creation grow and expand. They cultivate Eden, working in and through God to bring about a multiplication of life, with the goal of expanding the borders of Eden so that Mount Eden would cover the entire earth.

Lastly, our life with God culminates in *worship*. As Adam and Eve draw near to God and experience God's glory in the garden, they worship him and reflect his glory. God's glory envelops the worshiper, so much so that we can speak of Adam and Eve as being clothed in garments of glory.

LIFE ON THE MOUNTAIN

Genesis 2 introduces us to many of the key symbols that stitch together the Bible. Trees, waters, and garments are all images that reemerge throughout the biblical story. They will continue to disclose to us the depths of the biblical story and continue to invite us into a deeper life with God. But the most prominent image given to us is of the mountain, Mount Eden. The image of Eden is reflected in Sinai, in Tabor, and in Zion, and the events chronicled upon it are meant to be foundational for how we imagine our own life with God. Mount Eden gives us an account of personal growth and life with God that is free from the burden of sin, and hence it is one that the Bible will return to after the effects of sin are finally and definitively addressed by Jesus. At the end of this story we will discover that life on Mount Zion is in many ways a return to and fulfillment of life on Mount Eden.

Adam and Eve are placed in the middle of Mount Eden and are given the opportunity to continue to grow in their love and knowledge of God, with the goal of eventually reaching full maturity in their relationship with God and partaking of the tree of life. Ideally, the biblical story would continue by chronicling their uninterrupted growth. However, things go terribly wrong, and the lives and goals of Adam and Eve become thwarted through their own decisions, leading to a fall off Mount Eden and a descent into sin and death.

Had Adam conquered,
he would have acquired
glory upon his limbs,
and discernment of what suffering is,
so that he might be radiant in his limbs
and grow in his discernment.
But the serpent reversed all this
and made him taste
abasement in reality,
and glory in recollection only,
so that he might feel shame at what he had found
and weep at what he had lost.

—*Ephrem the Syrian*

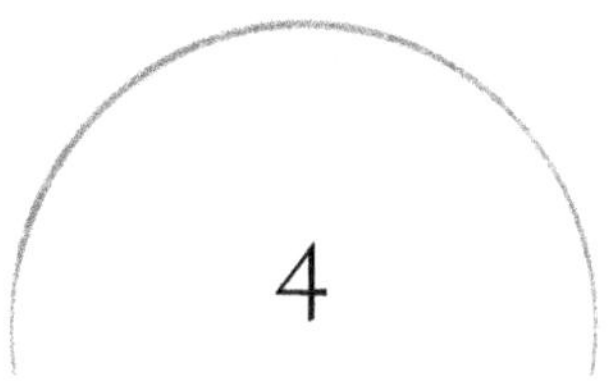

4

THE FALL FROM MOUNT EDEN

On Genesis 3 and Psalm 51

As we hike up a mountain on a calm autumn afternoon, we might imagine we are on Mount Eden. The brilliant sunshine reminds us of God's glory, the white oaks of the tree life, and the swirling streams of the river of life. But beneath the surface of this mountain climb lies danger and hardship. The hike becomes tiresome, and our bodies are susceptible to insect stings and sun exposure. The very same animals that give life to the mountain can also threaten the life of the hiker. Deadliest of all these animals is the poisonous snake, whose venom can bring about a sudden and quick death. While trees and rivers can carry our hearts to Eden, the pain of sunburn, the sting of an insect, and the bite of a snake remind us of the blunt reality that we are not there. The world is beautiful but broken.

Genesis 2 paints a beautiful picture of a creation in harmony with itself and of humankind in a harmonious relationship with God. But things go terribly wrong. Adam and Eve disobey God by eating of the tree of knowledge before God has granted them permission. Satan, an angel who himself chose to disobey God, twists God's command and persuades Eve to disobey. Eve then takes of the fruit and gives some to a nearby Adam, who partakes of the fruit and thus participates in the first sin of humankind. As a result, this joyful story goes off the tracks, and the beautiful harmony of life on Eden becomes broken and distorted.

The source and cause of this brokenness is what Christians call sin. Genesis 3 chronicles the first sin and its consequences. Because Adam and Eve represent all of humankind, it tells us about the nature of our own sin as well. Specifically, their story tells us why we sin, how we respond to it, and the resulting consequences.

WHY DO WE SIN? THE NATURE OF SIN AND THE FIRST SIN

Most, if not all of us, want to be good and do good. Few set out to intentionally do wicked or evil things. I do not wake up in the morning wanting to lie or be bitter, and yet, despite my best efforts, I often find myself massaging the truth and thinking terrible things about others. If we do not want to do wicked things, why do bad things still happen? What lies at the root of human sin? Genesis 3 helps us to understand these questions by describing the circumstances surrounding the first sin of humankind.

According to the Letter of James, sin begins with an assent to temptation, which leads to desire, and finally action (James 1:13–15). And we see in Genesis 3 all three of these stages at work in the first sin on Mount Eden. The chapter begins by telling us about the craftiness of the serpent, and a dialogue ensues between the serpent and Eve concerning God's commands. The *serpent* is a symbol of temptation and sin. This serpent on Eden is no ordinary snake, but instead a reptile that is being inhabited and used by Satan. Satan is himself a fallen angel who rejected God's commands and exists to tempt others to likewise turn away from God. How does Satan go about tempting Eve? He twists the commands of God to entice her to put her desire for the hidden knowledge of good and evil above her desire to obey God. This is key to understanding the nature of sin and evil, which is *disordered desire*: we want something that is good, but we want it on our terms, not God's. Satan does not try to tempt Eve to commit murder or to lie. Instead, he tempts Eve to do something good in a disordered way.

Sometimes it is the good things in life that tempt us most. Whenever something great happens to someone in my family, I want to celebrate with ice cream. Ice cream is meant for special occasions like this. But whenever a carton of ice cream is sitting in my freezer, I am tempted to eat it for every meal. I will be tempted to place my enjoyment of ice cream above my health, and if I give in to this temptation too often, I will slowly have less energy to spend on my family and others. There are more serious examples in our life of good things twisted and distorted. One can easily place a desire to watch football above their need to parent, or leisure above spending time with God. Similarly, the tree of the knowledge of good and evil is a good thing, created by God to give Adam and Eve wisdom, but only when God believed the timing was right.[1] Its fruit was meant to be savored on a special occasion rather than ravished on a whim. The goal of Satan was to convince Adam and Eve to disorder their desires, placing the love of earthly wisdom above the love of God.

But a simple dialogue between the serpent and Eve did not have to culminate in a sinful act. To be tempted is not to sin. Adam and Eve could have passed by the tree of knowledge for years, or even centuries, without ever desiring to disobey God. The serpent could have whispered these words to Eve hundreds of times before, but those words could have simply bounced off her ears. But one day, the words of the serpent become enticing, and that which was innocently ignored suddenly becomes seductively alluring.

One way to picture this scene is to think of advertising billboards. Billboards that promote products that do not interest us are generally ignored as we pass by. I have very little desire for automobiles, so passing by giant car advertisements each day has little to no effect on me. However, billboards that promote something that I do desire—a new phone or computer—entice my eyes and push me towards spending money on things I don't need. We can be flooded each day with these kinds of temptations, but can choose whether to ignore them or to entertain them in our hearts. If we give in to these temptations, we begin to *desire* sin, and our evil actions follow.

The key sentence in this passage lies in Genesis 3:6, where it states that Eve saw "that the tree was *desirable*" (NASB95, emphasis mine). Adam and Eve placed their desire for knowledge above their desire to obey God, and the action of taking and eating the fruit naturally flowed out of this twisted desire. All sins of humankind bear a resemblance to this primordial sin. Behind every sinful action is a disordered desire, a desire to place the good things in life above delighting in and obeying God.

In eating the forbidden fruit, the condition of sin became encoded in the DNA of Adam and Eve and was passed to their offspring, and thus all of humanity. In consuming the fruit, Adam and Eve ingested the venom of the snake, and this venom continues to poison the entire human race to this day. We are all now born with wayward hearts and all experience moments of thinking and acting in ways that go against God's good will for us. We love the good things of the world—food, pleasure, leisure, and money—above God and others. The actions that spring from these disordered loves result in an erosion of good in the world.[2]

OUR RESPONSE TO SIN: SHAME, BLAME, AND EXCUSES

Immediately after eating the fruit, Adam and Eve notice that something is wrong. They realize that they are naked, and they cover themselves up with leaves. The first sin in human history is followed immediately by these first feelings of guilt. Guilt is the discordant sensation we experience after we do something that we know we should not have done. As humanity has inherited Adam and Eve's sin, we have also inherited their guilt, and guilt remains for each of us today a sign that we were created to love and obey God, but that we all too often fall short of this goal.

The story of sin does not jump right from guilt to punishment. God does not approach Adam and Eve with a harsh reprimand, but instead calls out to them, asking them three questions. The purpose of these questions is to provide an opportunity for Adam and Eve to come clean, to acknowledge what they have done, and ask for forgiveness.

But instead of confessing their sin to God, Adam and Eve respond by hiding in shame, then justifying their actions by blaming each other and making excuses. The story of sin for all of humankind is, unfortunately, one that mimics their actions. First, Adam and Eve hide in shame. Rather than admit their sins, they hide from God, hoping that the whole affair will soon be forgotten and glossed over. How many times have we likewise attempted to bury our guilt and shame deep inside, quickly moving on to the next activity to distract us from the negative feelings? Of course, running from guilt does not make it go away, and only leads to a further erosion of our soul. We discover, when we run from our guilt, an increased proclivity to commit the same sin again and again. No one understands this better than recovering alcoholics: those who pretend they are not addicts only fall further into addiction. In fact, the first step to recovery according to *Alcoholics Anonymous* is to admit that you are an alcoholic.

While they are hiding in shame, God approaches Adam and Eve, again questioning them in order to provide space for confession. While Adam and Eve acknowledge what they have done, they refuse to take responsibility for their actions. They point the finger at each other and at the serpent in an attempt to deny personal responsibility. Adam blames Eve, Eve blames the snake, and neither acknowledge that their actions are a result of their own selfishness. The history of sin for all of humankind has thus been marked, not by honest confession, but by obstinate self-justification. We sin, and immediately begin crafting a story in our minds that minimizes our guilt and places the responsibility of our failings on others. One of the main perpetrators of the Holocaust, Adolf Eichmann, was arrested and tried for crimes against humanity. Through his conviction and execution, Eichmann continued to deflect his own guilt, blaming his superior officers, and insisting that he was just following orders. His denial of sin should not surprise us. Each and every one of us has the spectacular ability to justify and minimize the effect of our sinful actions. This is because we have all inherited the venom of sin, and with that comes the desire to hide our sin from God.

THE CONSEQUENCES OF SIN: DISHARMONY, LABOR, NAKEDNESS, AND EXPULSION

Adam and Eve were created to have their desires for home, harmony, work, and worship fulfilled in a living and vibrant relationship with God on Mount Eden. Instead, their sin created a rift in their relationship with God whose consequences fatally permeated their entire existence. One way of understanding this damage is to see how these four longings became distorted once Adam and Eve's relationship with God was severed.

First, instead of *harmony*, there is *disharmony*. Adam and Eve were the caretakers for all of God's creation, living in harmony with one another and all living creatures. But now, because of sin, they are unable to care for this creation as they should. As a result, all of creation falls into disharmony and disrepair. I once spent a year as a substitute teacher at a high school, and quickly discovered that I was terrible at it. Students would never do their work when I was in the classroom, and behavioral issues occurred nearly every time I taught. I even had a spontaneous pillow fight erupt in one of the classes I was teaching! As the head of the class, my ineptitude reverberated to those below me. We see a similar dynamic in other areas of life: bad coaches create poor sports teams, and dysfunctional parents create dysfunctional families. Since Adam and Eve were the caretakers of all of creation, their dysfunction reverberated throughout the entire world.

Genesis 3 describes the full extent of this disharmony. We see that there is enmity between creatures and humans—the snake will bite the heel of Eve's offspring, and Eve's offspring will step on the serpent's head (Genesis 3:15). This symbolizes the animosity we now experience with animals. The created world is still beautiful, but it is now a world that can harm us as well. Furthermore, there is now animosity between human beings. Adam and Eve no longer get along perfectly. Instead of taking care of each other, Adam now rules over Eve. The long history of oppression of women begins at this moment, as does our whole human history of failed, fractured, and broken relationships. Instead of being at peace with one another, we fight, ignore, dominate, and oppress; sometimes in small ways, such as gossiping, and other times in large ways, as in the case of war and violence. Despite our best intentions, we cannot seem to get along with *anyone* perfectly.

There is even disharmony within the human body itself. Childbearing, the joyful ability to bring forth new life, is now tinged with pain and difficulty. For a premodern world, in which women often died during labor, this curse would have been known all too well. Furthermore, there is disharmony in the mind. Adam and Eve are confused at their nakedness, covering themselves with fig leaves. Confusion and neuroticism are the results of a mixed-up mind, in which even our own internal dialogue is off kilter.

Second, instead of *work*, there is arduous *labor*. The disharmony that exists between human beings also extends to the ground itself around Mount Eden. Instead of joyful and fruitful work on Mount Eden, Adam and Eve must garden in the thistles and thorns outside of Eden. This work is harsh, requiring pain and sweat. It is tedious, requiring much labor to produce meager crops. From this point onward, our history of work is also tinged with ardor and pain. The cool waters of the river of life are replaced by the salty sweat on our brows. Work is exhausting, tedious, and boring. We labor away at difficult tasks only to find precious little time remaining for other things in life.

Third, instead of *worship*, there is *nakedness*. The greatest self-inflicted malady experienced by Adam and Eve comes in the sudden realization of their nakedness. This is not only a sign of their confusion and loss of innocence, but most importantly, it is a sign that they no longer reflect the glory of God—they have "divested themselves of the glory surrounding them."[3] The radiance which once enveloped and clothed them has been lost as they move away from God's presence. They have lost their heavenly garments and can only see the nakedness that lies underneath. The brightness of God's glory no longer envelopes them, and they see in detail what that glory was covering: naked, frail bodies.

The removal of God's glory reveals the fragility of the human body. Adam and Eve have removed themselves from the source of being, existence, and life. If I pull the plug out of my laptop, its power will slowly diminish until it dies. Adam and Eve have similarly removed themselves from the power source of life, and they instantly see their glory fading, their life slowly draining away. Not only is their life now marked with the tedium of labor, it has also lost its source of vivacity. Life is now marked less by God's glory and more by death. And so it is for us today. We experience the pain of lost loved ones, and the pain of our own bodies breaking down, all because we are no longer connected to God who is the very source of our life.

Lastly, instead of *home*, Adam and Eve experience *separation* from Eden. The story told in Genesis 3 is often simply called "the fall." We can see the story as a literal fall from the mountain of Eden. Adam and Eve lose the ability to be in God's presence and must leave the mountain. God declares that they must be kept off of this mountain lest they eat from the tree of life while still possessing sinful hearts. The issue underlying this declaration is God's holiness. God is perfectly good, true, and beautiful, and as such he cannot be united to that which is imperfect. God cannot be 99 percent good; he cannot be diluted. Imagine if someone were to draw a large black line across the *Mona Lisa*. No matter what portion of the original can still be seen, the piece as a whole has been irreparably damaged. The black line must be removed. It cannot simply be ignored.

Adam and Eve must be removed and separated from the mountain, since God cannot be contaminated. They are cast out of the mountain, separated from Eden by water and a flaming *sword*, which symbolize the barrier that now exists between humankind and God. We can think here of a medieval thief, kicked out of a castle and banished to the harsh wilderness outside of the kingdom. He is prevented from reentering by the castle moat and the swords of the guards. Adam and Eve are banished from the safety of their home on Mount Eden, and must live their lives in the wilderness, the place of chaos, the place of barrenness and toil, the place of disharmony, and the place of death.

A SPLIT BETWEEN HEAVEN AND EARTH

As we have seen, sin creates separation for Adam and Eve. That separation involves both a physical separation from Mount Eden, which is represented by the flaming sword, but also a spiritual separation from God. Adam and Eve can no longer walk in God's presence in the garden of Eden, they cannot speak to God with the same intimacy they once shared, and their bodies no longer reflect God's glory. One of the ways to think about this separation is to consider a split between the physical and the spiritual, the earthly and the heavenly, and the sacred and the secular. On Eden, there was a unity between these things: the ground of Eden radiated with the heavenly presence of God. The physical bodies of Adam and Eve felt the spiritual presence of God in their bodies and heard the heavenly voice of God with their ears. The ordinary, secular activity of work was honored as sacred labor (see sidebar on senses).

Now, due to sin, there is a separation. The ground east of Eden does not radiate with God's presence. Work takes place in ordinary, secular time. Furthermore, there is a split in Adam and Eve's senses: they can still hear, but can no longer fully hear God's voice. They can still touch and feel, but they can no longer feel God's presence around them. Sight, touch, taste, hearing, and smelling are now ordinary and earthly, no longer imbued with heavenly adornment.

As a result, God feels more distant and separate, residing far away in heaven as opposed to being present on Eden. One of the ways the Bible speaks about this distance is to describe God as residing in his heavenly temple (or heavenly tabernacle). This is the place of God's pure presence and, because of sin, it cannot contain the presence of any human being. The sun in the sky still reminds us of God's pure glory, but now it also reminds us of just how far away from God we are. Just as our bodies are millions of miles away from the sun, our souls are light years away from God. As we will discover, God's mission to save the world will involve not only dealing with the problem of sin, but also creating a way to have heaven and earth, the spiritual and material, come together as one. Just as God's glory shone on Mount Eden, the Bible promises that his glory will shine once again on Mount Zion.

LIFE EAST OF EDEN: SIN AND MERCY

As the rest of the Old Testament will chronicle, life east of Eden is marked by a continuous struggle with sin, yet also by the continual mercy of God. We are given glimpses of both humanity's struggle and God's mercy in the final sentences of Genesis 3.

Humanity's struggle with sin is seen in the wrestling between Eve's offspring and the serpent. Humanity will continually attempt to trample out evil and bring about goodness and justice in the world, but evil will always reoccur on earth, popping up in new and unexpectedly wicked manifestations. This continual struggle is a sign that the venom of sin has infected humanity to the core. No number of good deeds can bring about its end. Instead, humanity must wait for a whole-scale cleansing of sin from the inside out. The poison must be removed, not just from our arms and legs, but from our hearts and our souls.

While this struggle with sin and evil now characterizes human existence, God does not abandon his good creation. While Adam and Eve can no longer return to Eden, they are still loved by God. God still shows Adam and Eve mercy, making for them garments to care for them amidst the harsh wilderness east of Eden.

Physical and Spiritual Senses

Human beings have five physical (outer) senses: seeing, hearing, feeling, smelling, and tasting. But they also have five corresponding spiritual (inner) senses related to these physical ones. We see with our physical eyes, and we see pictures in our mind's eye. We hear words with our ears, and we hear words in our head. We can feel a hand on our shoulder, and we also have inner feelings in our heart. We even have an inner smell and taste: all we have to do is think of the best meal we have ever had and we can have an inner sensation of its aroma and flavor.

Human beings are designed to have all of these senses, both inner and outer, attuned to God. We are created to hear God out loud and to hear God's word in our hearts. We are all created to one day see God with our physical eyes just as we see God with our mind's eye. We are created to taste of God's goodness in our souls just as we are created to one day taste of the trees in paradise.

On Mount Eden, we see that Adam and Eve had their senses aligned to God: they were able to physically hear God and get a physical glimpse of God as they walked with him in the garden. However, after the fall, they lost their outer, physical ability to see God as they were banished from God's presence on the mountain. Furthermore, their inner, spiritual sense of God grew weaker and weaker. God's voice became only a faint whisper in their hearts, and they no longer felt his love as they once did on Eden.

The story of the Bible is in part a story of God restoring these senses by rescuing us from sin. As we will see, the various symbols in the Bible appeal to our senses: we hear the howling wind, smell a fragrant oil, and taste a fine wine. Through the Holy Spirit we can have our inner, spiritual senses renewed right now, and have assurance that both our inner and outer senses will be fully attuned to God when we reach Mount Zion.

However, these garments are not the brilliant white robes of his glory, but instead the blood-stained skins of animals. As we will see, the mercy that God shows Adam and Eve in this simple act of provision is indicative of a greater love and mercy that he has for his creation. Adam and Eve are expelled from the mountain and God's presence, but God is still at work in the wilderness. The land outside of Eden is now sinful and broken as well as chaotic, but God still chooses to sustain this life, as damaged as it may be. God's creation is broken, but not destroyed.

As God's love continues to sustain life outside of the mountain, God will continue to pour out his love and mercy, eventually initiating a rescue mission to enable a path for humanity to return to his mountain. This rescue mission will culminate in God's Son falling on the sword that separates us from Eden, thereby taking us through the waters of death to plant us firmly in paradise forever. But before we can get to this rescue mission, we must first turn to a fuller depiction of the sinful and broken life outside of Eden, a sinfulness that reaches its culmination in the man-made creation of the false mountain of Babel.

Notice how the human race, instead of managing to keep to their own boundaries, always longs for more and reaches out for greater things. This is what the human race has lost in particular, not being prepared to recognize the limitations of their own condition but always lusting after more and entertaining ambitions beyond their capacity.

—*John Chrysostom*

5

THE FALSE MOUNTAIN OF BABEL

On Genesis 11 and Psalm 2

God has given us these symbols to lift our hearts toward him. He has given us trees to lift our eyes to the tree of life, and water to remind us of the gift of life in Christ. But because of sin, we fail to look to God and behold his glory, choosing instead to look downward, fixating on our own dusty feet. We exchange the beauty of creation for the blunt dullness of man-made things; brick and mortar become our mountains. Rather than longing to return to the mountain of God, we've made our home in this sinful world, worshiping material things and glorifying ourselves. Such is life east of Eden.

EAST OF EDEN: INCREASE IN HUMANITY, SIN, AND DISTANCE

Sin expands and multiplies with the expansion of humankind. Over the past few centuries, we have seen a remarkable explosion in the numbers of people that populate the earth, and enormous technological advancements that make life easier and more comfortable for millions. And yet, along with such expansions have come new and more brutal ways to kill others. The more cities grow and expand, the more crimes seem to multiply. Each technological advancement that helps humankind brings with it a new technology of war that enables us to destroy one another more efficiently.

This is no coincidence. The Bible tells us that the expansion of humankind also brought with it an expansion of human sin. After Adam and Eve are banished from Mount Eden, they begin to populate the earth with their offspring. However, since sin is now encoded into the human soul, each addition to the human race multiplies the damaging effects of sin. We see this vividly in the story of Cain, the first son of Adam and Eve. Cain's murder of his brother Abel shows how much more devastating the effects of sin have become. As a result, Cain is banished further from God's presence and further east of Eden. The ensuing chapters of Genesis continue to reveal this pattern, as increasing population increases human sin. The culmination of humanity's sinful journey east of Eden comes when human civilization bands together to build a technological wonder: the Tower of Babel.

THE TOWER OF BABEL: THE MAN-MADE MOUNTAIN

The Tower of Babel is the peak of human sin in the Bible. Upon first glance, the building of this tower appears to be rather innocuous: human beings have one language, and they have decided to join together to build a tall building. We typically think of skyscrapers as objects of wonder, rather than the product of nefarious activity. But when we look more closely at this passage, the sinister motives of its creators begin to emerge. We can see this by examining the materials used for its foundation, the labor employed for its erection, and the reasons given for its construction.

First, the tower was constructed through the production and placement of enormous quantities of bricks for its foundation. In order to make these bricks, stones were pulverized into dust, and then reformed and heated in an extensive firing process. As it is today, this process was arduous and tiresome, more so in societies that lack modern machinery. Furthermore, the formation of these bricks required a massive destruction of that area's topography, most likely leading to soil erosion and flooding. As it is today, the construction of large structures often requires the harvesting and devastation of the land.

You can tell quite a bit about structures by looking at their foundations. As a demolition contractor, my father can easily discern the quality of a building by a simple inspection of its ground floor. Before I purchased my first home, my father took one look at the basement and knew instantly that it was built to last. In the Bible, *stones* are symbols for whatever is foundational in our lives. The contrast between the foundation of Eden and the foundation of Babel informs us of their quality: the foundation of Eden is adorned with precious stones of bdellium and onyx that speak to the beauty of God's creation. They were opulent, radiant stones, handcrafted by God to vivify the ground on which Adam and Eve walked. Babel, by contrast, is built upon dull bricks formed through the destruction and reformation of stone. The contrast between Eden and Babel is striking: the beautiful God-crafted stones of Eden are pulverized, powdered, and burned in order to make the man-made stones of Babel. The foundation of Babel is made through the ugly degradation of Eden. Humankind grinds the stones of Eden to dust, refashioning it into brick to serve their own ambitions. It is a sign that God is no longer the foundation of human life.

The making of these bricks and the construction of this tower also necessitated an extraordinary amount of labor. The difficulty of this work meant that slaves were conscripted and forced to carry the burden of the tower's construction. Hundreds, if not thousands of lives were lost in this agonizing and burdensome process. While we may ask ourselves why human beings would risk so many lives for the creation of a physical structure, to this day, numerous laborers die each year in the construction of skyscrapers and stadiums. This was perhaps most visible in the recent construction of Qatar's World Cup stadiums, which led to the deaths of at least 6500 workers, most of whom were poorly paid immigrants. The risking of cheap labor for the construction of man-made wonders is still a practice very much alive today.

And so, what on the surface appeared to be a peaceful joining together of humanity for a building project, was actually the joining together of the rich and powerful to exploit their fellow humans and devastate the environment. Why would people ever decide to partake in such a venture? In order to understand this compulsion, we must look to what this tower signified, and then look at the ultimate purpose behind its construction.

The tower of Babel was a man-made mountain modeled after Eden. Since human beings are now far away from Eden and are incapable of returning to its heights, they decide to build their own mountain in order to get closer to God. The tower is meant to rise to the heavens (Genesis 11:4). Human beings attempt to force God to meet them by creating a marvel that he must acknowledge as great. If they cannot climb Mount Eden, they will create their own structure capable of reaching its heights, forcing God to descend.

So much of our own work is predicated on a similar desire to be recognized, which is rooted in our own insecurities. When we feel separated or detached from the love of a friend or a parent, we will attempt to earn their love by some great deed or accomplishment. Recently I was a finalist for a prominent job position that had a high salary and a lofty title. While part of me wanted to get this job out of a desire to serve and provide for my family, there was another part of me that wanted this job in order to impress my father. Even after forty years of life, there is still a part of me that is not secure in my father's love, and as such, my achievements are rooted in a desire for him to look upon my accomplishments and shout "well done."

The builders of Babel are separated from a loving relationship with their heavenly Father, and out of that insecurity they long desperately to compel God to come down from heaven and shout "well done." But what Babel's builders refuse to acknowledge is that it is their sin, not their lack of achievement, that separates them from God. The tower of Babel is both a symbol and warning to each and every one of us: there is imbedded deep in our sinful souls a desire to reach God through our good and marvelous deeds while simultaneously ignoring our sin which is the very reason we *cannot* reach God.

Much like ourselves, the builders of Babel are fixated on their goodness and need to display their greatness for the world to see. This is seen most vividly as they disclose the purpose of Babel's construction: "let us make a name for ourselves" (Genesis 11:4).

When we convince ourselves of our goodness, and when we convince ourselves that our achievements have merited the attention of God, we become people who ultimately desire *our* glory rather than God's glory. When we fail to acknowledge our need for God, we set out to make ourselves God's rival. Babel is in this way a complete perversion of the mountain of God. If Eden is the place of God's glory, where human beings can encounter God, Babel is the mountain of human glory, where human beings challenge God.

THE CONSEQUENCES OF THE SIN OF BABEL

My wife grew up watching classic black and white movies and admiring the legendary actors and actresses from the 1940s and 1950s. When we watch movies like *White Christmas* and *It Happened One Night*, I am prompted to read more about some of these famous people from the silver screen. What I often find is that these performers had sad and miserable lives. Nearly every one seemed to struggle with depression and addiction, divorce and abuse. These were people that were idolized and admired. Millions of people would give anything in the world to dance like Vera Allen or sing like Bing Crosby. These people had the world but couldn't acquire internal happiness. The actor Jim Carey once summed up this dilemma by remarking: "I hope everybody gets rich and famous and will have everything they ever dreamed of so they will know it's not the answer."

There is an ironic component to human sin. In sin, we seek to fulfill our own desires on our own schedule apart from God's will. But the irony of our sin is that we often *get* what we desire, but find that it was not all that it was cracked up to be. We see this effect of sin from its inception: Adam and Eve desired the knowledge of good and evil on their own terms, rather than on God's terms. The irony is that, when they ate of the tree, they actually received the knowledge of good and evil, but this knowledge only made them anxious and fearful.

Human beings constructed Babel in order to force God to descend and acknowledge their great deed, and they got what they wanted. God does descend in response to the completion of Babel, but instead of elevating them to greatness, he scatters them. The tower was built out of a false sense of unity—the rich and powerful believed they had united the world, when really, they had merely united the rich in oppressing the weak—and the consequence was not further unity, but disunity. Human beings are scattered across the earth and their languages multiply. Ever since Babel, human history has been marked by confusion and hostility amongst various languages and cultures. As we will see, in order to bring about true harmony amongst people, God must act, and human beings must confess their sins in order to be vessels capable of receiving his unifying Holy Spirit. The fire that hardened the bricks of Babel and the hearts of its builders must be countered by the fire of the Holy Spirit received by the followers of Jesus at Pentecost.

BABEL AS THE PERVERSION OF HOME, PEACE, WORK, AND WORSHIP

If the mountain of God is the place in which our desires for home, peace, work, and worship find their fulfillment, it is on the man-made mountain of Babel that we find the full perversion and denigration of these desires. If we find these images distorted and twisted after Adam and Eve's sin, we find this distortion magnified to its highest extent at Babel.

Babel is a false home. If the mountain is meant to be the place where we are at home with God our maker, Babel is an attempt to find our home entirely apart from God. It is a home built entirely by human hands and human stones, far away from God's glory on Mount Eden. This is a sign that human beings have plunged so far into the depths of their sin that it has begun to feel like home. They are so far removed from the glory and splendor of God that they think mud and brick is beautiful. We are similarly tempted to make our home in the brick and mud of our lives, giving up our struggle with sin and delighting in our waywardness. Rather than fighting the serpent, we are energized by its venom. The politician who boasts of their power, the alcoholic who gleefully goes on a bender, the lothario who brags about their sexual conquests, are all making their home in Babel.

Babel is a false peace. One of the consequences of sin is disharmony instead of peace. Adam and Eve experience this in their relational animosity and their difficulty in interacting with the animal kingdom. Babel takes this one step further: the builders of Babel *believe* they are at peace with one another even while they are exploiting slaves. There is only here the illusion of peace. To this day, human beings are quick to declare a peace that ignores injustice. The politicians of the small country of Bhutan often declare that it is one of the most peaceful and happiest countries on earth. These statements often overlook the deportation of over 100,000 ethnically Nepalese citizens who were expelled from the country and forced into refugee camps in the 1990s. Peace and unity is maintained only at the expense of the vulnerable. But such declarations of false peace are not limited to countries. Any time we proclaim harmony without acknowledging our own sins, we are partaking in a false peace. Anytime we declare an end to relational conflict without acknowledging our role in that conflict, we participate in the peace of Babel.

Babel is a false work. Instead of work being a joyful cultivation of God's creation, Adam and Eve must work through sweat, labor, and toil. Babel magnifies this malady. Slaves toil not just to the point of sweat, but to the point of death. Instead of cultivating God's creation, the labor of Babel destroys God's creation. The product of labor is not the production of necessary things such as food or clothing, but a meaningless tower. Ever since, the history of humankind has involved the destruction of the environment and the exploitation of labor to produce frivolous material goods. Such devastation occurs on both large and small scales. The coal miner contracts black lung to produce coal that will pollute the air, all to power pocket sized LED screens which display violent and sexual images. Our consumption of energy in these ways participates in the false work of Babel.

Finally, *Babel is false worship.* Adam and Eve are prevented from entering Mount Eden for the rest of their lives, and it is a source of constant sorrow and weeping. Now, human beings have made their home in the sinful, chaotic world, and no longer mourn the loss of Eden. Instead of desiring to enter the mountain to worship God, they build a tower so that God might worship them. Sin reached its pinnacle in Babel and continues to this day. Human beings no longer desire to worship God, but instead desire for God to worship them. We do not long for God's mountain, but instead long for human towers built on crushed stone. At its core, sin is the desire to place ourselves above God and above others, and it is at Babel where human beings are finally honest about their sinful intentions: they want to make a name for themselves. In our sin, we long desperately for recognition and accolades and are driven by the desire for others to marvel at us. We want others to admire our accomplishments, so we place work above friends and family. We want others to appreciate our sense of humor, so we make fun of others. We want others to marvel at our physical bodies, so we engage in sexual seduction and immorality. We worship ourselves, and desire for others to worship us, and in so doing, we participate in the false worship of Babel.

Each touch of a rough brick façade is a reminder of the illusion of the greatness of our works. We all wish that our lives would stand out like a large skyscraper, but deep down we know that, just as those bricks will one day turn to rubble, so will the memories of all our accomplishments.

THE NEED FOR A NEW COMMUNITY

Babel reveals the depths and heights of human sin. Our sin has magnified and multiplied, moving from an individual bite of forbidden fruit to a civilization-wide exercise in false worship. In the wake of Babel, the peoples scatter and become confused and hostile to each other and God. It is at this point, in the full manifestation of sin, that God decides to begin his rescue mission. Humanity has become so depraved that God decides to begin his saving mission by creating a new nation and a new community from scratch. Starting with Abraham, God will begin the slow process of forming a people capable of seeing and knowing him in a world marked by darkness and confusion. This people will be called Israel. Their story begins with Abraham and reaches its apex on Mount Sinai. And so, the tragic story of Mount Eden ends with the tower of Babel in Genesis 11, but this is also where the redemptive story of Mount Sinai begins.

PART 2:

THE STORY OF MOUNT SINAI

Abraham offered God a mortal son who was not put to death;
God delivered to death an immortal Son for humanity.

—*Origen*

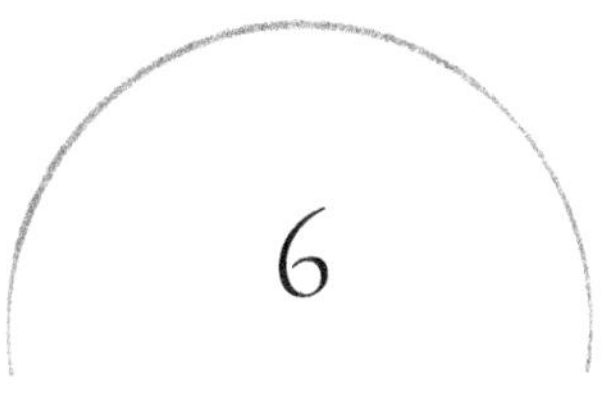

ABRAHAM

On Genesis 11–25 and Psalm 105:1–15

Deep in every human soul, there is a longing for the mountain of God. In moments of great joy and quiet beauty, we sense that there is more to life than the material things of the world. These longings often emerge as pictures in our imagination. We get glimpses of some hoped for future, but the images are random and disjointed. We can only contemplate the mountain of God as a sneak preview, a glorious glimpse of coming attractions.

OBEDIENCE AND FAITH

Obedience for many of us in a four-letter word. Few of us like to be obedient, and fewer still are willing to obey without putting up a fight. As the owner of a demolition company, my father would find himself shorthanded from time to time. One week during Christmas break he needed extra help demolishing a hotel in Dubois, PA, and so at the dinner table that night he gave my brother and I a simple command: get ready to wake up at 4 a.m.

to help tear down this hotel. Not wanting to give up a relaxing holiday break with my friends, I put forth every excuse possible to try to get out of working, but to no avail. I went to work the next morning, mopey and grumbling, and spent the rest of Christmas break knee-deep in dust and grease.

Our aversion to obedience should come as no surprise, since all the sin and brokenness in the world began with one act of disobedience by Adam and Eve. This is one of the reasons why God begins to reverse this curse of Eden by inviting a simple herdsman to a life of obedience. He calls this herdsman, Abraham, to pack his bags, take his entire family and possessions, and head west. God's simple call is met with simple obedience: "Abraham went, as the Lord had told him" (Genesis 12:4). There is no lengthy interrogation or bargaining session. Abraham simply leaves his home country without questioning God's rationale for this command. Of all the people living in the world, God called Abraham; a rancher living in an obscure part of the world with no apparent education. We are given no indication that he was a particularly intelligent, noble, or shrewd individual, nor that he had accomplished notable deeds before his encounter with God. He seems so very *ordinary*. And yet *this* is the person God chose to begin to reverse the curse.

Why did God choose him? The answer to this question can be found in Abraham's response to God. God asks Abraham to radically uproot his existence—to leave behind his homeland and his father, to journey to an unknown land, to risk his physical and financial security, without any explanation. Abraham does not quarrel or question this instruction. Instead, he believes God and obeys. We call this act of belief and obedience *faith*.

To have faith is to share in Abraham's act of trusting in God. God calls each and every one of us to believe and trust in him, and, like Abraham, we can choose to listen and obey, or ignore and delay. For some of us, the challenge to having faith is listening: we are too busy to stop and hear God calling us. We spend every waking hour of our lives caught up in the affairs of the world and lack the time and space to hear God calling our name. Our hearts resemble the crowded chaos of Babel and not the open and serene pastures of Haran.

For others, faith can be difficult because we have trouble obeying God. Following God may mean leaving behind some of our favorite comforts and pleasures. Rather than responding like Abraham, we easily come up with excuses to delay responding to God. When I was a youth group leader, I had a conversation with a high school student who was just introduced to Jesus. He was excited to hear about the life he could experience with God right now, but he was hesitant. He knew he would have to give up drinking and partying, and maybe even some friendships in order to be obedient to God. And so his answer to God's call was "someday when I'm older." I have had this kind of conversation with many people, and for most of them "someday" never comes.

Abraham stands as the model of faith and a consistent challenge to all of us to have simple hearts set to obey God. While Abraham's simple obedience to God's calling challenges us, his humble origins should also comfort us. Abraham was an ordinary person. We do not have to be special in the eyes of the world to be called by God. We do not need to be intelligent, wealthy, or successful to have faith. God is not waiting for us to perform some great, pious deed before approaching us. Instead, he calls us where we are at, in the midst of the trials and challenges of everyday life, and asks us to believe, trust, and follow him.

A SNEAK PREVIEW

I remember as a kid seeing a sneak preview for the 1989 movie *Batman*. The preview was filled with images of Batman and the Joker, and snippets of scenes from the movie cut and pasted together to grab the viewer's attention. I was captivated and could not wait to visit the theaters to see the full story that had been teased in that brief preview.

Abraham's journey with God is sneak preview of the rest of the biblical story. It introduces images and symbols that will emerge again at Sinai, Tabor, and Zion. God arranges Abraham's life so that we begin to get a glimpse of these symbols and get excited about the continuation of the story of God's redemption. In these experiences, Abraham enters sacred time, and is thus able to experience some of the future in the present (see sidebar on Sacred Time).

But just like a movie preview, the stories in Abraham's life have a kind of cut and paste quality to them. We do not get the full plot of the movie, only a series of scenes meant to capture our imaginations and make us excited for more. Abraham himself does not seem to grasp the sinews between the events in his life; he is merely trusting in God through life's twists and turns. However, as we read the story of Abraham millennia later, we can discern the connective tissue between his life and the story and symbols of the entire Bible. As we will discover, Abraham's adventures are simultaneously stories about Jesus. We see in these stories early encounters with the recurring symbols of *altar*, *bread*,

Sacred Time

Time is different on the mountain than in the rest of the world. We normally think of time as linear, something that always moves forward like the days on a calendar. What is in the past is forever gone and cannot be revisited. However, when we enter into God's presence, we are approaching the one who is above and outside of time, because God created time.

To encounter God is thus to enter into what is known as sacred, or heavenly time. God is capable of drawing together events from the past and future for us, enabling us to experience them in the present. Throughout the Bible, when people climb the mountain and draw near to God, they enter sacred time. In this chapter, Abraham is able to experience the future death and resurrection of Jesus through the near sacrifice of his son Isaac on Mount Moriah. Later, prophets will receive visions that draw together past, present, and future. The culmination of sacred time comes in Jesus's death and resurrection, where he will heal past, present, and future sin.

When we read the Bible, we too can enter into sacred time. We experience the past of Abraham and Moses as if they were present to us, and get a taste of our future life on Mount Zion when we are lifted up into the heavenly visions in the book of Revelation.

wine, and *lamb* that draw us to Jesus. God desires to teach us about Jesus's death and resurrection and our life in communion with Jesus through the ups and downs of Abraham's life. We will proceed by taking a brief snapshot of these various scenes from Abraham's journey, showing how his story and the symbols he encounters invite us to see Jesus and ourselves in the pages of Abraham's life.

MOUNTAINS AND ALTARS

As humankind is pushed further east of Eden, they are also pushed further away from God. By the time we get to Abraham, he is far away in Haran, and God has to ask him to pack up his bags and move west, back towards Eden. During his travels he frequently scales mountains in order to be with God. Abraham hungers intuitively for the mountain of God and knows that climbing these mountains offers opportunities to connect with him. What does Abraham do when he climbs these mountains? He builds *altars*, a symbol of worship and fellowship with God. We see this most vividly when Abraham scales a mountain east of Bethel, where he "built an altar to the Lord and called upon the name of the Lord" (Genesis 12:8). Abraham makes altars on top of several of these mountains in order to meet God, calling on God's name in worship.

These mountains were for Abraham the premier location through which he could encounter God. On one of these occasions, God even refers to himself as El Shaddai, which means "God of the mountain." Since mountains are the meeting place between God and humanity, we should not be surprised that God refers to himself in this way. Jesus will even refer to himself in a similar way, calling his body the temple, the mountain in the flesh.

Just as Adam and Eve ascended and descended Mount Eden, Abraham took special time during his journeying to climb mountains, create altars, and meet with God. Christians likewise follow in the footsteps of Abraham every time we take a break from our sojourning in the world and enter church. Church is meant to be a respite from the cares and concerns of the week, a time to both receive peace from God and engage in the worship of God. As Abraham ascended the mountain to approach God at the altar, so Christians ascend the pews of the church to approach Christ at the altar for communion.

BREAD AND WINE

We often celebrate big events with friends, food, and drink. Birthdays, weddings, and anniversaries are moments to gather with those we love around a table for food, fellowship, and merriment.

An altar is a table set aside for the worship of God, and so it should come as no surprise that one of the principal things we do at an altar is have a celebration with God over food and drink. Abraham is given the opportunity to have one of the first of these special feasts with God after he wins a dramatic victory over evil kings and rescues a group of captives. After this victory, Abraham is approached, seemingly out of nowhere, by a mysterious priest and king from Salem named Melchizedek. Melchizedek brings out bread and wine to celebrate, blessing Abraham and praising God Most High. Abraham responds by giving this enigmatic figure a tenth of his possessions (Genesis 14:13–24).

Ever since this day, *bread* and *wine* have been symbols of celebration and the worship of God. Just as fresh bread and fine wine are partaken of at wedding banquets on Saturdays, each Sunday Christians around the world gather together to celebrate the victory of Jesus over evil, bringing bread, wine, and a tenth of their earnings to the altar as they sing praises to God Most High. Like Melchizedek, Jesus our king joins us at this table, as this bread and wine become his body and blood. When we gather at the altar, we stand alongside Abraham in praise and thanksgiving for the victories of God. We celebrate not only Abraham's victory over the wicked kings, but also Jesus's ultimate victory over the wicked serpent.

TREES AND VISITORS

At the top of Mount Eden stood the tree of life, and with it the promise of a deep and mature relationship with God, a full experience of his dazzling glory. As part of his rescue mission, God wants to let humanity know that he still desires for them to join him under this tree. One day, God calls Abraham to camp out under a beautiful oak tree at Mamre. As Abraham rests underneath its shade, he is reminded of the eternal peace and rest that is promised him under the tree of life.

While underneath this tree, Abraham is approached by three mysterious visitors. Although Abraham sees three visitors, he speaks to them in the singular tense, referring to them collectively as one Lord. This is because Abraham knows he is having an encounter with God's glory. Recall from previous chapters, God's glory shines more brilliantly than the sun, engulfing those who encounter it. It is difficult to discern the details of a person when they are standing in front of the sun, and, likewise, when Abraham encounters God's radiance, he cannot tell whether he is speaking to three persons or one.

In this encounter, Abraham is having a vision of the Trinity, the unfathomable mystery that we worship one God in three persons: "In the fact that he saw three ... he understood the mystery of the Trinity; but since he adored them as one, he recognized that there is one God in the three persons."[1] Abraham continues to dialogue with one of these three, which many believe to be Jesus. Since Jesus is referred to in the Bible as the Word of God, it is Jesus who exchanges words with Abraham under the tree at

Mamre.[2] Later in the Bible, Jesus himself will refer to this conversation that he had with Abraham long before he took on flesh (John 8:56).

What Abraham experiences at Mamre is a sneak preview of Mount Zion, the final and eternal mountain of the Bible. He has an experience in sacred time, a moment where the future hope of Mount Zion is brought into his present. Abraham encounters God the Father, Son, and Holy Spirit, and has a personal conversation with Jesus underneath a tree. The hope for all humankind is to have this same experience: to one day be surrounded in God's glory and have a conversation with Jesus underneath the tree of life on Mount Zion.

SWORD AND SACRIFICE

While God gives to Abraham a sneak preview of the end of the biblical story, he also wants Abraham to know that this story is not just about victories and celebrations. These victories must come at a cost, and that God must first save humankind from the terrible consequences of sin. For this reason, God begins to educate Abraham and his descendants about the problem of sin, and what must ultimately be done to deal with this problem.

As we will see, the solution to the problem of sin is sacrifice—someone must fall on the sword separating us from Eden; someone must pass through the waters of death and bring us to new life in God. And so, in order to prepare humankind for what must be done, God calls Abraham to ascend a mountain with his son Isaac. Like many other trips up the mountain, Abraham is called to approach an altar for worship. But this time, God asks Abraham to do something more on this altar: use his sword to sacrifice Isaac (Genesis 22).

We can only imagine what was racing through Abraham's mind during this journey up the mountain. God was asking him to relinquish the life of his beloved son without any explanation. But, like so many other points in Abraham's life, he believes and trusts in God without fully understanding God's plan.

Isaac is also in the dark. As he is carrying wood up to the altar, he asks his father a simple question: "Where is the lamb for the burnt offering?" Abraham responds to his son with words of hope: "God will provide for himself the lamb." While Abraham is fully trusting and obedient with this extraordinarily difficult command of God, he also has hope that God will provide a way out of this terrible situation.

Just as Isaac places the wood on the altar, Abraham snatches Isaac and places him on the pile of wood. He then ties him up and pulls out his knife, ready to plunge it into Isaac's side. It is at this moment that God's angel yells "stop!" Abraham has passed the test. Isaac is taken down from the altar and a ram is found to take his place. Why does God test Abraham in this way? First, God wants to reveal to Abraham and his descendants that the seriousness of sin requires a sacrifice. Someone has to absorb all of the pain of human sin, and someone has to fall on the sword that separates us from the mountain of God. Second, God wants to show Abraham that no human being can take on this burden. A person may be able to give their life to save a friend or two, but no person is strong or pure enough to take upon themselves all the sins and evil in the world. As we will see in chapter 9, in the Old Testament, God provides a temporary solution to the problem of sin through the ritual sacrifice of animals. But this solution only creates a yearning for a full, permanent, and perfect sacrifice to take away the sins of the world forever.

Abraham cannot fully grasp the details of these future events. But as he descends down the mountain with his son Isaac, he gets an inkling of what needs to happen. As he reflects on this terrible ordeal, he recalls the words he spoke to his son while traveling up the mountain, and so he names this hill Mount Moriah, which means "God will provide."[3] What Abraham understands is that God will have to provide the true sacrifice, the true answer to sin. God will make Abraham's proclamation come true thousands of years later, by providing His own Son, Jesus. Like Isaac, Jesus will carry the wood of the cross up a mountain called Golgotha.[4] Jesus will be bound to this wood and raised up to the top of Golgotha as if on an altar. But unlike Isaac, Jesus will die on the cross, and the sword will pierce his side: "Great is the mystery, and utterly glorious, which Abraham's son performed on the mountain: he carried the wood with which to be burnt, he went out to die, unaware. A great act of discernment, and much to be wondered at, did the Son of God perform on earth: He carried the wood on which He was to be crucified, and He went forth to die, to deliver all."[5] It is thus on Mount Golgotha that Abraham's prediction will come true: God will provide.

THE PROMISE OF ZION

A promise invites faith. If someone promises something to me, I must have faith that one day they will fulfill their end of the bargain. I once met an elderly woman who grew up in a small village called Aboud in the West Bank north of Jerusalem. Her grandfather was the Christian pastor of this tiny community, a man loved by all who knew him. One day, soldiers from the Ottoman Empire came into town and arrested him for the sole reason that he was a Christian. Rather than executing him on the spot, this pastor negotiated his imprisonment in Turkey. Just before leaving, he promised to one day return to his wife and his community. The wife believed her husband's promise and never remarried. Then one day, years later, the pastor walked back into town, embraced his wife, and began pastoring his church again as if nothing had happened. Somehow, he had escaped from an Ottoman prison and walked all the way home from Turkey to Aboud. Despite great hardship and uncertainty, his wife had faith in his promise and was rewarded with a reunion and an unforgettable embrace from her husband.

Abraham was a flawed and imperfect person, yet he is nevertheless held up as the paragon of faith in the Bible, and this faith is directly tied to a promise that God gave to Abraham: that he would be the father of a great nation whose descendants would be as numerous as the stars and the sands. This nation would dwell in a promised land. Abraham sees the first seeds of this promise come true in his lifetime: his wife bears him a son named Isaac and he gets to walk on top of this promised land. But Abraham does not live to see it inhabited by a great nation. He dies long before his descendants would multiply and prosper. As Abraham lived his life in faithful obedience to God, he entered into death remaining in faith, trusting that God would keep his promises thousands of years later. As the biblical story progresses, the prophets begin to refer to the future gathering place of this great nation as Mount Zion. Mount Zion becomes the term used not only for a plot of promised land, but a land full of Abraham's descendants.

We can now see why Abraham is the model of faith in the Bible. Abraham is called to trust in the promises of God, knowing full well that he will die before seeing those promises fulfilled. This is a challenge for us, as we live in a world obsessed with instant gratification. We are used to getting what we want quickly, like a McDonald's cheeseburger. As such, we grow frustrated when others do not promptly accede to our demands. How often do we lose our patience when we must wait for a friend or stand in a line? It is easy to be just as demanding and impatient with God. When we pray, we expect instant results, and quickly blame and question God when we do not see our prayers answered in what we would consider a timely manner.

But God often works in centuries rather than days. In fact, the promise that God gives us of eternal life with Jesus on Mount Zion is the same promise given to Abraham thousands of years ago. Jesus promises that he will return and that we will one day embrace him. And just like Abraham, we must be willing to trust that God will fulfill this promise to us. We all stand with Abraham in between Mount Eden and Mount Zion. We trust in God throughout the trials and tribulations of life, stopping along the way to come to the altar, to worship God and celebrate his victory with bread and wine. We all long to stand under the tree of life and behold God's glory on Mount Zion. But we know that this longing will most likely be fulfilled long after we die. And so, we are asked to have the faith of Abraham, believing in the promises of God while we live, and trusting in those promises as we perish.

No one who hears this should be ignorant of the mystery of the water. He who has gone down into it with the army of the enemy emerges alone, leaving the enemy's army drowning in the water.

—*Gregory of Nyssa*

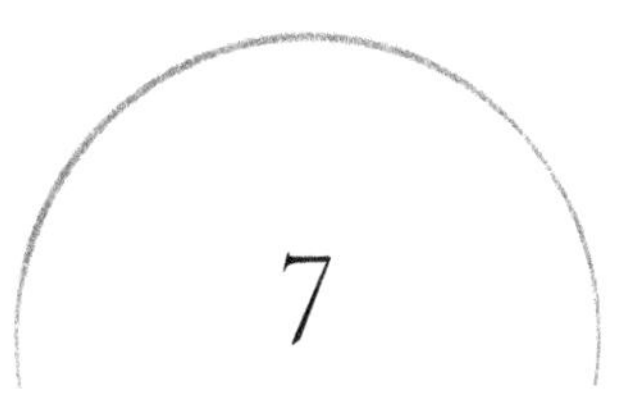

OUT OF SLAVERY AND INTO THE WILDERNESS

On Exodus 1, 4, 14–18 and Psalm 68:1–20

We all experience moments where we feel trapped in our sin. We all experience a sense of helplessness, that pull between wanting to obey God but also wanting to obey ourselves. For every stomp on the snake, there is a bite at our heel. The inescapable nature of sin is a kind of slavery, like being submerged in water without being able to swim to the surface. We know that escape cannot come on our own: we need to be rescued. Someone must enter the waters of our temptation and bring our souls safely through to dry land.

FROM ABRAHAM TO MOSES

The Old Testament continues by chronicling the history of Abraham's descendants from Isaac down to Jacob. Jacob fathers twelve sons and is given a new name by God: Israel. Israel becomes the name given to the nation that grew from Abraham, Isaac, and Jacob. Jacob's twelve sons form twelve tribes within this country.

But sin still remains. And sin manifests itself in continual hardship and devastation, culminating in a severe famine that forces the Israelites to work for food as slaves in the foreign country of Egypt. Their life in Egypt involved tiresome labor with little food or rest. They were forced by Pharaoh to work ruthlessly (Exodus 1:13), making the same kind of bricks that were used to construct the false mountain of Babel. Furthermore, this life in bondage was one of constant temptation, as the Israelites were surrounded by the false worship and false gods of the Egyptians. The ruler of Egypt himself, Pharaoh, wore a crown topped with a gold serpent—a constant reminder that their life in bondage was a life under evil.

Slavery is one of the devastatingly ironic consequences of human sin. Human sin is predicated upon a magnificent exertion of independence: Eve uses her freedom to eat the fruit and disobey God. However, one of the consequences of this grand act of freedom is that Adam begins to rule over Eve. In exerting her will to disobey God, Eve loses her ability to be truly free. Slavery is the large-scale manifestation of the oppressive consequences of sin: human beings use their independence to suppress the freedom of others. As W. E. B. Dubois once remarked: "Most men today cannot conceive of a freedom that does not involve somebody's slavery."[1]

The roots of slavery lie in human sin. The Bible uses the term to describe both the physical captivity of the Israelites in Egypt and *all* of humanity's captivity to sin. Physical slavery is but one of the many wicked manifestations of humanity's spiritual slavery to sin. From time to time, all of us experience sin as a kind of spiritual slavery. We feel spiritually oppressed and helpless in the face of an onslaught of temptation. We give in to desires that we know are harmful, yet we are powerless to resist them. This slavery to sin is most evident in our addictions—to alcohol, pornography, or even television. We experience both the desire to refrain from these activities and the inability to reform our behavior. In a famous passage later in the Bible, Paul laments his own experience of being seemingly trapped in sin: "I do not understand what I do. For what I want to do I do not do, but what I hate I do" (Romans 7:15, NIV). This helplessness is a signal that we need rescue from outside of ourselves. Slaves do not need improved conditions, they need *emancipation*. Slaves to sin do not need helpful tips to become better or nicer people, they need *salvation*. For this reason, God began his great rescue mission through the miraculous emancipation of the Israelites out of slavery, in turn showing us that he is a God that has the power to free anyone from physical and spiritual slavery.

God invites us to view the Exodus of Israel out of physical slavery as our own exodus out of spiritual slavery. We are invited to read ourselves *into* this story. We are called to experience the Israelites' *past* exodus out of slavery in Egypt as our *present* exodus out of slavery to sin. Here we will discover that salvation comes through a person, through blood, through water and through bread.

SALVATION THROUGH A PERSON

God loves starting small. In creating the world, God gave tiny seeds the capacity to grow into voluminous trees. He gave two small human beings the ability to tend and nurture a mountain full of animals and agriculture. And when the sin of humanity reached its apex on Babel, God decided to begin his rescue mission by calling a simple herdsman named Abraham to come to the mountain and worship him. When God initiates salvation, he begins with an individual person. And this is precisely how God begins his rescue of the Israelites. Just as God called Abraham up a mountain, God invites an individual person, Moses, up to a mountain called Horeb. Just as God spoke to Abraham at Mamre, God speaks to Moses on Horeb. He tells Moses that through him he will lead Israel out of slavery and into the promised land. In response, Moses asks God to identify himself, and God reveals his name, calling himself the great "I Am."

The exchanging of names is a crucial first step in a relationship. It's nearly impossible to have a deep friendship with someone if you do not know their name. In college, my wife Allison frequently encountered a mutual friend who could never seem to remember her name. One day out of frustration, she told him that her name was Grace. And sure enough, this fraudulent name was the one he finally remembered! He spent a full two years of college calling her Grace. Needless to say, they never became close friends.

This is one of the reasons why God reveals his name to Moses on Mount Horeb. God tells Moses his name because he wants to establish a more intimate and personal relationship with him. And through Moses, God wants to establish a personal relationship with all of God's people. This is why, as we will see in the next chapter, remembering and honoring God's name becomes an important part of this relationship.

In this brief exchange of names on Horeb, God reveals the purpose of his great rescue mission. While God promises Moses that he will emancipate his people from slavery, he wants to emancipate them *for* friendship with him. Freedom is not the ultimate goal, but rather freedom for the sake of friendship. As we will discover, this is also the goal of God's spiritual rescue mission. Jesus will go to the cross to rescue us from our spiritual slavery to sin, but this is not the final goal. Jesus wants to rescue us from sin so that he might also take us to the top of Mount Zion to be friends with him forever.

While Moses begins his friendship with God on Mount Horeb, it quickly becomes clear this is not like other human friendships. This is no relationship of equals. God is still the Almighty Creator of heaven and earth, and he reveals to Moses that he alone has the power to bring salvation. He alone has the ultimate power of life and death. God does this by working a number of miracles through Moses. First, Moses is told to throw his wooden staff on the ground. It instantly turns into a snake, and Moses runs away. God then instructs Moses to pick up the snake by the tail, and it turns back into wood. God is revealing that he has the power to conquer sin and evil. It is God alone who has the power to ultimately subdue Satan and all his serpentine forces. Second, Moses is told to place his hand in his shirt twice. The first time, his flesh appears to be dead and rotting. The second time, it turns back to normal. What God demonstrates in these actions is that he has power not only over sin, but also over the consequence of sin: death. He has the power to conquer the serpent and the power to heal those who have died by the serpent's venom.

What Moses experiences on Horeb is a confirmation that he is entering into a relationship with the God of the universe. But Moses is also experiencing in these interactions the death and resurrection of Jesus. It is no coincidence that the snake is killed by the lifting up of a wooden staff. Years later, Jesus will be lifted up on the cross to conquer evil, "as Moses lifted up the serpent in the wilderness" (John 3:14). The wood of the cross will be raised to the top of Mount Golgotha to bring about the decisive victory over the serpent. Furthermore, in seeing his dead flesh restored, Moses is experiencing "an anticipation of the resurrection of humankind," initiated by Jesus.[2] Shortly after the wood of the cross is lifted high on Golgotha, the decaying flesh of Jesus will be resurrected, restored, and glorified. Even today, when we experience the healing of a small cut on our hand or a bruise on our leg, we can catch a glimpse of the eternal healing that is made possible through the resurrection of Jesus. Just as Moses is called to be the one person to lead Israel out of physical slavery, Moses learns that it will be through one person, Jesus, that God will lead humanity out of spiritual slavery.

SALVATION THROUGH BLOOD

God taught Abraham the terrible lesson that sin requires sacrifice: someone must fall on the sword and spill their blood in order to absorb the pain and wickedness of sin. For this reason, God will bring about the salvation of the Israelites through the symbol of *blood* to reiterate the need for a sacrifice to deal with the manifold effects of sin.

After Moses is called by God on Mount Horeb, he confronts Pharaoh on numerous occasions, begging him to let God's people go and promising a series of plagues if Pharaoh refuses. After each encounter, the Bible states that Pharaoh's heart was hardened; even after seeing numerous, miraculous plagues, he is unconvinced of the power of God. Pharaoh is synonymous with those today who refuse to acknowledge and follow God despite overwhelming evidence to the contrary.

Finally, God initiates one final plague to convince Pharaoh. Moses warns him that, one terrifying night, an angel will sweep through Egypt, killing every firstborn human and animal in the country. In this great act, Pharaoh will realize the ultimate consequence of sin and disobedience: death. While Moses believes that this terrible event will indeed come to pass, there is a problem: the Israelites are still in Egypt. They too will experience this destruction unless God intervenes. Fortunately, God gives Moses instructions on how to avoid death: each Israelite household is commanded to slaughter a lamb, placing its blood on their doors. Then, they are to roast this lamb and eat a ceremonial meal with bread and wine. As God passes through Egypt, every household marked with the blood of the lamb is passed over (this is why this event is called the Passover), and their household is spared death. Not only did the blood of the lamb spare the Israelites from death, it also ensured their release from captivity. Pharaoh finally caved to Moses's demands after the Passover and allowed the captive Israelites to be set free from Egypt and slavery.

Since the day of the Passover, the symbols of *lamb* and *blood* have been signs of salvation for all of God's people. In the Passover, God revealed an eternal truth: the blood of the lamb saves. It is the blood of the lamb that rescues Israel from slavery, and it is the blood of the Lamb of God, Jesus, that rescues humanity from our slavery to sin. "It is not difficult to interpret the spotless lamb of Christ and his sacrifice made to free the slavery of our death," wrote Martin of Braga, "For, marked by the sign of his cross as by the sprinkling of blood, we shall be saved from the angels of destruction even to the consummation of the world."[3]

The Israelites remembered this incredible day of Passover with an annual meal of lamb, bread, and wine. At this Passover meal, they celebrated salvation through the blood of the lamb and fellowship with the God. Each time Christians gather to celebrate salvation through Jesus, they do so over a table of bread and wine. When they eat this food, they join together with the Israelites in eating that first Passover meal in Egypt.

SALVATION THROUGH THE WATERS

In our training to become foster parents, my wife and I learned about the devastating effects that an abusive home can have on a child. Often, when a child lives in a dysfunctional environment, they experience various developmental disorders. For many of these issues, there is little that can be done for the child while they are still in an abusive environment. In these tragic situations, the child must be removed from their home and placed in a different one so that they can begin to experience true healing.

Salvation and healing often require a change of location. For a gambling addict to recover, they need to stop frequenting casinos. For the alcoholic to be free of their slavery to liquor, they need to remove themselves from bars. The salvation of Israel also required a change of location. Israel would never be free from slavery while they tread on Egyptian soil. And so, the Passover culminated in an exodus, an escape out of Egypt. Even though Pharaoh had permitted this departure, he quickly changed his mind, amassing an enormous army to pursue the Israelites and force them to return to slavery. As they fled, Moses and the crowd hit a dead end at the Red Sea. With the Egyptian army in rapid pursuit, the Israelites are given a choice: they can either trust in God's ability to control the waters, or they can turn back to slavery in Egypt. The Israelites decide to put their trust in God, and God controls the waters to enable their safe passage through.

In creation, God brought about life through the taming of water, and in this passage, he brings the Israelites into new life by controlling the waters of the Red Sea through the wooden staff of Moses. The same wood that flattened the snake is now used by God to control the chaotic sea. Moses lifts his wooden staff, and a strong east wind, the same wind of the Holy Spirit which hovered over the waters of creation, causes the sea to split in two. Wood and wind enable a full rescue of Israel from slavery. Here, God is teaching all of us that true salvation can only come through the outstretched arms of Jesus. It is through these outstretched arms that the wind of the Holy Spirit can enter into our hearts, releasing us from our bondage to sin, evil, and death.

After the Israelites pass safely through the waters, a harrowing and gruesome picture follows. The Egyptian army attempts to pass through the turbulent Red Sea, but just as they are making their way through, God releases the waters. Soldier, horse, and chariot are swallowed up and crushed, and the Israelites see battered remains of the Egyptian army wash up to shore. It is at this moment that the Israelites erupt into celebration and song, for they realize that the army is no longer in pursuit and that they are truly free from the Egyptians. In this passage, they discover the deep meaning of the symbol of water. While water absorbs and demolishes evil, it is also a pathway to salvation. What Israel experiences in the Red Sea is a baptism. In baptism, God controls the raging waters, using them to both destroy sin and bring about new life. Christian baptism is itself a spiritual crossing of the Red Sea. God is calling us to have faith in him as we approach the waters. He invites us to trust that in stepping through the water, he will cleanse us of our sin. He invites us to emerge out of that water and breathe the first breaths of new, eternal life. But for water to hold this power, Jesus must first enter into it for us. Just as the wood of Moses's staff tamed the Red Sea, the wood of

Jesus's cross must tame the spiritual waters. Just as the wind split the sea in two, the Spirit of Jesus must move through the water to enable a spiritual salvation.

SALVATION SUSTAINED BY BREAD

As we saw with the revelation of God's name, salvation is not an end in itself. The goal of a prisoner is not just to get out of prison, but to be freed so they can start a new life of freedom. Similarly, God has set Israel free *from* slavery *for* life with him. God brings about salvation and simultaneously gives to Israel a mission: they are to travel to Mount Sinai and Mount Zion, learning how to live with God along the way. This journey, however, was through a still broken and sinful world, and so the Israelites had to journey with God through the wilderness, a place of hardship and exhaustion. They are asked to forge ahead, with the hope that God will bring them to the promised land.

The most rewarding experiences in our lives do not come easily. Learning an instrument requires tedious repetition of scales. A beautiful camping experience in the woods entails insect bites, sweat, and discomfort. As the Israelites traveled through their own wilderness on the way to Sinai, they experienced hardship. Life on the other side of emancipation was free, but not easy. Despite a firm knowledge of what God had done for them at the Red Sea, they began to waver in their confidence that there was something better ahead. They were tempted to return to Egypt, to exchange the promises of God for the more certain life of slavery. This desire to turn around was brought to a fever pitch when their food supplies began to run out, and their minds were filled with images of Egyptian fleshpots, a kind of meat stew. They longed, like so many migrants, for the comfort foods of home. In their hunger and weariness, they forgot about their desire to reach their new home and considered turning back to their old one.

This is no less true for those who have come through the waters of baptism. Baptism brings freedom from sin, but it also initiates a lifelong journey to the promised land of Mount Zion. This journey in a sinful world is often a slog, a wilderness of trials and temptation. Amidst these challenges, it is easy to think of life before God, to long for the comforts of the past, even when we know that these comforts are not what is best for us. We long to return to the comfort of a bad relationship or the security of an addiction rather than pressing forward with Jesus through the wilderness of life.

Fortunately, God responded to the cries and moans of the Israelites by giving them special food to eat while they journeyed in the wilderness: manna. Each morning, flakes arose from the ground which were gathered and made into a dense calorie rich bread. This bread from heaven had a special quality to it: it could not be stored for long periods of time. God gave the Israelites this bread not only to sustain them physically on their journey, but also to nourish them spiritually. The Israelites had to trust that God would provide this food from heaven each and every morning. Each sunrise presented an opportunity to believe and trust in the promises of God.

God continues to give this bread of heaven to Christians today through Jesus: "the manna from heaven fell and, with a prefiguring of the future, showed the nourishment of heavenly bread and the food of the coming Christ."[4] For those who walk through the waters of baptism, Jesus offers manna in the form of communion bread, a sign of his body. As the Israelites gathered manna, Christians gather around an altar, ready to receive this bread. Each time we eat it, we are taken up into heaven, into sacred time, where we can experience something of this past manna meal in the desert.

This communion bread is also meant to nourish our spiritual journey to Zion just as manna nourished the Israelites on their physical journey to Sinai. As we journey through the wilderness of life, we will no doubt experience hardships, and may even question whether our journey with Christ is worth the trouble. We may be tempted to go back to the sinful comforts of our old lives. Fortunately, we are granted the privilege of receiving bread from heaven each and every Sunday, which strengthens our trust in Jesus and renews our hope that we will reach the end of our journey in the future promised land of Mount Zion.

As they journeyed through the wilderness, the Israelites slowly learned to trust God and trust in his provision. But they still had much to learn. They had to get to know this God who rescued them and learn why they were still prevented from having a full and intimate friendship with him. This, they will learn when they reach the base of Mount Sinai.

As regards this life, Moses is told, "Nobody has seen the face of God and lived." You see, we are not meant to live in this life in order to see that face; we are meant to die to the world in order to live forever in God. Then we won't sin, not only by deed but not even by desire, when we see that face which beats and surpasses all desires. Because it is so lovely, my brothers and sisters, so beautiful, that once you have seen it, nothing else can give you pleasure. It will give insatiable satisfaction of which we will never tire. We shall always be hungry and always have our fill.

—*Augustine*

8

LIFE AND LAW ON MOUNT SINAI

On Exodus 19–20, Leviticus 19, and Psalm 1

While we are invited to delight in God's creation and see, in trees and streams, a semblance of our paradise lost, none of these created things can match the beauty of gazing into the eyes of a loved one. To truly behold the face of a loved one is to partake in the depths of their inner beauty. When we behold the beauty and glory of another image bearer of God, it stirs in us our deepest longing of all—to gaze upon the face of our Lord on Mount Zion.

LEARNING TO BE WITH GOD AGAIN

Release from captivity is not the end of life, but the beginning. A prisoner who is released from captivity begins a long and difficult process of reintegration. They must reconnect with their loved ones and relearn how to live as a free individual. But this reintegration process is difficult. The free life awakens deeper problems, ones that were kept under wraps in prison. An end to physical captivity can bring with it the reemergence of spiritual and emotional captivities: angers and addictions, disordered desires, and deep depressions.

It is at Mount Sinai that God begins this reintegration process with his people. When Israel is set free from physical captivity, they begin a long process of reintegration with God. They must reconnect with God and relearn how to live life under God. However, life in the wilderness brings to the surface remnants of their spiritual captivity to sin. It is at Sinai that God will reconnect with Israel by revealing his character and holiness. However, through the giving of the Ten Commandments, God will also reveal to Israel the deep recesses of sin in their hearts. What began as an outward exodus from physical slavery must continue with a spiritual exodus out of sin and evil. In effect, Israel must learn that they are spiritually enslaved, and that they need to be saved from the inside out. God initiates this reclamation process at Mount Sinai through *fire, trumpet,* and *cloud.*

Figure 2: Mount Sinai—Exodus 19

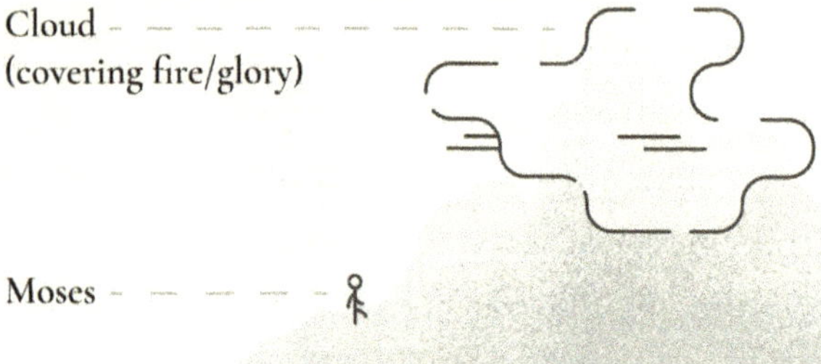

FIRE: GOD'S HOLINESS AND HUMANITY'S SINFULNESS

The pivotal moment in Exodus comes when the Israelites reach the foot of Mount Sinai. God has brought the Israelites out of slavery through the waters to the mountain of God so that they might encounter him. One might think, as perhaps the Israelites did, that Mount Sinai marked the end of the biblical story. Perhaps this mountain symbolized a return to Mount Eden, and the people of God could now ascend the mountain and be with God for eternity. However, it quickly becomes clear that they are not able to ascend the mount to be in the presence of God. This must have been extraordinarily difficult for Israel: imagine traveling to your destination, only to find a large *Do Not Enter* sign.

Why is it that the people of God cannot ascend Mount Sinai? This question is answered when God descends on Sinai with fire and smoke and gives Moses the command to "set limits around the mountain and keep it holy" (Exodus 19:23, NRSV). Because God is present on Sinai, the mountain is holy ground, and the impure will die as soon as they start their ascent.

What does it mean for God to be holy? To call God holy is to acknowledge his perfection and purity: God is fully good, perfectly wise, and always just. There is no shred of evil or imperfection in him. Because God is holy, he cannot permit any imperfection or sin to approach him, and it is for this reason that the Israelites cannot climb Sinai.

A symbol of God's holiness is *fire*. Fire purifies and consumes all impurities. The dirt and dust of a gold nugget is eliminated when thrown into a scorching fire. Medical tools are placed over fire to consume and eliminate harmful bacteria. Fire is "destructive of evil things and preservative of what is better."[1]

Sin is dirt on our hearts, a harmful bacterium that pollutes our soul. Because of this stain, we cannot approach the fiery holiness of God without being consumed. There is no room in God for our sin, and so a pure encounter with him necessitates the elimination of our sin.

Imagine you are a firefighter approaching a burning building. You cover every inch of your body with protective equipment but fail to recognize a large opening in the back of your suit. While you believe you are ready to enter the fire, once inside the building, you instantly realize that you are unprepared. The small opening in your suit is just enough to let the consuming fire in. Sin is like a tear on the back of our soul. Because we live in a sinful world, our personal sin doesn't always stand out to us. However, if we were to enter into God's pure presence, his holiness would quickly reveal that tear on our soul. His pure radiance would burn up this sin, and in turn burn us alive. For that reason, the Israelites cannot ascend into the pure and holy air of the summit of Sinai.

God wants to be with his people on Mount Sinai, but his holiness and their sin prevent this relationship from happening. In response, God creates a way for the Israelites to have *limited* access to him, and in turn God begins a process of instructing his people on how they might live lives of holiness.

First, God creates a way for the Israelites to have limited access to him through a ritual act of washing and bathing. If sin is dirt on our souls, this act of washing is a kind of symbolic cleansing—one washes their garments and their skin as a sign that they want their souls cleansed of sin. In so doing, the Israelites demonstrate that they take their sin seriously and take seriously this opportunity to encounter God. Later, we will see these rituals expanded to include the sacrifice of animals. While these actions may seem strange to our modern sensibilities, ritual preparation is still very much part of our culture. Special occasions call for special preparations. If I am going out on a date with my wife, I shower, shave, and wear my best outfit. This preparation signals to my wife that I value her and the special time we get to spend together. If, however, I show up to a date dirty, smelly, or unkempt, it signals to my wife that I am not taking our relationship seriously. In a similar way, the Israelites are called to perform these cleansing rituals as a sign that they view their encounter with God on Sinai as an important and special occasion.

In addition to granting these purification rituals, God begins the process of instructing the Israelites on how to live lives of holiness. As God is holy, so human beings—created in the image of God—are called to reflect God's holiness. For this reason, God called Moses up to Mount Sinai and, through him, gave Israel the Ten Commandments: a guide to holiness.

TRUMPETS: THE TEN COMMANDMENTS

On Mount Eden there was only one command: do not eat of the tree of knowledge. However, thousands of years later, humanity is far from Eden and far from God. They know little of this God who commands and have little awareness of the sin that prevents them from knowing him. And so, when the voice of God rings out from the mountain to give a command, it begins with the sound of a loud *trumpet*. This trumpet sound is a symbol of God's word and God's judgment. To those steeped in sin, the sound of God's voice is like a booming warlike bugle call, a sign that God will not be surrounded by evil. However, to those who are holy, the sound of the trumpet becomes the pleasing melody of divine teaching, beckoning the listener to ascend the mountain to hear more of these heavenly words. While Adam and Eve heard God's word as a pleasing melody on Mount Eden, the sin-sick Israelites hear the booming word on Sinai and tremble.

As one commandment rang out from the top of Mount Eden to humankind, God gives Ten Commandments from the top of Mount Sinai to reintroduce humanity to his holiness. These commandments revealed both the character of God and the nature of human sin. What do the commandments reveal to us today? First, they reveal the saving and merciful heart of God. The Ten Commandments do not begin with a list of dos and don'ts, but a simple statement from God: "I am the Lord your God who brought you out of the land of Egypt, out of the house of slavery" (Exodus 20:2). God reminds the Israelites that he is the God who rescued them from slavery and calls on them to obey him in *response* to this great act of salvation. Similarly, Christians follow God's commands as a response to Jesus for rescuing us from slavery to sin and death.

This is a crucial point. It tells us that God desires to save us *while* we are sinners and *before* we are holy. The Ten Commandments are not given to Israel before the Exodus, as if God was waiting to reward their good works with the gift of emancipation. The same is true for Christians today: Jesus does not see our good deeds and reward us with forgiveness, instead he offers salvation as a free gift, asking us to obey him in response. If we turn the Ten Commandments into a kind of ladder to gain access to God, we will be left in despair. God is not waiting for us to perform the commandments perfectly. Instead, he wants us to respond to his goodness by realizing that we need his son, Jesus, and must depend on the help of the Holy Spirit to obey God.

Second, the Ten Commandments tell us how to love God and others. They are part of a larger set of laws in Exodus and Leviticus, which are summarized in Leviticus 19: *Love God and love your neighbor as yourself.* The Ten Commandments give us specific examples of how we are to love God (the first four commandments) and love others (the last six commandments).[2] In fact, every law given in the Old Testament can be boiled down to a request to love God and neighbor.

One way to approach the Ten Commandments is to think of them as a blueprint, or an instructional manual for human living. They are "for the whole inhabited world a sacred school of the knowledge of God and the conduct of the soul."[3] Through them, God is telling us how he designed humanity to live and love in this world. On Mount Eden, God only needed to give one command to Adam and Eve—they were so close to him that these commands were intuitive. However, since then, sin has multiplied east of Eden, and we need a more detailed manual. In the same way we use instruction manuals when we forget how to operate a machine, we need God's commandments when we forgot how to live righteously. Throughout Exodus and Leviticus, God teaches us how to orient every aspect of our life around the love of God and love for our neighbors. Work, rest, food, sex, and speech are all meant to be oriented around the love of God.

Third, the Ten Commandments reveal our sin. Once we accept these commands and attempts to obey them, it will become readily apparent that we cannot keep them on our own. We see this most clearly in the last commandment: *thou shall not covet.*

Coveting relates not to our actions, but our desires. To covet is to desire what is not ours. It speaks to a disordered heart that desires one's self above God and others.

This last command prevents us from thinking that we can fully obey the Ten Commandments on our own. These are not commands that we can check off a list and be done with. Jesus reminds us of this when he gives his Sermon on the Mount, a definitive interpretation of the law. Here, Jesus shows how each of God's commands involves our hearts even more than our actions. I may be able to refrain from murder for eighty years, but it feels almost impossible to go eighty minutes without being bitter toward someone, or to go eighty seconds on social media without being envious of another.

The Ten Commandments reveal God's goodness, how we should live in response to this goodness, and our inability to fully live into this goodness. They are the words of life, God's sweet instructions to us. Yet they are also the sounds of a thundering trumpet, causing us to tremble in our sin. They make us realize that we cannot keep these commands through our own power, and that we are in need of help to fully love God. In this way, they prepare us for the coming of Jesus, who will make a way for us to enter back on the mountain and perfectly love God and others. The Ten Commandments are thus "a kind of schoolmaster to those who by it were appointed to be led to Christ and to be instructed and trained in order that after their training in the law they might be able with greater facility to receive the more perfect precepts of Christ."[4] But before that great descent of Jesus to earth, the Israelites must relate to God in an indirect way, which is symbolized on Mount Sinai by a cloud.

THE CLOUD

Exodus 19 ends with God descending and covering Mount Sinai with fire and smoke. The cloud remains on top of Sinai for the duration of the Israelite's time there. The *cloud* symbolizes the limited relationship that now exists between God and Israel. It both reveals and conceals. When I see a smoke cloud, I know there is something burning nearby. However, that same cloud is a barrier to my sight.

Similarly, the cloud on Sinai alerts Israel that God is present, yet concealed. The Israelites can hear from God, but they cannot get close to him. One way to conceive of this relationship is to think of it as an informative, but not intimate, relationship. Imagine a relationship that only takes place over email. You could learn quite a bit about another person through this exchange of information, but it would never come close to an in-person, face-to-face relationship. It is this kind of remote and limited friendship with God that is made available to Israel at Sinai.

One person alone is allowed to enter this cloud: Moses. As leader and representative of Israel, Moses is called to be the mediator between God and his people. For Moses, the trumpet blasts on Sinai are an invitation to ascend the mountain. As he climbs higher and higher, he is able to hear God's word with greater clarity, the sound of the trumpet changing from a harsh noise to a pleasing melody with each step higher. Moses is constantly ascending and descending—he goes up the mountain to be close to God, and goes down the mountain to give God's people instructions on how to live. During these moments of ascent, Moses is able to converse with God and have the kind of personal, one-on-one interaction with God that the rest of humanity desperately needs. But Moses wants even more.

LONGING TO SEE HIS FACE

If God granted you one wish, what would you ask for? Perhaps you would ask for peace on earth and an end to fighting and famine. Or perhaps you would turn to more personal matters, asking God to repair a fractured relationship or to return a departed loved one.

Throughout the story of Mount Sinai, we have seen that Moses is both extraordinarily blessed by God and extraordinarily faithful to him. Moses believed that God would bring his people out of slavery in Egypt and trusted that he would provide bread in the wilderness. In turn, Moses was given extraordinary access to God—it is Moses alone who scales Mount Sinai and converses with God. In Exodus 33:17, God declares his love and approval of Moses by stating he knows Moses's name. In so doing, God demonstrates the personal relationship he has with Moses. Furthermore, God states that Moses has found favor in his sight. He not only knows Moses, but delights in him, and it is for this reason that God decides to grant Moses one wish.

Moses replies with a request: to see the glorious face of God. Moses could have asked for anything. He could have asked God to perform another extraordinary miracle or for God to destroy an evil adversary. And yet, Moses shows the "flame of his desire" by requesting to see God's glorious face.[5] We can understand Moses's desire if we think of how faces are the primary point of intimacy between two persons. I remember those first few months falling in love with my eventual wife. We would spend hours simply looking deeply into each other's eyes and studying the curves and lines of one another's face.

There is a need for an eye-to-eye, face-to-face encounter in all close friendships. While friendship often begins with an exchange of names, it is cemented in face-to-face fellowship. My closest friends are those whom I desperately want to see in person. They are the ones that, when I see them, I immediately embrace with joy. This, perhaps, explains the reasons for the dramatic increase in loneliness in our modern world: we increasingly spend more of our time having mediated relationships over text messages and iPhones rather than unmediated, eye-to-eye friendships in the flesh. How much alienation and isolation are due to the simple fact that we look down at glowing screens more than we look up at another's eyes?

Moses wants this immediate encounter with God's face and his glory. He desires deep and personal intimacy with God as his best friend.[6] This should also be our deepest desire. All too often, our desires are only for the things of the world—we want peace and health, freedom and security. Moses witnessed God miraculously provide all of these earthly things—freedom for his people, peace from Pharaoh, and the comfort of heavenly manna. And we are called just like Moses to set our sights higher, asking not only for these things, but to behold the glorious face of God. This should be our ultimate and highest desire—to know the God of the universe as the closest of friends, to physically look into the eyes of God and behold his glory. We should be willing even to give up earth for this heavenly vision.

Despite Moses expressing his deepest desire, God does not grant him his wish. Moses cannot see the glorious face of God and live. Though Moses is able to get closer to God and higher up the mountain than anyone else in the Old Testament, he is still a sinner. His DNA is infected with the same proclivity to sin that is the hallmark of all children of Adam and Eve. His sin still prevents full intimacy with God, and just like anyone who ascends the mountain, a pure encounter with God's glory would consume him.

However, God still desires that Moses would one day be free of sin and see him face-to-face, so God gives Moses a sneak preview: as Moses hides behind a rock, God passes by and Moses is given a vision of Jesus, the Son of God.[7] Moses is given a preview of the awesome events of the New Testament, where God will become a human being in Jesus Christ. It is revealed to Moses here that he is in fact speaking to God the Son, and in this vision he is given the hope that he will be able to one day look deeply into the eyes of Jesus, and as such be able to see the glorious face of God.

Moses's deepest desire is our deepest desire: "Home is not home without Thy Blessed Face."[8] It is our ultimate goal, waiting for us at the summit of the mountain and under the tree of life. In viewing God's face, we will be surrounded by his radiance and wear his glory as a heavenly garment. Our deepest desire should be to behold the glorious face of God in Jesus. But in order for this to happen, we need Jesus to come down from the mountain and swallow up our sin so that we might ascend the mountain of God once again.

Original sin could not have easily been forgiven, if a victim had not been offered for it, if that sacred blood of propitiation had not been shed. Even then the words in Exodus were not vainly said of our Lord: “I shall see the blood and shall protect you.” That figure of the lamb represented this passion of Christ our Lord. Blood is given for blood, death for death, a victim for sin, and thus the devil lost what he held.

—*Caesarius of Arles*

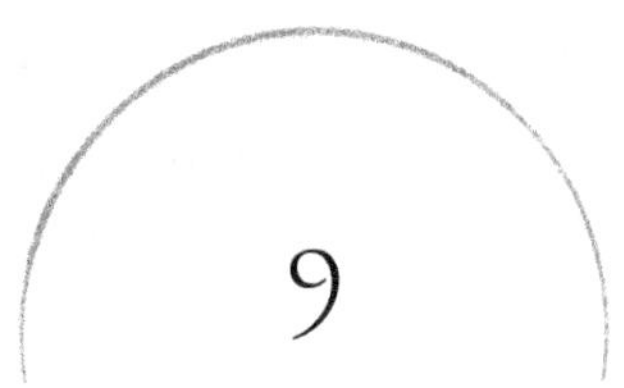

9

THE TABERNACLE

On Exodus 40, Leviticus 1–9, and Psalm 66

Few things are more stomach churning than the sight of blood. To witness an animal bleeding—or worse yet, a loved one, is to witness the draining and exhaustion of life. In Scripture, to bleed is to bear the burden of sin, which is death. We long to escape such a fate, hoping that someone will exhaust their own life and shed their own blood so that we may live.

THE PORTABLE MOUNTAIN

Israel quickly discovers that Mount Sinai is not the end of their journey. Due to the persistent problem of sin, they cannot scale the mountain and enter God's pure presence. Thus the Israelites must continue their sojourn to the promised land. But one question remains: will God go with them? The mountain is a special, holy place of encounter with God. Does their departure from Sinai mean a departure from God's presence?

Fortunately, God decides to go with the Israelites on their journey by making a way for them to continue to have this mountain-like encounter with him as they travel. He does this by giving

Moses a vision for the construction of the tabernacle. While on top of Mount Sinai, Moses is taken up into the heavens and is given a glimpse of the heavenly temple. Heaven is God's dwelling place, the place of his pure presence. Since God is above creation, he is capable of being everywhere and in one place at the same time.

Ever since the sin of Adam and Eve, heaven and earth have been split apart. While human beings could still experience some of God on earth, access to God's pure heavenly temple was strictly forbidden. But God longs to one day make a space for human beings to enter this temple and into his presence. For this reason, he takes Moses up to the top of Sinai yet again, but this time he gives him a vision of the heavenly temple, with angels and archangels constantly worshiping God. God then instructs Moses to build a copy of this temple on earth. He gives Moses the blueprints for constructing the earthly tabernacle, which will become the meeting place between God and humankind on earth. It is the touchstone, the intersection, of heaven and earth. As we will discover, the church today carries on as a living tabernacle every time Christians gather together in the name of Jesus.

Throughout the Bible, the meeting place between God and humankind has occurred on mountains. Since the tabernacle is meant to be the continuing meeting place between God and humankind, it is modeled after these mountains, particularly Mount Eden and Mount Sinai. It is, in effect, a portable mountain.[1]

As the Israelites continued their trek in the wilderness, they could now stop when needed to set up this portable mountain and meet with the living God. This tabernacle was also called the "tent of meeting" to highlight this point. What happened inside this tabernacle? First, one entered and performed a ceremonial washing with water. We have already seen water at the base of Eden, which was a sign that Adam and Eve could not cross over and back to the mountain. Israel's passing through the Red Sea served as a kind of movement through these waters, enabling them back into God's presence at Mount Sinai. As such, when one wanted to enter the portable mountain of the tabernacle, they had to first *cross the waters* through an act of ceremonial washing at its entrance. Just as the Israelites needed to wash before reaching the base of Sinai, they also needed to wash before entering further into the tabernacle. In washing, one was reenacting the movement through the Red Sea, passing through the waters of death and into life in God's presence.

After passing through the waters, one entered the main court of the tabernacle, which corresponded to the base of Mount Sinai.[2] To stand in the court was to stand on the mountain and to stand in God's presence, albeit still far away from the summit. In effect, one stood looking up to the cloud on top of Sinai, getting to know God but still lacking intimacy with God.

Just as the top of Sinai was hidden in a cloud, the back of the tabernacle was shielded by a *curtain (veil)*. Like the cloud, this curtain existed as a barrier to keep Israel away from God's pure presence.[3] And just as Moses was the one person capable of entering into the cloud on Sinai, the High Priest was the one individual appointed by God to go behind this curtain at specific times of the year.

The architecture of the tabernacle thus communicated to Israel both the good news that they were able to be with God, and the hard news that this access was still limited and veiled due to sin. One relived the parting of the Red Sea with each splash of water, but with each glance at the curtain they were reminded of the consequences of their perpetual sin. As Israel continued to journey in the wilderness, they would gather in the tabernacle to worship and fellowship with God, and, most importantly, to address the problem of sin. These activities were carried out through an elaborate system of sacrifices.

SACRIFICES

While entrance into the tabernacle would remind Israel of Mount Eden and Mount Sinai, the activities performed during their time in the tabernacle would remind them of their need to be a holy and sinless people. For this reason, God instructs Moses to inaugurate a system of sacrifices that would take place in the tabernacle and (eventually) the temple, in which animals were to be ritually sacrificed. The book of Leviticus highlights a number of different sacrifices which we can classify as *fire, food, and blood* sacrifices.

FIRE

First, there was a fire sacrifice. Before entering the tabernacle, a worshiper would offer a pristine animal to be burned on an altar. This pure and unblemished animal would then be entirely burned up, with the smoke and aroma lofting up into the heavens. The fire on the altar reminded one of the fire of the Holy Spirit; God's pure holiness. In watching the innocent animal burn, one was reminded of their deep desire to access this fire.

The point of this sacrifice was to demonstrate that one was serious about this profound opportunity to enter into the tabernacle for worship. From an earthly perspective, this sacrifice was pointless—the expensive animal was completely consumed by the fire, and nothing was left to be eaten. It would be the equivalent of lighting a one-hundred-dollar bill on fire. However, from a heavenly perspective, it was a sign of love and respect. One of the many ways that I show my wife that I love her is by gifting her flowers on random occasions. But these flowers do not really do anything or have any utility. In just a few days they will wither away to dust and ashes. But it is the unnecessariness of the flowers that make them so special. They are nothing *but* a beautiful sign of love. These tabernacle fire sacrifices were meant to be a similar act of love. The Israelites would spend a large amount of money and get nothing physical in return for their expense. But by this act they showed how much they loved God and wanted to just be in his presence for a little while.

Churches today perform this sacrifice when they pass around an offering plate, giving members the opportunity to give money to the church. The point of the offering is not principally to pay the salary of the pastor or to help with a building project. Instead, it is an opportunity for individuals to sacrifice their hard-earned money as a demonstration of honor and devotion to God. The money offered is supposed to be the first they earn each week, as this is their most valuable and precious earnings, as valuable as the precious livestock of an Israelite. One gives this money like a bouquet of flowers, expecting to get nothing back in return. These offerings are meant to be a sign that the giver loves Jesus and is grateful for the opportunity to stand in his presence. As one approaches the doors of church, one should ask how much they are willing to give to simply be in the presence of God each Sunday.

FOOD

After one washed and sacrificed an animal with fire, one entered into the holy place, where another altar stood as a marker of continued worship. Altars are both places of sacrifice and places of fellowship. Abraham placed Isaac on an altar as a sacrifice, and also feasted at an altar with bread, wine, and praise. In the tabernacle, there were sacrifices that produced food meant for a similar kind of fellowship meal. In eating the food, Israel enjoyed fellowship with each other and with God in his dwelling. Sharing a meal is the most common way we experience fellowship with our friends: families gather for Thanksgiving, weddings are celebrated with banquets, and couples go on dates at expensive restaurants. When we eat together, we commit ourselves to being around each other. Likewise, the tabernacle meal was a time for the community to draw close to each other and to God, and for that reason it has become known as comm-union (community + union with God). Christians gather today in the tabernacle of the church to share a similar communion meal of bread and wine associated with the sacrifice of Jesus. Here, the bread and wine become the sacrificed body and blood of Christ, and to partake of this food enables one to draw near to Jesus and all other Christians who share in this heavenly feast.

BLOOD

We have already seen the damaging effects of sin throughout the Bible, including how sin prevented humankind from fully encountering God. With the construction of the tabernacle, God begins to specifically deal with this problem of sin through the institution of blood sacrifices.

Leviticus gives us a detailed account of the significance of the symbol of *blood*. While reading Leviticus, one is struck by the omnipresence of blood in the tabernacle. Why does the remediation of sin require these bloody, painful sacrifices? Why doesn't God just pronounce forgiveness of sins, or wave a magic wand and make everything better again? We must remember that God is holy, perfectly good, *and* perfectly just. His justice requires that sin be taken seriously as an affront to himself that damages our relationship with him. If God did not take our sin seriously, if he just shrugged it off, it would be an act of neglect, not of love, and it would certainly not be just.[4]

Imagine that you discover that your best friend has been spreading false rumors about you behind your back. What should you do? You could attempt to shrug off the offense, but if you do, you will have to accept a diminished friendship. Your expectations for friendship will have to be lowered in order to accommodate these lies. You will have to eliminate truthfulness as an essential component of friendship. If, however, you truly love your friend and value their friendship, you will fight for a higher friendship, one predicated on goodness and truth. This will require that you take the path of reconciliation, which is a road paved with confrontation, tears, anger, and pain. Reconciliation requires hard conversations in which the damage inflicted by those lies is addressed. At some point, you will have to absorb the pain of those lies, swallowing them up so that it is no longer a barrier to friendship. This is what we call forgiveness. In forgiveness we *sacrifice* our anger and absorb the hurt in order to reestablish friendship.

This is precisely what is going on in these blood sacrifices. Our sins cause a rupture between us and God, and justice requires that those sins be painfully forgiven. In many ancient cultures, human sacrifice was required to deal with communal sin. But we have already seen how God, in sparing Isaac, has provided a temporary solution to sin through animal sacrifice.

These sacrifices began with the sinner offering their best animal, one that was clean and unblemished. The purity of such animals was meant to represent innocence: "an animal's being whole and sound, without blemish, served to symbolize the morally blameless life."[5] From here, the worshiper pressed their hands firmly on the animal, signaling that this pure innocent animal was representing them, just as the ram took Isaac's place on Mount Moriah. The animal, often a lamb, thus took the place of the sinner. From here, the animal was cut with a knife, with blood pouring out—the lamb's life poured out on behalf of the sinner.

In performing these blood sacrifices, the Israelites acknowledged the gravity of their sin and the need for their guilt to be mitigated. The lamb's blood was spilled so that a relationship with God could be restored. As sin tears through the life of the community, the animal's body is torn in two by the blade of the sword. The pain of sin is born on the flesh of the lamb, its life exhausted so that the life of the sinner might be preserved.

These sacrifices remain an ever-present reminder of the seriousness of our sin. God will not downgrade himself, or downgrade the definition of friendship, to be with us. God wants us to have *more* of his friendship, not less. The sight of blood remains for us a constant reminder of the life that pours out as consequence for our sin. When we fall into sin, we are invited to see ourselves standing in the tabernacle, our guilty hands in search of something—or *someone*, willing to bear the bloody consequences of our sin. We pray in those moments for someone to carry our guilt on their shoulders, and fall on the sword and shed their blood on our behalf.

VEILED AND CLOUDED

After Moses completes the construction of the tabernacle according to God's blueprint, the book of Exodus ends with God radiantly filling the tabernacle with his glory. The presence of God on Sinai now moves to the portable mountain. From now on, God's presence will go with the Israelites as they continue their journey in the wilderness. The tabernacle becomes the continual meeting place between humans and God, as well as the place where sacrifices are performed to address the perpetual problem of sin.

Through the tabernacle, God has enabled an opportunity for individuals to have an ongoing relationship with him. But this relationship is limited. It is a relationship in veil and cloud. It is a relationship of constant sacrifice and the constant spilling of blood. It is a relationship limited to a small nation in a remote part of the world. While the remainder of the Old Testament chronicles the history of God's people, with all its ups and downs, this community never gets any closer to God. And so, God begins to send prophets to prepare his people for what lies ahead, to grant them hope that he will provide a final and complete victory of sin, a final and perfect sacrifice that will open the veil to his glory forever.

Isaiah should be called an evangelist rather than a prophet, because he describes all the mysteries of Christ and the church so clearly that one would think he is composing a history of what has already happened rather than prophesying what is to come.

—*Jerome*

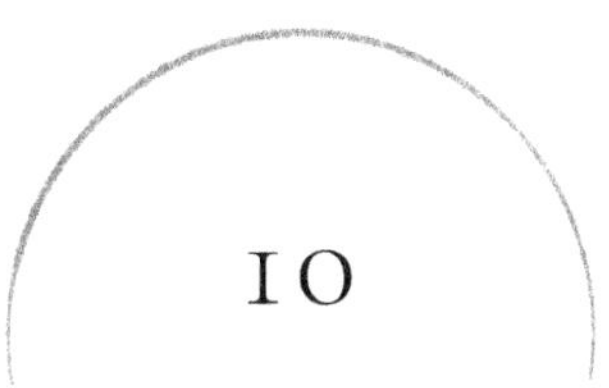

10

THE PROPHETS PREPARE

On Daniel 7, Isaiah 11, 53, Ezekiel 36–37, and Psalm 126

So much of our life is goal driven. We long for a sense of completion, whether it is accomplishing a vocational milestone or seeing our children graduate college. These goals come to us as pictures in our minds, visions of a perfected and glorious future. Such visions give us hope for the future and push us to strive in the present.

FROM LEVITICUS TO KINGS

The remainder of the Old Testament chronicles the ups and downs of the Israelites as they strive to keep God's commandments and faithfully worship him in the tabernacle. However, sin remains a persistent problem, and as such, there are continual cycles of faithfulness and unfaithfulness, holiness and wickedness, orthodoxy and heresy. As the Bible continues, Joshua will take over for Moses and lead God's people into the promised land of Israel through a series of military victories. But the Israelites cannot resist the allure of the false gods of their enemies, and they again turn away from God. Eventually, God anoints a line of kings in order to help Israel maintain peace and order in a still sinful world. The greatest of these kings was David, who composed numerous Psalms and was a man "after [God's] own heart" (1 Samuel 13:14). Yet even David succumbed to iniquity, abusing his power to commit sexual sin and murder.

During a particularly intimate encounter with God, David offered to build God a permanent dwelling place called the temple, which would bring an end to the portable mountain tabernacle (2 Samuel 7). But from the beginning, the significance of this temple is clouded in ambiguity. God answers David by stating that he has no need for a permanent dwelling, since he has already been at work in and through Israel. The temple is eventually built by David's son Solomon on Mount Zion in Jerusalem. But from the outset one can see that it lacks the heavenly inspiration of Moses's tabernacle. While Moses received instructions for the construction of the tabernacle directly from God, God is conspicuously absent from the construction of the temple. Indeed, it seems as though the temple is built according to *Solomon's* plans, rather than God's.[1] Solomon builds an enormous and opulent temple out of imported stone, but he also builds a number of equally large structures for himself. One might rightly question: Was the temple built for God's glory or Solomon's?

Unfortunately, soon after the temple is finished, Solomon falls deeply into sin. He takes for himself hundreds of wives and concubines from the surrounding areas, in turn importing the false gods of these areas into the temple. Solomon begins worshiping these false gods and drifting away from the true God. One is left wondering whether the enormous stones of the temple are the holy stones of Eden or the man-made stones of Babel.

It becomes clear soon after Solomon that the temple did not bring an everlasting reign of peace and prosperity to Israel. Instead, the country falls into factions and civil wars. God needs to remind his people that he called them out of slavery in Egypt with the goal of bringing them out of spiritual slavery to sin. He needs to remind them that he wants to give them a heavenly kingdom rather than just an earthly kingdom. In order to remind Israel of their true and final goal, and to encourage them to live towards this goal, he gives a series of visions to prophets.

VISION AND IMAGINATION

My father had an uncanny ability to predict the future careers of his children. Growing up, he would give each of us nicknames based upon our interests and habits, helping to paint a picture in our minds of our future vocations. For instance, he nicknamed me the "Little Professor" when I was eight years old, based upon my penchant for reading. And it turned out that I did become a professor. My sister was nicknamed "Ms. Park Forest," which was a reference to the elementary school we attended. This nickname resonated deeply with her, and she began to daydream about her future life as a schoolteacher. In fact, at age nine she started her own school in her room, giving my brother and me lessons, homework, and quizzes (where I received my first B grade). And sure enough, my sister did one day become a schoolteacher, and even taught at Park Forest Elementary. Fifteen years after she was christened with the nickname, she had become Ms. Park Forest!

In giving us these nicknames, my father presented a picture of our future lives that changed the way we lived in the present. The expression we use to describe this phenomenon is *capturing our imagination*. A picture of our future life is presented to us—a vision as a schoolteacher, or professor, or athlete, etc.—and that picture takes hold of the image-making part of our brains. As it does, we begin to picture more and more scenarios related to this future, and in turn change the way we behave in the present to help make that future picture a reality.

These images of the future are not limited to our childhood. We continue to daydream about the future throughout our adult lives, often at a rapid pace. For instance, in just a handful of seconds, my mind can go from picturing a relaxing vacation at the beach, to thinking of a job promotion, to imagining my daughter's college graduation. None of these images give me a complete description of how the future will unfold, they are only snapshots of a potential future. But they have enormous power to motivate me in the present. A picture of a vacation prompts me to save my money now, and the image of my daughter's success motivates me to continue faithfully educating her in the present.

Visions of the future prepare us for the present. This is because God has given us imaginations, and God does not give us something unless it is intended for our good. God wants us to think in pictures, and these pictures are often more powerful than the words in our heads. This is one of the reasons why, when God wants to help us understand his ultimate future for us, he does so by giving visions to a series of prophets. Prophets are given glimpses of the future, and are instructed to write down these visions so that they might capture our imaginations. As these visions capture our imagination, we are invited to change the way we live, ordering our lives around the hope created by these pictures.

The visions of the prophets are meant to unfold the future of Israel as well as the future of all of God's people. They tell us not only about the events of Jesus's life, death, and resurrection, but also the content of our final life on Mount Zion. They tell us who, where, and how God is going to bring about salvation from sin. First, we will look at who will bring salvation (the Son of Man), then we will examine how the Son of Man will bring salvation (through suffering and from the inside out). Lastly, we will see how the prophets foretell the location of final salvation: Mount Zion.

SALVATION THROUGH A PERSON

Imagine you are drowning in the ocean during a raging storm. How would you survive? Someone—some person—must come to your rescue. This person must be stronger than you, capable of fighting back against the raging storm. And that same person must be willing to jump into the water, to draw near to you, securing your body and carrying you to safety. Someone who is strong must come from above, and that person must descend into the waters to complete this rescue mission.

The human predicament of sin is portrayed in scripture as both a spiritual drowning and a spiritual slavery. We are all drowning in the chaotic waters of our sin, powerless against its crashing waves. We are as helpless in our sin as the Israelites were helpless slaves in Egypt. What we need is someone strong enough to break the yoke of slavery, and someone willing to enter into the waters to bring us to safety.

For this reason, the prophets' visions of the future coalesced around a single person who would come to bring salvation. Just as a single person, Moses, led Israel out of physical slavery in Egypt, the prophets foretold the coming of a single person to lead God's people out of their spiritual slavery to sin. The problem, however, is that all human beings are infected with sin. No one, not even Moses, was able to live a perfect life. For this reason, the rescuer had to come from outside of creation, above and beyond the waters of sin. He had to be untainted by sin and thus capable of entering into the waters without drowning.

This person is identified by the prophets as the Son of Man, who is described vividly in a vision given to the prophet Daniel. In this dreamlike vision, Daniel is lifted up into the heavenly temple, where he sees God, the Ancient One, seated on his throne. Then suddenly, one "like a human being" appears, "coming with the clouds of heaven. And he came to the Ancient One and was presented before him. To him was given dominion and glory and kingship" (Daniel 7:13–14, NRSV). This tells us that the savior of humankind would descend out of the heavenly temple, like a stone rolling down from the mountain of God (Daniel 2:45) to bring an end to evil and restoration to humanity. This person is known as the Son of Man. Justin Martyr says of this person: "He would become man and appear as such but that he would not be born of a human seed. Daniel states the same truth figuratively when he calls Christ 'a stone cut out without hands,' for, to affirm that he was cut out without hands signifies that he was not the product of human activity but of the will of God, the Father of all, who brought him forth."[2]

Daniel reveals that this Son of Man must come from above creation in order to rescue it, and he will do so by entering *into* creation. While someone stronger can save me from drowning, they still must dive into the water to carry me to safety. For this reason, the prophet Isaiah continues to unpack this vision of the Son of Man by describing his entrance into creation from below.

While Daniel gives us the top-down vision of salvation, Isaiah fills out this picture by giving us the bottom-up vision. For Isaiah the Son of Man will have a human origin, having a human lineage from the "root of Jesse," which descends back to Solomon, David, and Adam. Furthermore, he will have a specific, earthly birthplace, David's hometown of Bethlehem. Yet despite these humble human origins, this savior will be fully anointed by the Holy Spirit.

We have already seen the Holy Spirit at work through Moses and other Israelite leaders. Later in the Old Testament oil will be used to anoint David as a Spirit filled king. For centuries, *oil* has been used as a medicine for the sick, as well as a perfume for those who want to look healthy and beautiful. Early Jews and Christians viewed anointing oil as a product of the olive branches of the tree of life. Oil thus became a marker of the Holy Spirit, the very life of God working to heal and empower individuals to do the will of God. Oil was used by prophets to mark someone as empowered by the Holy Spirit, however the Spirit was only made manifest on limited occasions in the Old Testament. But Isaiah foretells that the root of Jesse will *fully* receive the anointing of the Holy Spirit, and thus bear in him the fullness of God's glory, manifested in perfect wisdom, knowledge, and might (Isaiah 11:2). He will be given the added title of Son of God, or Messiah, the Christ.

What these visions from Daniel and Isaiah reveal to us is that the fulfillment of Old Testament prophecy will come through a specific person, and that this person will come from both above and below. They will be above and beyond human sin, but willing to enter into the depths of humanity. They will descend from the heavenly temple and yet be born as an infant in a small town. They will be both heavenly and earthly, fully human yet fully divine. It is this person that will have perfect wisdom and perfect power, capable of conquering the serpent and healing the world of sin.

SALVATION THROUGH SUFFERING

How will this Son of Man and Son of God heal the world of sin? Through suffering, abandonment, and blood. God cannot take sin lightly—he cannot shrug off sin any more than we can shrug off a grave harm done to us. However, God still loved humanity, and wanted to extend his merciful forgiveness to those who desired to be with him. The sacrifice of animals enabled this price to be paid without taking the life of the sinner.

However, this system of sacrifice could not bring about perfect justice or complete mercy. It was hampered by quantitative and qualitative issues that limited its efficacy. First, there was the quantitative issue—how could the sacrifice of animals ever be enough to compensate for the magnitude of human sins? An animal was simply not worth enough to bear the brunt of human sin. If I were to steal one million dollars and was only able to pay back ten dollars to my victim, justice would not be served. Similarly, if we were to add up all the sins and offenses perpetrated by humanity, what would be an appropriate sentence? Surely a few livestock could not be enough.

Second, there was a qualitative issue regarding the priests who would conduct these sacrifices. Since every human being was infected with sin, the priests themselves were also caught up in this web of continuous sin. As such their ability to perform an act of justice was compromised. We can think here of a corrupt judge who is guilty of the same crimes as those he is sentencing. This crooked judge could not be trusted to rule fairly. When it comes to dealing with the injustice of human sin, everyone is infected, priest and parishioner alike. All are drowning, so none can save.

We may scoff at this antiquated and bloody system of justice, but every man-made system of justice carries with it these same deficiencies. No system of punishment has ever been enough to redress the horrific atrocities perpetrated by humankind. No prison sentence can compensate for the Holocaust. No amount of punishment could ever bring back a departed loved one. Similarly, there has never been a perfect system of justice. Every day our news feeds are flooded with stories of prison sentences that are too long or too short. The scales of human justice will never balance, since sin has "set his sign on every one."[3]—judge and jury, victim and perpetrator, oppressor and oppressed.

The ultimate purpose of the tabernacle sacrifice was to reveal the gravity of sin and the limits of justice. The limitations of the animal and the limitations of the priest were meant to foster a longing for God's intervention. What was needed was a sacrifice capable of bearing the sins of the world and a perfect priest to initiate this sacrifice. According to the prophets, this longing for perfect justice and complete mercy would be fulfilled by the Son of Man, the Son of God, the Messiah.

The vision given in Isaiah 53 describes how the Messiah would fulfill the potential of the tabernacle by becoming a perfect sacrifice, describing him as a lamb. Since lambs are signs of purity and innocence, this vision tells us that, unlike the temple priests, the Messiah would be free of all sin and corruption and thus capable of bringing about true and perfect justice. However, unlike a lamb, this Messiah would not be a dumb animal. This lamb is the same Son of Man and Son of God, both human and divine. As such, this person who will later be called the Lamb of God will carry the entire weight of human sin on his shoulders.

Isaiah's vision states that this Lamb of God will absorb the burden of sin in all of its brutality. He will bear the emotional consequences of sin—being "despised and rejected by others" (Isaiah 53:3, NRSV). He will bear the physical consequences of sin, his body crushed and wounded. By accepting this wickedness on his body, this root of Jesse would carry upon himself the entirety of sin in the world (Isaiah 53:6).

And yet, despite carrying upon himself "the iniquity of us all," this innocent and suffering lamb will somehow live on after death. One of the most important verses in scripture, Isaiah 53:10, says of the suffering lamb: "Yet it was the will of the Lord to crush him with pain. When you make his life an offering for sin, he shall see his offspring, and shall prolong his days" (NRSV). God will lay upon the suffering lamb the weight of sin, and the suffering lamb shall die as an offering for the sin of the world. And yet, this same suffering lamb shall somehow live on, his days prolonged for eternity. The Son of Man will be shown to be stronger than sin and even stronger than death itself. His sacrifice will be enough to fully address the problem of sin, and the blood of the Lamb of God will be sufficient to blot out sin forever.

SALVATION FROM THE INSIDE OUT

Sin is a matter of the heart. It was birthed into humanity through a wayward act of desire on Mount Eden. While corrective action can mitigate some of the damage of sin, it cannot cure it. God graciously granted to the Israelites the Ten Commandments and the sacrifices as ways of addressing the exterior manifestations of sin. But neither of these good gifts could ever bring about a change of heart simply through their observance.

Good works and proper behavior cannot bring about love, yet it is love that we desire most out of our relationships. Yes, we want our friends to act appropriately towards us, to not harm or offend us. And yes, we want friends who will do things for us. But none of this matters if there is not love underneath. As St. Paul states: "If I speak in the tongues of men and of angels, but have not love, I am a noisy gong or a clanging cymbal … If I give away all I have, and if I deliver up my body to be burned, but have not love, I gain nothing" (1 Corinthians 13:1–3). The greatest deeds in the world are worthless if they are not undergirded in love. The same is true for our relationship with God. The mountain of God is more than a place of obedience and justice, it is a place of love. Its summit is not a cold encounter with a stern schoolmaster, but a face-to-face encounter with an intimate friend.

Because the sacrifice of the Son of God is perfect and complete, it alone can free us from our slavery to sin and create a restored relationship with God. Moreover, the one who accomplishes this sacrifice is the same man who is uniquely anointed by the Holy Spirit. As such, his death will enable a pouring out of the Holy Spirit on all his followers. The prophet Joel states that God will usher in an outpouring of the Holy Spirit, like oil, upon all flesh. (Joel 2:28, see also Zechariah 4:1–6). In the Old Testament, such a pouring forth was impossible due to sin. Moses yearned for a day when all might receive this Spirit, exclaiming: "Would that all the Lord's people were prophets, that the Lord would put his Spirit on them!" (Numbers 11:29) The prophets declare that Moses's supplication will come true through the Son of Man, and that the reception of this Spirit will enable a renewal of the heart. In Ezekiel's vivid imagery, the Spirit will wash clean the human heart and transform it from a heart of stone to a heart of flesh (Ezekiel 36:25–27). Our cold and rigid heart will be "softened and split up by the water of the Spirit," and thus capable of tenderly loving God.[4]

While this renewal by the Spirit will begin in the human heart, it will work its way out from the spiritual to the material. The cleansing of sin through water and the Spirit will heal every manifestation of sin, including the ultimate result of sin, death. Ezekiel describes the ultimate reversal of sin as a *resurrection*: dead and dry bones will be revived with flesh, blood, and sinew. The very breath of God, which we first saw in the formation of human beings, will enter these bones, a sign that the dead have new and eternal life through the Spirit (Ezekiel 37). What begins as a spiritual renewal also becomes a physical renewal of the human body. God says through Ezekiel these incredible words: "You shall live, and you shall know that I am the Lord." (37:6)

SALVATION'S FULFILLMENT ON MOUNT ZION

Finally, these prophetic visions tell us the specific *location* where this spiritual and physical renewal will occur: Mount Zion. When Isaiah was first given his vision, Zion was the place where the earthly temple was located. However, this temple on Zion was not the true mountain of God. Its stones had come to resemble the bricks of Babel rather than the onyx of Eden. Therefore, the prophets do not tell us to look to this current mound of dirt and rock for hope. Rather, they invite us to cast our eyes up into the heavens as we await the coming of the *eternal* Mount Zion, which will come at the end of history. Isaiah is granted a vision of one of the last great acts of the Son of Man, in which he will descend from heaven and bring the heavenly temple down with him onto Mount Zion. Heaven will physically descend to earth, making Mount Zion "the highest of mountains." (Isaiah 2:2) What will life look like on this eternal Mount Zion?

First, all sin, evil, and wickedness will be banished from its grounds. Isaiah 11:3–5 chronicles how the root of Jesse shall bring the fiery judgment of God over all wicked persons and look with favor upon the poor and oppressed. The social effects of sin are borne greatly on those with very little in the world, thus the reversal of sin that comes through the Holy Spirit will manifest itself in the healing of vulnerable communities. The Son of Man will complete this process by pronouncing a final end to sin, bringing relief to those who heavily bear its burdens. While this passage stands as a warning to those who continue to perpetuate injustice today, it also stands as a comfort for those who live under constant oppression. Through the vision of Isaiah, we now know that injustice has an expiration date, and perfect justice will permeate every inch of Mount Zion.

In order for perfect justice to reign on Mount Zion, there must be a complete end to sin and evil, including the demonic forces that bring forth death and destruction. Isaiah states that the root of Jesse will come not only to end worldly injustices, but also destroy the forces that help manifest them. He will judge both sin and the demonic powers that help to perpetuate it. In Isaiah 11:8–9, the prophet states that even in his childhood, the Son of Man will have power over the snake, and will keep the serpent from entering the mountain of God. The one who bore the weight of sin will be strong enough to subdue the serpent for eternity, banishing his presence from Mount Zion.

With sin banished from Zion, there will be everlasting peace. The imagery in the prophets brings us back to the harmony of Mount Eden. Mount Eden was a place of harmony between humankind and the animals, and Mount Zion will bring forth peace between animal life once again. Even lions and lambs will live in peace together. And as Mount Eden contained perfect harmony between Adam and Eve, Mount Zion will encompass perfect harmony between human beings, with people gathering from every tribe and nation to live in peace with God and each other. Isaiah 27:13 states that a sound of a great trumpet will awaken the oppressed, and they will stream to Mount Zion together. For the oppressors, the sound of this trumpet will be a warlike blast signaling a final judgment by the Son of Man. But for those who believe, the trumpet sound will be a wake up call, the sound of the Son of Man's voice inviting them to arise and gather together on Mount Zion and enjoy eternal peace.

Finally, the glory of the Lord, which has been limited to the tabernacle and veiled by a curtain and a cloud, will shine everywhere. In fact, the sun will no longer be necessary for illumination—God's very beauty will shine like a light. God's glory will spread forth from Mount Zion and cover the whole earth, stretching far enough to include peoples from every nation and tribe. The curse of Babel will finally be lifted, and human beings will worship God together in perfect harmony.

FROM THE OLD TESTAMENT TO THE NEW TESTAMENT

The need for God to descend from the heavenly temple is only made clearer throughout the remainder of the Old Testament. Solomon's kingdom and his temple devolve into sin and idolatry.

God's glory departs from the temple, as its stones had become the bricks of Babel. It is finally destroyed by the Babylonians, and the Israelites are sent into captivity once again. Though a remnant returns to build a second temple, this one is but a shadow of the first, and there is not a trace of God's glory to be found in it.

At the close of the Old Testament, the relationship that human beings can have with God is still *limited*, *veiled*, and *temporary*. It is limited to the people of Israel as the descendants of Abraham. God has still not opened the gates of his mountain to the rest of the nations. This relationship is also veiled through the cloud and the temple curtain. The Israelites can know God only indirectly, not personally and intimately. Finally, it is temporary. The temple sacrifices must go on and on in perpetuity, a reminder that sin is still an issue. Yet these sacrifices stoked in the hearts of worshipers a desire for God to bring a final and complete sacrifice, a once-for-all end to sin. The conquering of Israel and the destruction of the temple served as a constant reminder of this need, and sparked speculation as to when God would come to complete what he started.

The vision of the prophets was meant to capture the imaginations of Israel as it waited, often in harsh and difficult circumstances, for the completion of the redemptive story of the Bible and the future fulfillment of its symbols. While many of these visions have been actualized in time, others are still waiting for their fulfillment. And so all of us still turn to the prophets for hope in the future. They enable us to see hope in the symbols of the Bible. Blood is no longer a sign of death, but a hopeful sign of salvation. The clouds in the sky are a reminder that the clouds that separate us from God's glory will one day be no more. A simple act of pouring out olive oil from a bottle triggers in us a longing for the Holy Spirit to be poured out upon all human beings.

Centuries later, God will begin to fulfill the promises pronounced by the prophets, not through a grand display of power and might, but rather a shocking display of humility. He will take on human flesh, allowing himself to be born to a simple teenager in a working-class home in a small, remote village.

PART 3:

THE STORY OF MOUNT TABOR

Our own cause was the occasion of his descent and that our own transgression evoked the Word's love for human beings, so that the Lord both came to us and appeared among human beings. For we were the purpose of his embodiment, and for our salvation he so loved human beings as to come to be and appear in a human body.

—*Athanasius*

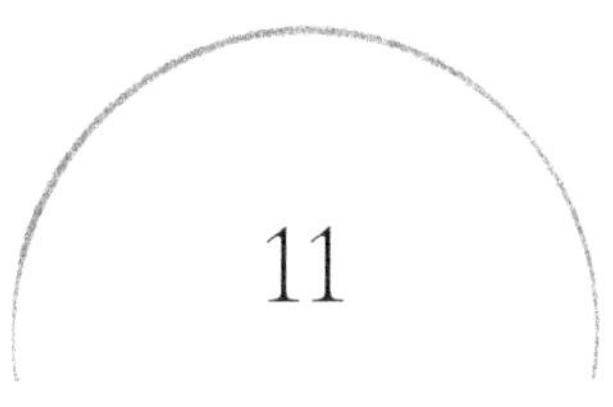

11

JESUS DESCENDS

On Matthew 3–4, John 6, 9, and Psalm 89

Love moves us towards our beloved. A lover does not wish to love their beloved from afar, but desires to draw near. When those we love are in trouble, we enter into their world, drawing near to them in body, mind, and soul. As his beloved creation, God likewise draws near to us in our despair, entering into our world by taking on human flesh to rescue us from the inside out.

ENTERING INTO THE STORY

The novelist Dorothy Sayers created a series of mystery novels centered around the detective Lord Peter Wimsey. The character was astute, and clever, but also lonely. Sayers loved this character that she created and longed to provide him a cure from his loneliness within the world of her novels. So she did something extraordinary: she decided to write herself into her novels, creating a character based on herself named Harriet Vane. Vane enters into Peter Wimsey's world, saves him from his loneliness, and they eventually get married.[1] In order to save her creation, she wrote herself into the story, rescuing Peter Wimsey from within.

The Old Testament story ends with humanity stuck in their own loneliness and brokenness. God enters back into a relationship with his creation through Abraham and Moses, but this relationship is much like that between an author and their story: it is one of distance. But the prophets tell us that God will complete his rescue mission through one person—the Son of Man will descend from the heavenly temple and enter into the world—just as Sayers entered into the pages of her own novel to save Peter Wimsey.

The prophets foretold that this savior of humankind would enter the world from both above and below: the Son of Man would descend from heaven, and yet would also be born in Bethlehem from the lineage of Jesse. These prophecies come to fruition in the birth of Jesus: He was conceived by the power of the Holy Spirit and yet born of the humble Virgin Mary. On one hand, his life was ordinarily human: he was a simple carpenter from a remote, backwater town called Nazareth. On the other hand, his life is extraordinary: he is God incarnate living in perfect obedience to the Father. In Jesus, God enters into humankind to save it from the inside out. Jesus does this by first bringing to fulfillment the stories and symbols of the Bible.

FULFILLING THE STORY, FULFILLING THE SYMBOLS

As we read through the Gospel of Matthew, we see the word *fulfilled* peppered throughout. Matthew is quick to point out how the words and actions of Jesus fulfill the Old Testament. Fulfillment is a complex word that means both "to satisfy" and "to develop to full potential." First, fulfillment means to satisfy an obligation. For instance, if I have agreed to rake my neighbor's lawn, I have not fulfilled my obligation until the final leaf is removed. Second, fulfillment means to reach one's potential. We can think here of a young choir student who desires to perfect her craft by becoming an opera singer. She fulfills her hopes and dreams by one day singing at the Royal Opera House.

When the Bible states that Jesus fulfills the Old Testament, it is claiming that he satisfies its stories and brings to full potential its symbols: "the whole Divine Scripture speaks of Christ and is fulfilled in Christ."[2] Jesus is capable of this because he is fully God and fully human. As the only perfect man he is able to fulfill the stories of Mount Eden and Mount Sinai by living a perfect life. As we have discovered throughout the Old Testament, no human being lives up to their full potential. Despite moments of great faithfulness, Adam, Eve, Abraham, Moses, and all of Israel messed up. And so, when God enters into history in Jesus, he wants to show us what human life is supposed to look like. He wants to show us how every moment of human life—from childhood to adulthood, from moments of celebration to moments of temptation—are meant to be lived in perfect obedience to the Father. For this reason, every single one of Jesus's actions fulfills some part of the Old Testament.

Human beings have in themselves a desire for perfection, a desire to see even the most trivial activities performed without fault. I can still remember winning my first video game when I was six years old. As soon as I finished *Super Mario Bros*, I immediately began a number of successive run throughs of the game, in which I attempted not only to win, but to win perfectly. Decades later I discovered the term *speedrunning*, in which individuals attempt to play perfectly through video games as fast as they can, with zero faults.

We can think of Jesus's life and ministry as a kind of perfect speedrun through the key events of the Old Testament. Throughout the Old Testament, we see human beings falter and mess up as they attempt to live in relationship with God. In the New Testament, Jesus relives these same events, demonstrating what perfect obedience and faithfulness look like. He does so as the perfect human, a representative of all of humankind. In so doing, he "recapitulated in himself everything that pertains to our salvation," showing us how to live holy lives in relationship with God.[3] This enables us to relive the events of the Bible through and with Jesus. Jesus stands as our perfect guide through the Old Testament, taking us through the waters of the Red Sea in his baptism, saving us from temptation by Satan in the wilderness and guiding us up the mountain to God the Father on Mount Tabor.

In addition to fulfilling the story of the Old Testament, Jesus fulfills all of the symbols in the Bible. He does this by bringing these symbols to their full potential. Every single sign in the Old Testament comes to completion in the person and work of Jesus Christ. One of the ways we can understand this fulfillment is to think about the performance of dramatic stories. There is a writing concept called Chekhov's Gun, which states that "every element in a story must be necessary, and that unnecessary elements should be removed. If an element is introduced, it must be resolved by the last act."[4] So, if a character or object is introduced early on in a story, its purpose must be disclosed by the end of the story. For instance, if I go to a play and see a gun on a table in Act I, I should expect someone to pick up that gun in Act II or III.

As God is the author of the Bible, he has given symbols throughout the Old Testament that hint at something more, something greater than themselves. For instance, we have seen the reconciling power of blood in the book of Leviticus, but this blood stands as a reminder that we need a fuller, more lasting sacrifice to take away human sin. In the New Testament, we discover that each of these symbols is fulfilled in Jesus Christ. We discover the fullest meaning of water in his baptism, the fullest understanding of bread in his body, and the fullest meaning of blood in his death on the cross. We can then reread the Old Testament and see Jesus at work through these very same symbols. Jesus, in a sense, becomes the main musical note in the Bible. He is the root, or bass note, of a harmonious chord that allows us to intertwine his life with the stories and symbols of the Old Testament.

In the following three chapters, we will walk through the major events in the life of Jesus, showing how he fulfills the stories of Mount Eden and Mount Sinai and the symbols associated with them (see Figure 3). In fact, Matthew arranges his account of the life of Jesus to show us how his ministry is the spiritual fulfillment the story of Moses. The story of Mount Sinai is fulfilled in the story of Mount Tabor:

- As Moses led the Israelites through the waters of the Red Sea, Jesus begins his ministry by passing through the spiritual waters of baptism.
- As Moses and the Israelites struggled with earthly temptation in the wilderness, Jesus resists spiritual temptation in the wilderness.
- As Moses banned the Israelites from ascending Sinai because of their impurity, Jesus descends the mountain to cleanse and heal the people of their impurity.

- As Moses encountered Jesus on top of Mount Sinai, Jesus encounters Moses on Mount Tabor.
- As Moses built the tabernacle and instituted the sacrifices after Mount Sinai, Jesus calls his body the tabernacle and offers it as a final sacrifice on the cross after the events of Mount Tabor.

While the Gospel of Matthew follows the general shape of the story of Mount Sinai, it should be noted that Jesus fulfills all the Old Testament, and as such we will also see the stories and symbols of Mount Eden, of Abraham, and the prophets also fulfilled as we examine the life, death, and resurrection of Jesus. The remainder of this chapter will describe the ministry of Jesus as one characterized by the waters of baptism, his temptation in the wilderness, and his healings as he approaches the mountain of his transfiguration. The next two chapters will discuss his journey to Mount Tabor and his journey to the cross.

THROUGH THE SPIRITUAL WATERS: JESUS'S BAPTISM

Jesus begins his earthly ministry to rescue us from our spiritual slavery to sin by passing through the waters of the Jordan River in his baptism. What was this baptism that Jesus participated in? We are told its original meaning by John the Baptist, who called people out into the wilderness for the repentance of sin (Matthew 3:11). This ceremony was akin to the ritual washing that was performed by the Israelites before they entered into the tabernacle: one washed the dirt off their bodies as a sign of one's desire to wash the sin off of their souls. Jesus, however, had no need to be cleansed, since he had never sinned. Instead, Jesus enters into his baptism as the representative of humanity itself. Like Moses, he

Figure 3: Jesus Fulfills the Stories and Symbols of the Old Testament

MOSES	crosses the Red Sea	complains when tempted	bars Israel from ascent due to impurity	gives Ten Command-ments	receives glimpse of God's glory	given earthly tabernacles/ temple blueprint	institutes food sacrifices	institutes continuous blood sacrifices
JESUS	crosses waters of baptism	resists Devil's tempatation	performs healings of the impure	gives Sermon on the Mount	God's glory shines through him	revealed to be the true temple	institutes Communion	offers final sacrifice on the cross
SYMBOLS FULFILLED	Water	Snake	Oil	Trumpet	Sun, Cloud, Garmets	Stone	Bread, Wine, Altar	Tree/Wood, Lamb, Sword, Blood, Curtain

spiritually leads each of his followers through the waters, enabling our souls to be cleansed through his baptism. Jesus takes upon himself the dirt of our souls, and drowns it in the waters, so that we might pass safely through.

Jesus's baptism thus reveals and fulfills the deepest meaning of water as the source of eternal life for those who have faith in him. His immersion in the Jordan River sanctified water, allowing us in turn to have our souls cleansed in the waters of our own baptism.[5] When we believe in Jesus and are baptized, the same water that the Israelites passed through in the Red Sea, the same water that Jesus passed through in the Jordan, surrounds our bodies and our souls. Our souls lock arms with Jesus, plunging into the deathly depths of the waters, only to reemerge from the waters with new life in him. Paul will later say that those who are baptized share in the death and resurrection of Christ. (Romans 6:3–4). They participate in Jesus's baptism in their own baptism, and thus participate in his death and resurrection as well. In baptism, we die to our sins and are resurrected to new life, allowing our souls to pass through the waters of Eden and back onto the mountain of God.

THROUGH THE SPIRITUAL WILDERNESS: JESUS'S TEMPTATION

While the exodus through the Red Sea meant salvation for Israel, it was not the end of the story, but the beginning of new life with God in the wilderness. The wilderness was a time of hardship and temptation. Though the Israelites were free from physical slavery, they continued to grumble and complain, yearning for their cruel yet comfortable homes in Egypt.

And so, just as the Israelites endured forty years in the wilderness after crossing the Red Sea, Jesus spent forty days in the wilderness after his baptism, where he endured many trials and temptations. However, Jesus's temptations were not merely the physical temptations of hunger and comfort that Israel faced. Because Jesus's mission is to save us from the inside out, to free us from our spiritual slavery, he had to endure the *entirety* of human temptation—physical, emotional, and spiritual. His temptation in the wilderness was a kind of speedrun through every kind of temptation depicted in the Bible—those of Eden, those of the wilderness, and those of Babel.

In order to defeat temptation at its core, Jesus goes up to a mountain to be tempted directly by the master of wickedness, Satan. He goes up to Mount Eden, to the birthplace of human sin, to do battle with the same serpent who tempted Adam and Eve. This battle begins with Satan asking Jesus to turn stones into bread. Jesus is hungry, and he is tempted to forsake God's provision in order to satiate his bodily desires. It is a temptation that many of us face daily—to put our love of food and comfort ahead of our desire to be with and trust God. Fortunately for us, Jesus resists this temptation, creating an example for us to follow whenever we are tempted.

Second, Jesus is tempted to disobey God. On Mount Eden, Satan twisted the words of the Father to convince Eve to eat of the tree of knowledge. And so, on this mountain, Satan similarly tempts Jesus with the very words of Scripture, misquoting psalms to convince Jesus to disobey the Father and throw himself off the temple. This is a temptation that we too will face from time to time. Rather than trusting in God's word, we will be challenged to twist the meaning of the Bible into a pretzel to convince ourselves that we are not being disobedient. While Adam and Eve succumbed to this conceit, Jesus resists, allowing us to similarly resist this temptation and firmly trust in God's word.

For the third and final temptation, a desperate Satan takes Jesus up to the peak of the mountain to look down at all the kingdoms of the earth. Satan offers Jesus rulership over all of these kingdoms and the opportunity to become the greatest and mightiest king to have ever walked the earth. Satan attempts to split God the Father from God the Son by tempting Jesus to establish his own rival kingdom on earth to compete with heaven. Just as Babel is the culmination of human sin in the Old Testament, the culmination of Jesus's temptation is the offer of Babel—the offer of a rival mountain through which to rule and oppress. We are similarly tempted whenever we seek out power over others for the sake of our own gain.

Fortunately, Jesus resists this final temptation, rejecting earthly power and banishing Satan from his sight. In so doing he fulfills the vision of Isaiah: he is the one capable of casting the serpent from the mountain of God. We can see in Jesus's resistance to temptation the beginning of the reversal of the curse of Eden. In fact, in Mark's account of the temptation, it states that after Jesus resisted the devil, he dwelled with the wild beasts (Mark 1:13). This harkens back to the peace of Mount Eden before the fall, where Adam lived at peace with the entire animal kingdom. It is the first sign that the consequences of sin are slowly being reversed in and through Jesus.

Jesus experiences the entirety of temptation, and resists. In him we have "one who in every respect has been tempted as we are, yet without sin" (Hebrews 4:15). While Christians are given the privilege of entering into new life in Jesus by passing through the waters of baptism, this does not prevent us from being tempted. Life on the other side of baptism is still life in the spiritual wilderness, where we face trials and temptations. The temptations we face today are no different than those of Jesus: we are tempted with base physical urges, with the deceitful twisting of words, and with the lure of power and greatness. But now in Jesus we have an antidote to the poisonous venom of the snake. In Jesus we have the power to resist the devil (James 4:7). Whenever we are tempted, we ought to "emulate and imitate His victory"[6] over Satan, drawing strength from Jesus to similarly battle the serpent, trusting that we will be victorious if we fight with Jesus.

TO THE SPIRITUAL MOUNTAIN: JESUS'S HEALINGS AND MIRACLES

Moses's arduous journey through the wilderness is halted by the presence of Mount Sinai, where the Israelites are informed of their inability to ascend due to their sin. God reveals himself in the cloud at Sinai, but places a large *Do Not Enter* sign at its base. Limited access to God is granted through the institution of elaborate purity rituals, which were a constant reminder that, due to sin, God was still largely unapproachable.

After Jesus's arduous spiritual journey in the wilderness battling the temptations of Satan, he immediately descends down the mountain and begins a ministry of healing, curing the poisonous venom of sin and all of its pernicious manifestations. In so doing, he begins to erode this barrier that was erected at Sinai, enabling people to begin to encounter God's presence once again.

The purpose of Jesus's healing ministry can be summed up in the first few interactions he has after he is tempted by Satan. First, Jesus enters into a synagogue and declares that the words from

Isaiah are now fulfilled in him: "The Spirit of the Lord is on me, because he has anointed me to proclaim good news to the poor. He has sent me to proclaim freedom for the prisoners and recovery of sight for the blind, to set the oppressed free, to proclaim the year of the Lord's favor" (Luke 4:18–19 NIV). Jesus declares that he is the anointed Son of God prophesied by Isaiah. He is the Messiah and true king of Israel, the one who is fully anointed with oil and the Holy Spirit. Jesus has declared that his kingship will be one marked by freedom for the oppressed and healing for the sick. In this passage and the healings that follow, Jesus is fulfilling the symbol of oil. He discloses that he alone has power over life and death, and that he will use this power to heal the sick and downtrodden. Oil now stands as a royal mark of Jesus's kingship. At baptism, Christians are marked on their foreheads with oil: a sign that they reside in Jesus's kingdom and live under his reign. But this same oil is also an oil of healing. As Christians grow sick and weary, they can pray for each other and anoint each other with oil as a reminder that Jesus can heal them now, and Jesus *will* eternally heal them at their resurrection (James 5:14). Like a soothing aloe or restorative lotion, Jesus is the one capable of healing us from the inside out. Now, every time we smell a fragrant oil or feel a cool balm on our skin, we can be reminded of the eternal healing that will come through Jesus.

After this announcement, Jesus begins this healing ministry by exclaiming, "Repent, for the kingdom of heaven has come near" (Matthew 4:17 NIV). In Jesus, God is no longer far off at the top of the mountain, but has instead come near in his very person. Jesus in effect comes down to the base of Sinai and performs these healings as a sign that God is now approachable through him. In the person of Jesus, the sinner and the unclean are finally able to see him, touch him, and to experience healing. Thus begins a reversal of sin and its manifold deleterious consequences. What kinds of healings does Jesus perform?

First, Jesus heals the demon-possessed. The demon possessed are those who have lost control over large portions of their mental or physical capacities and have somehow become vessels of demonic forces. Sometimes these possessions are the result of individuals willfully and unrepentantly acceding to evil desires over a long period of time. But other times the sources of these possessions remain difficult to understand. We still see demon possession at work today in some individuals whose hearts, minds, or bodies are no longer fully under their control. As Jesus battled the prince of these demonic forces on the mountain, he now descends to do battle with these forces in the valley. In Matthew 8:28–34, two demon possessed men leap out of an empty tomb to confront Jesus. At that moment, the demons inside of them begin to tremble at the presence of the anointed one. They beg Jesus to send them out of the men and into a group of pigs! The demons then flee from the two men, a sign to all that Jesus has power even over the demonic spiritual forces.

Jesus continues to heal in this way today. He does so in the small ways he forgives our sins and empowers us to leave behind our sinful lives, and he does so in larger ways like healing our deeply engrained addictions. In more dramatic ways, Jesus continues to heal the demon-possessed amongst us. I once encountered a nursing home resident named Lily who suffered from a number of psychological and physical ailments. When we started a church service in her nursing home, she would periodically interrupt the service with loud curse words and screams. Over the ensuing months, we began to pray for healing for Lily, and watched as the screams and curses lessened over time. One day, as we were singing *Come Thou Fount of Every Blessing*, Lily began shouting, but this time, she was not cursing. Instead, Lily had begun to sing along to the words of this hymn. After the song had ended, Lily began to converse with others at this church service. It was the first time in years that she had had a cogent conversation with anyone. The fount of Jesus's blessing continues to heal those sick with sin to this very day.

In addition to healing the demon possessed, Jesus descended the mountain to heal the sick and disabled. As we have seen, life east of Eden is marked by constant decay and atrophy. The final curse of Genesis 3 is death, the breaking down of the human body. From that time on disease and illness have reigned. From the moment we are born, we are on borrowed time, awaiting our inevitable expiration. However, since Jesus has come into the world to reverse the entirety of the curse of Eden, he begins to show that even death can be reversed.

Throughout his earthly ministry, Jesus draws near to sick and broken bodies, touching them and bringing about physical healing. While Jesus performs these miracles as a deep outpouring of the love that he has for the wounded and downtrodden, these miracles are also meant to be signs of the deeper, inner healing that Jesus will bring about. Jesus has come to heal not only our physical senses, but also our inner, spiritual senses as well. As we saw in chapter 4, Adam and Eve's fall from Eden, into sin, created a split between heaven and earth, and a degradation of their inner and outer senses. They could still see the earth with their physical eyes, but their spiritual eyes were blinded to heaven. They could hear each other's voices with their physical ears, but they could no longer hear God with their spiritual ears.

Since Jesus has come to save us from the inside out, his rescue mission involves not only the healing of physical senses, but a healing of our inner spiritual senses as well. And so many of Jesus's miracles are given as signs of the inner healing that he desires to bring about. The physical miracle becomes a sign of a deeper spiritual miracle that is made possible for those who turn to Jesus. For instance, on one occasion Jesus heals a man that was born blind (John 9). While this man is ecstatic over his ability to physically see the world around him for the first time, Jesus uses this opportunity to reveal that he has the power to heal our inner sight as well. Jesus tells this man that, just as he has lifted the dark curtain that covered his physical eyes, he has the power to remove the curtain on his spiritual eyes. This is the veil that is blocking us from seeing God in our mind's eye. Those who believe in Jesus will have their inner eyes opened. They will begin to see Jesus in their mind's eye, and this inner opening will be brought to full physical sight one day on Mount Zion.

On another occasion, Jesus miraculously multiplies a small number of loaves of bread and fish in order to feed thousands of his hungry followers. While this miracle was meant to provide a physical meal for the crowd, it also served as a springboard for Jesus to reveal to the world that he desires to heal our inner, spiritual sense of taste. Jesus declares, after this miracle, that he is the "bread of life" (John 6:35). Those who hunger for righteousness and goodness will find these inner spiritual longings satiated by him. He is inviting us to hunger for him in our gut. Just as God gave to the Israelites bread from heaven in the wilderness to satisfy their physical hunger, Jesus has come from heaven to give us himself as the spiritual bread of life. In him we will find all of our deepest desires fulfilled.

Jesus performed a number of other miracles that revealed to the world that he is the fulfillment of the ancient Scriptures. All of these miracles were signs indicating that God desired to heal us from the inside out. Jesus has descended from above so that he could begin to heal us from below. But the effect of these miracles was limited: none of them created a permanent change. Each and every person whom Jesus healed would eventually succumb to death. Jesus performed these miracles to prove to the world that he is God and to foreshadow what life with him will look like for those who believe. But as signs, these healings could only point to a fuller healing yet to come. His death, resurrection, and the sending of his Spirit will enable this full healing of both the inner and outer senses. But first, Jesus had to reveal his power to fully defeat sin. He had to show the world that he was more than a miracle worker: he was in fact God incarnate. For this reason, Jesus continued on the path of Moses, taking us up to Mount Tabor to reveal his full, divine glory.

Christ today is the one who reveals this divine light, and shines forth ineffably. Let us shine along with him, transfigured, as far as possible, by the light of God. Christ, on the mountain, makes the glory that is inaccessible available to the disciples. Let us be lifted up to the height of contemplation, and let us join them in gazing on the Mystery.

—*Leo the Great*

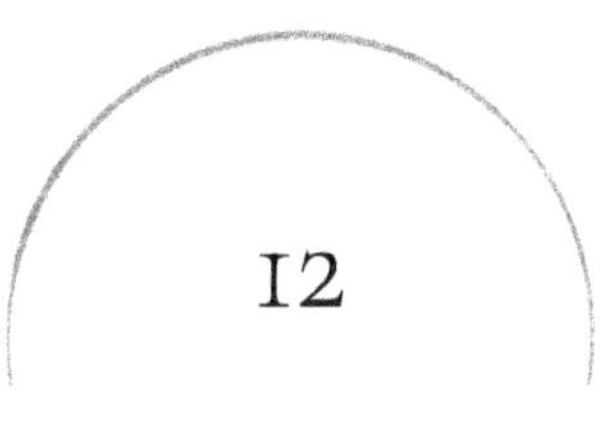

12

JESUS ASCENDS

On Matthew 5–7, 17:1–3, John 2:13–22, and Psalm 27

We all journey with a picture of our final destination in mind. As we hike up a mountain, a vision of the view from the top spurs us to climb higher and higher. Similarly, we want to look forward to the finale of our travels with God at the top of his mountain. When the clouds cover the sun, they remind us that something brighter lies ahead. We want a clearer picture of this final goal. We want this picture to capture our heart and imagination in the present, in order to give us hope for our eternal destination on Mount Zion.

FROM DESCENDING TO ASCENDING

As Jesus begins performing miracles, speculation runs rampant regarding his identity: Is he really the Messiah foretold by the prophets? Or, is he just another miracle worker in a long line of holy persons that had come before? At this point of the gospel story, the full divine glory of God had not yet been revealed in Jesus. Jesus claimed to be the Son of Man and the Son of God foretold in Isaiah and Daniel and had begun to prove this by *descending* to earth as a baby, and healing the sick and demon possessed. He then goes on to show that he is God by *ascending* the mountain, giving perfect teaching through the Sermon on the Mount and revealing his divine glory on Mount Tabor.

ASCENDING TO INTERPRET: THE SERMON ON THE MOUNT

God's command rings out from the top of the mountain. On Mount Eden, one simple command was given to Adam and Eve. On Mount Sinai, God thundered the Ten Commandments to the people of Israel. Unfortunately, each of these commands were eventually violated and misunderstood by God's people. For this reason, in Matthew 5–7, Jesus climbs a mountain and gives the Sermon on the Mount. Near the beginning of this sermon, he tells his audience that in his very person, the fullness of these commandments is revealed. He states "Do not think that I have come to abolish the Law or the Prophets; I have not come to abolish them but to fulfill them" (Matthew 5:17). Just as Jesus fulfilled the Old Testament through his baptism and miracles, he now fulfills all of the teachings of the Old Testament by giving their definitive interpretation. In so doing, he reveals to the crowd that he is God—he is the same God who shouted the Ten Commandments from Sinai, and he is the same God who gave the command to Adam and Eve to not eat of the tree of knowledge.

What Jesus proves in his Sermon on the Mount is that he is both the author of the Ten Commandments and the source of every law in the Old Testament. While the Ten Commandments were bellowed from far way, Jesus allows the crowd to draw near to God, to meet the author of these commands. In this way he fulfills the promise of the trumpet call on Mount Sinai. On Sinai, the trumpet noise was a warning that no one except Moses could scale the mountain to hear God's voice. Now through Jesus all are granted the possibility of climbing the mount to hear God's voice. Through belief the trumpet blast becomes the pleasing timbre of Jesus' voice, bestowing on its hearers the words of everlasting life. The ancient writer Chromatius summarizes this best when he says that Jesus:

> Is the One who had once handed down the Mosaic law on Mt. Sinai, showing that he was the author of both laws. ... When the law was first given on the mountain, the people were forbidden to draw close. But now, as the Lord was teaching on the mountain, no one is forbidden. Rather, all are invited that they may hear ... In the former case, terror is instilled in the unbelievers. In the latter case, a gift of blessings is poured out on the believers.[1]

Through belief in Jesus one can now scale the mountain and hear the author of all biblical teaching. There is a difference between reading a book and meeting its author. While a book communicates the ideas of its author, a personal encounter provides the opportunity to discuss those ideas and clarify any misconceptions or misunderstandings. Furthermore, a personal encounter can shed further light on the meaning of the words written.

Karen Russell was one of my close college friends who was known for composing hilarious emails to our friend group in North Mid Quads dorm. She had this knack for creative narration, and could describe a simple walk to the dining halls in ways that made one laugh out loud. Though we lost touch after graduation, I found out later that Karen had become a famous author, writing short stories and novels, winning awards, and being interviewed on NPR. Because I know her personally, I can read her work with added depth, hearing her quiet, cheerful voice narrating each line of prose.

Similarly, Jesus stands up on a mountain to let the crowd meet the author of the law and to help further clarify the content and meaning of the whole Bible. We can connect the person of Jesus with the teachings of the Bible, and we can picture Jesus reciting these teachings with raised hands and intoned voice. We can now know the person behind the words, and this gives us a deeper understanding of all biblical instruction.

In many ways, Jesus's teaching is an extension of the Ten Commandments. As we saw, the commandments are summarized in two statements: Love God with all of your heart, mind, and soul, and love your neighbor as yourself. A large portion of the Sermon on the Mount involves Jesus boiling down the entirety of Old Testament laws into two simple commands. His goal is to demonstrate that every single law, at its core, is about the love of God and neighbor, and to prove to the prideful that following the law is not enough to make one a loving person. Two examples from the Sermon on the Mount vividly demonstrate Jesus's approach.

First, Jesus addresses the commandment against adultery. This command is straightforward and easy for most people to obey. But Jesus proceeds to explain that anyone who looks at another person with lust in their heart has committed adultery (Matthew 5:28). Jesus pushes this command to the extreme to get to the heart of the law: loving other people means that we respect their bodies and refuse to use them to fulfill our sexual desires. Even a fleeting sexual fantasy can dehumanize another image bearer of God, turning them into an object we use for our own satisfaction.

Second, Jesus addresses the commandment against murder. Again, this command is simple and easy for most people to follow. But Jesus raises the stakes when he adds that anyone who harbors hatred in their heart has committed murder (Matthew 5:22). At its root, murder is the elimination of another person that we hate. And so, any moment in which we fantasize about getting vengeance on another person, or telling another person off, is a moment in which we desire the diminishment or extinction of another. Instead, Jesus says that our love must extend even to our enemies.

If we understand the teachings of Jesus, and all the teachings of the Bible in this way, it should quickly become clear to us that we cannot treat God's law like a checklist. There is no way for anyone to perfectly obey each law. Like the commandment against coveting, the Sermon on the Mount is meant to break us of our pride, forcing us to admit that we cannot climb our way to Mount Zion by our good works. Jesus sums up his teachings with this devastating statement: "Unless your righteousness exceeds that of the scribes and Pharisees, you will never enter the kingdom of heaven" (Matthew 5:20). The Pharisees were well known for their devotion to following every single commandment. And Jesus says that not even this is sufficient.

Jesus is reminding the crowd that sin makes it impossible to fully follow the law. Instead, we need forgiveness and new hearts, capable of fully loving God and others in purity and truth. If we are not made new in Christ, no amount of law will make us good. In fact, every rule will be received as a burden. When I was little,

I fought often with my older brother, and my mother would set forth a number of rules to try to curtail our bad behavior. But since neither of us had any intention of respecting each other, these rules were received as burdens. We would quickly search for loopholes. If we were told not to hit each other, we would smash each other's GI Joes instead. If we were told to not destroy each other's toys, we would tease each other mercilessly. No rule could make us respect one another. What we needed were new hearts that were set on loving and respecting each other. What Jesus is revealing to the crowd is ultimately that they need new, loving hearts in order to lovingly obey God. They need hearts of flesh to replace their hearts of stone (Ezekiel 36:26). The awareness of this reality should instill in the crowd, and in us, a desire for Jesus to give us new hearts capable of such love.

After Jesus finishes his teaching, "as one who had authority, and not as their scribes" (Matthew 7:29), the crowd reacts with astonishment and amazement. With this teaching, Jesus demonstrates to the crowd that he is God, the very author of the Old Testament, and that its teachings find their fulfillment in him.

JESUS ASCENDS TO REVEAL GOD'S GLORY: THE TRANSFIGURATION

The deepest longing in the human soul is to see God face-to-face and behold his brilliant and illuminating glory. This was Moses's one wish, yet even he was denied the chance to see God's glorious face, having to settle for a quick and awesome glimpse of a passing-by God.

It was Jesus whose partial glory was revealed to Moses on top of a mountain. And it is this same Jesus that took his closest friends Peter, James, and John, up to another mountain, Mount

Tabor, to similarly experience God's glory. Peter, James, and John are given access to God's glory on Tabor just like Adam, Eve and Moses on Eden and Sinai. Except, something new happens in this glorious encounter on Mount Tabor. We can see three new aspects of this encounter, centering on the fulfillment of the symbols of *garments, glory,* and *face.*

First, on Mount Tabor, Jesus's clothing became dazzlingly white. When human beings are able to get close to God, they are described as surrounded and clothed in his glory. On Mount Tabor, Jesus's garments radiated this glory, but in a way that far surpassed the reflective glory of Adam and Moses. In Mark's account of the passage, it states that Jesus's garments became whiter than any one on earth could bleach—a pure whiteness that is purer than anything made by human hands (Mark 9:3). What these white robes tell us is that Jesus is the one, true, perfect human being. He is the only human capable of being fully in the Father's presence, because he is the only one without sin. On Tabor, Jesus fulfills the symbol of garments, enabling us to long for our future heavenly garments each time we put on our earthly clothing.

Second, on Mount Tabor, Jesus reveals God's glory. Not only do Jesus's garments radiate God's glory, but God's glory emanates *in* and *through* Jesus: "Glory did not come upon this body from outside itself, but from within."[2] Jesus's divine glory was now revealed to his disciples in all its beauty and wonder. In case there was any doubt left with Peter, James, and John, in this scene Jesus's identity becomes crystal clear: he is God. The same one who created light now reveals himself as true light.[3] This light was inaccessible to human beings because of their sin. Any attempt to enter that light would lead to certain death for sinful man. Now, however, "Christ, on the mountain, makes the glory that is inaccessible available to the disciples."[4] Access to God's glory is now possible through the person of Jesus Christ. Just as we can have a share in the sun's warmth and brightness each time we step outside on a hot summer day, we can now share in the radiant goodness and beauty of God through Jesus Christ.

Finally, Jesus fulfills the promises of scripture by revealing his face. While Jesus is transfigured, Moses and Elijah appear and begin to converse with Jesus. Why does Moses, all of the sudden, make an appearance on Tabor? It is because Tabor is the place where God decides to finally make Moses's wish come true. More than anything else, Moses longed to see the very face of God, to look into the eyes of God and experience deep relational intimacy with his creator. Now, thousands of years after he died, Moses is lifted up to Tabor to have a face-to-face conversation with Jesus. In Jesus's face shines the splendor of God's radiant glory. All partial glimpses of God's glory that Moses experienced on Sinai are now brought to fulfillment at Tabor as "Moses gazes on Christ as God."[5]

Mount Tabor reveals our destiny and the object of our deepest desire: Jesus. He is the joy of man's desiring. At the top of Mount Eden next to the tree of life, at the top of Sinai through the cloud, and at the top of Mount Tabor in full glory, stands Jesus. We long to encounter the awesome, powerful, and almighty God in all his pure, radiant glory. We also long for this encounter to be face-to-face. As the only one who is fully divine and fully human, these desires merge and coalesce in the very person of Jesus. In Jesus, we can know the God who created heaven and earth, and in Jesus we can know this God on a person-to-person, face-to-face level. To see his radiant, glorified body is what human beings were created for— a sight that, according to Thomas Aquinas, not even angels are fit to behold.[6]

Figure 4: Mount Tabor—Matthew 17:1–13

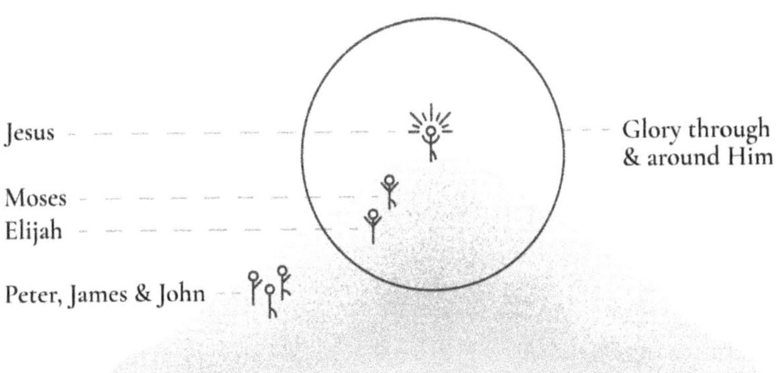

COMING DOWN FROM MOUNT TABOR: THE TABERNACLE AND TEMPLE OF JESUS

While Jesus is transfigured on Mount Tabor, a cloud surrounded Peter, James, and John. As they entered the cloud, the voice of God the Father called out "this is my beloved Son, with whom I am well pleased; listen to him" (Matthew 17:5), and the disciples fell down in worship of Jesus as their God and Lord. However, at this precise moment, the clouds drifted away and the lights began to dim. The glorious radiance of God retreated, Moses and Elijah disappeared, and the ordinary flesh of Jesus remained.

Peter, James, and John were given the fullest picture of what lies behind the cloud. Moses entered the darkness of this cloud in order to view the heavenly tabernacle, the place of God's perfect dwelling, and to model the earthly tabernacle on this vision. But this glimpse was only a preview, a foreshadowing of the mystery that is now revealed on Mount Tabor. As Peter, James, and John entered the cloud, what they discovered was Jesus alone. What they learned through this experience was that *Jesus is the true tabernacle and true temple*, the fulfillment of all the promises of the Old Testament tabernacle. Gregory of Nyssa summarizes: "This tabernacle would be Christ who is the power and the wisdom of God, who in his own nature was not made with hands, yet capable of being made when it became necessary for this tabernacle to be erected among us."[7] The heavenly tabernacle of Christ's divinity and the earthly tabernacle of his body are united in the one person of Jesus Christ.

Jesus makes this very claim about himself early in the Gospel of John, when he confronts those who were operating markets within the temple: "Jesus answered them, 'Destroy this temple, and in three days I will raise it up.' The Jews then said, 'It has taken forty-six years to build this temple, and will you raise it up in three days?' But he was speaking about the temple of his body" (John 2:19–21). The temple and tabernacle, modeled after the mountain of God, was the place where human beings could encounter God. It was the one location in which heaven came down to earth. It was the one place where human beings could encounter a glimpse of God's presence. The events on Mount Tabor show us that the fulfillment of the tabernacle and temple have come in the very person of Jesus Christ. In Jesus, there is a union of humanity and divinity, and of heaven and earth. In Jesus, the very presence of God radiates.

This assertion had profound implications for those who were worshiping in the temple in Jerusalem: if Jesus was the true temple, then their current, physical temple was no longer necessary. After Jesus's transfiguration on Mount Tabor, he makes this explicitly clear by pronouncing the impending destruction of the temple: every one of its stones will break apart (Matthew 24:1–2).

Furthermore, Jesus predicts that he will be rejected by the religious leaders, and that his body will become the cornerstone of a new temple built upon himself.[8] We see in these passages how Jesus fulfills the symbol of stone in the Old Testament. The true stone of Mount Eden was crushed to make the bricks of Babel. The earthly temple had, in turn, devolved into a kind of Babel. It is through Jesus the rock, the cornerstone, that the false worship of Babel can finally be put to an end. He is called stone because he is capable of destroying all false worship: "No one who stands upon him will fall victim to deceitful charms or be moved by the storms of persecution."[9] He is called the cornerstone because it is upon his body that the foundation of a new community called the church will be built, a community centered fully on the worship of God.

How will this be possible? How will true worship of God be accessible through Jesus Christ? As we have seen in the Old Testament, temporary and limited worship of God was accessible in the tabernacle and temple through the blood sacrifices of animals. As Jesus has come to fulfill the entire Old Testament, he must come to fulfill, to bring to completion, this system of sacrifice. As the tabernacle and temple were the location of sacrifices to God, Jesus will thus offer up his own body, the one true temple, so that all those who believe in him will have full access to the living God.

This sacrificial offering will take place through the horrific ensuing events of Jesus's arrest, trial, and execution. Peter, James, and John have just seen Jesus's heavenly exaltation. Now they must witness his earthly humiliation. But now they have hope. What has been revealed on Mount Tabor is a clear picture of the final goal of humankind. The tree of life was hidden from Adam and

Eve on Mount Eden. God was concealed by a cloud on Mount Sinai. For the first time, humanity has been given a clear picture of the top of the mountain of God: Jesus Christ. It is his body that radiates the very glory of God. It is his illuminated face that is waiting for us at the top of the mountain. It is Jesus who stands ready to converse with us, just as he conversed with Moses on Tabor. This is the goal and destination of every believer. Every thought in our mind, every word on our lips, every action we take, should have this goal at its center. All activity is meant to move us further up this mountain, to draw us closer to the transfigured Son of God. But first, before we can even begin our ascent, Jesus must complete his descent, breaking the bonds of sin and evil once and for all, and enabling us to finally draw near to God.

Blessed be the Merciful One
who saw the sword beside Paradise,
barring the way to the Tree of Life;
He came and took to Himself a body
which was wounded so that,
by the opening of His side,
He might open up the way into Paradise.

—Ephrem the Syrian

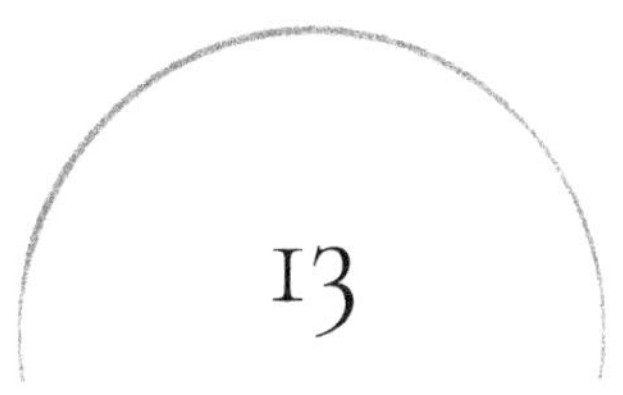

THE CRUCIFIXION

On Matthew 21: 1–11, Matthew 26–27, John 19:31–37, Hebrews 9–11, and Psalm 22

So many of our relationships in this world are marked by fragility. We live in fear that our friends will abandon us when our weakness is revealed and we can no longer hide our flaws. One thoughtless word or one regretful action is enough to sever a relationship. We all long for intimacy as well as security. We want deep, personal friendships, and we want assurance that those friendships will endure despite our sins and imperfections.

We also long for intimacy and stability in our relationship with God, but curtains and clouds remind us of our sinful separation. The sight of a fragile lamb reminds us that our paltry sacrifices are never enough to overcome this barrier. We need a sacrifice strong enough to clear the clouds and cut the curtains forever.

CHRIST THE KING: MATTHEW 21:1–11, 26:1–13

After finally revealing himself to the disciples as fully God and fully human, Jesus descended from Mount Tabor and headed towards Jerusalem, where he would reveal himself to the world as its true king. The prophets foretold that salvation would come to the world through the messiah, the king of Israel: Isaiah stated that the savior would descend from the line of king David, and that he would be anointed by the oil of the Holy Spirit to fulfill his mission to rescue God's people.

Jesus entered Jerusalem to great fanfare and praise. He was greeted by the crowds as the great and triumphal king of Israel. But what kind of king is Jesus? A mighty warrior king who vanquishes powerful adversaries? A wise political king who shrewdly builds alliances? A rich king who ushers in an age of prosperity? Two scenes from Jesus's entrance into Jerusalem reveal to us that he was a different kind of king than people expected. First, Jesus rode triumphally into Jerusalem on a donkey, with scores of commonfolk praising him. Whereas an earthly king would ride into town on a war horse surrounded by the rich, Jesus entered Jerusalem on a humble ass, surrounded by the poor. He came not to exercise power over others, but to exercise his power and mercy for the sake of others: "Now there was never any king, simultaneously just, a redeemer, gentle and seated on a donkey, who came to Jerusalem, unless this is he who alone is King of kings, God and Redeemer, Jesus. He is kind, gentle and abundant in mercy for all those who call upon him."[1]

As a sign of worship for the triumphant King, many in the crowd took off their outer garments and laid them down at the feet of Jesus as he rode by. Clothing is not only what surrounds us and protects us, it is also a sign of socioeconomic status: rich people wear fine clothing and kings wear opulent robes. In the case of uniforms, clothing also reveals that we are under someone else's authority. For instance, a military outfit indicates that one serves a particular country and is under the command of a superior.

Thus, when this crowd removed their garments and placed them under the feet of Jesus, it was a sign that they were disavowing themselves of their own power and status to serve Christ as king. They longed not for the fine clothing of high society, nor the prestigious uniforms of the military, but rather the transfigured white robes of Jesus. They longed to be surrounded by the glory of God. What they wanted was not the physical and temporary protection of an emperor, but the spiritual and eternal protection of Jesus.

After his entrance into Jerusalem, a poor woman anointed Jesus's body with expensive oil. The prophets foretold that the Son of Man would come with the full anointing of the oil of the Spirit, a king capable of ruling in perfect wisdom and knowledge. This anointing was thus an announcement of Christ's kingship, but a kingship unlike any other. Rather than a rich and powerful king crowned by nobility, Jesus was quietly and meekly anointed by a lowly woman in the midst of his disciples.

We see in these passages that Jesus has fulfilled the role of the king foretold by the prophets and he fulfills the hopes and promises latent in the symbol of oil. When Christians are anointed with oil today, they share in this kingly power of Jesus. The oil poured on Jesus runs down from his head and beard and onto his followers. They are marked with the oil of the true king and thus commit themselves to serve this king by exhausting their power for the sake of the downcast. The sight and smell of oil awakens us to the power of Christ working in us, but this power is not meant to build ourselves up, but rather to be exhausted outward for the benefit of the lost and weak. To be anointed with the oil of Christ is to be emboldened to lay down our own garments of wealth and status for the sake of others and long instead to be clothed with the heavenly garment of Christ's glory.

THE PASSOVER MEAL: MATTHEW 26:17–29

Food breaks downs barriers and brings people together. A vivid portrayal of the power of a meal is featured in the Danish film *Babette's Feast*, in which a Parisian refugee named Babette becomes a live-in cook for two elderly sisters who oversee an aging and dying church in a small town. The town, as well as the congregation, is rife with quarrels and tinged by decades of old animosities. One day, Babette discovers that she had just won the lottery, but rather than making plans to leave the small town, she spends the fortune preparing an opulent Parisian dinner. The feast brings together the entire town, and in the joyful atmosphere old enemies are reconciled. At the end of the story, the one sister Philippa embraces Babette and tells her that she will be a cook at the Lord's feast in heaven, where her cooking will "enchant the angels."

God uses food to bring people together to worship him and to be reconciled to him and each other. After his military victory, Abraham celebrated a sacrificial meal of bread and wine with Melchizedek. Later, food sacrifices in the tabernacle included meals meant to indicate fellowship between Israel and God.

On the night before Jesus was handed over to be executed, he participated in the celebratory Passover meal, the meal meant to commemorate the rescue of Israel from physical slavery in Egypt. Here, Jesus revealed the true meaning of this meal. He takes bread, blesses it, and says "Take, eat: this is my body broken for you." Here, the fullest meaning of *bread* is revealed. The manna that nourished the Israelites in the wilderness is also the spiritual bread of Jesus's body, nourishing our souls as we journey with him. The bread that is broken into pieces in a sacrificial meal is now the body of Jesus Christ, which is broken on the cross for the forgiveness of sins. Each time Christians gather, they obey the words of Jesus to continue this celebration, eating of this one bread, and thus having fellowship with each other and with Jesus.

When the Passover meal was concluding, Jesus took a cup of wine, saying "Take, drink: this is my blood poured out for the forgiveness of sins." Wine is a sign of opulence and celebration, as well as a symbol of the blood of the lamb that was placed on wooden doors during the Passover. In blessing this cup of wine, Jesus reveals how the symbols of *wine* and *blood* intertwine and culminate in himself. As the blood of the lamb was smeared on the wooden posts in Egypt, the blood of Jesus, the Lamb of God, will be spilt on the wood of the cross. This blood which rescued Israel from physical slavery is now the blood that will rescue God's people from the spiritual slavery of sin. Furthermore, this wine is now revealed to be the "fruit of the vine," a sign of the eternal heavenly banquet that we will have with Jesus on Mount Zion. When Christians gather today at the communion altar, they are taken up to heaven, into sacred time, to celebrate this meal. The past blood of the Passover and cross come together with the future wine of the heavenly banquet. The wine that is a sign of Jesus's death becomes the very same wine that will be poured out for us in heaven. Wine now reminds us of our final heavenly destination, while also reminding us of the blood of Jesus which enables us to get there.

In this Passover meal, Jesus reveals the full meaning of the *altars* constructed by Abraham and erected at the back of the tabernacle. In the Bible, altars were locations of sacrifice, as well as places of worship and communion with God. All these Old Testament altars foreshadowed the table of the Last Supper. They are now to become places of remembrance for Jesus's sacrifice on the cross, as well as sights of table fellowship with him. The wine on the communion table is an ongoing reminder of that sacrifice and that fellowship with Jesus. We enter church as people coming to a feast, sharing in this meal of bread and wine that Jesus has prepared for us. Even the sight of an ordinary table at home can stir in us a longing to be at the altar on Sunday and stoke in us a desire to one day partake in that heavenly feast with Jesus on Mount Zion.

THE WAY OF THE CROSS: MATTHEW 26:30–27:32

While many welcomed Jesus into Jerusalem as the true and final king, others were angered and alarmed by his entrance. Some religious leaders were threatened by Jesus's popularity and worried that he would usurp their authority. Others were disappointed because they had been hoping for a king who would wield power over others and lead a political revolution to punish Israel's enemies. They did not want a humble carpenter riding into town on a donkey! Others were simply annoyed by his goodness and humility. As is often the case, those who are good remind us of our flaws and insecurities. Those who seem to live wholesome and perfect lives provoke our envy. In response, we attempt to diminish their standing in order to make ourselves look better. As Jesus's goodness and perfection stroll through Jerusalem atop a donkey, the imperfections of the weak and the wicked are brought to the surface, and many react with jealousy and envy.

For these reasons, a group of powerful leaders conspired to have Jesus arrested and tried for blasphemy and sedition. As their conspiracy advanced, more and more people lined up against Jesus. First the religious leaders condemned him for claiming to be God. Then a political leader, Pontius Pilate, sentenced Jesus to execution by crucifixion. Then, the same crowd that cheered Jesus on as he entered Jerusalem turned against him, shouting back at Pilate a demand to have him crucified. Later, blue-collar soldiers beat and mocked him, and even more devastating, Jesus's own friends, the disciples, abandoned him for fear of their lives.

It seems as if the whole known world lined up against Jesus. As Isaiah foretold, the Lamb of God would come into the world to take upon himself "the iniquity of us all" (Isaiah 53:6). Jesus has come as the final tabernacle sacrifice, and this involves the absorption of the full range of human sin perpetuated by the full range of human beings. He is the lamb who can carry upon himself every kind of human sin performed by every kind of human person. We see this in the story of the cross: the rich and poor, the weak and the powerful, the blue collar and white collar, all line up to reject Jesus. Furthermore, Jesus is rejected in *every way* imaginable: he is betrayed, mocked, abandoned, denied, scorned, beaten, and battered. He became an object of envy, hatred, and humiliation. Fortunately for us, Jesus bears all this punishment for our sake. He stands like a lamb at the slaughter, patiently absorbing every blow, bearing in his body the physical and emotional torment.

When we observe the world turning on Jesus in every way imaginable, we are invited to read ourselves into this narrative, to see ourselves as one of the participants in Jesus's death. Jesus takes upon himself the sins of the whole world, and that includes *our* sins. Each and every time we sin, we are standing on the side of those who executed Jesus. Every time we are jealous, we participate in the jealously of the Pharisees. Every time we seek power for our own ends, we participate in the corruption of Pontius Pilate. Every time we mindlessly follow wicked people, we participate with the crowd shouting "crucify him." Every time we fail to be obedient to God out of fear or cowardice, we participate in the cowardice of Peter. Every time we sin, we place a hand on Jesus's innocent body, knowing that our sin has had a part in the killing of the Lamb of God.

The good news, however, is that Jesus stands ready and willing to bear our sin for us, and he is able to bear it all as true God and true man. Because he is human, he can fully carry the burden of human sin. Because He is God, he has the strength to carry its full weight to completion, fulfilling the sign of the lamb by dying for our sins and the sin of the world.

THE DEATH OF JESUS—MATTHEW 27:32–56

There is no other event that fulfills more stories and symbols of the Bible than the crucifixion of Jesus. The method of his execution, the apparatus of his death, and the location of his last breath interweave the stories and symbols of Mount Eden and Mount Sinai, while also pointing forward to Mount Zion.

We see this first in the location of Jesus's death: Mount Golgotha. Jesus is sentenced to die on the top of a mountain. Jesus carries the wood of the cross up to Golgotha as Isaac carried the wood up to Mount Moriah. His walk up the mountain is a walk to the top of the tabernacle, to the holy of holies to sacrifice himself in the presence of the Father. He climbs to the top of the mountain to show that he alone is able to fully enter into God's presence to heal our sins.

Second, we see the apparatus of execution: a wooden cross. At the top of Mount Eden is the tree of life. Abraham encountered Jesus under the trees of Mamre. Blood smeared on wooden posts protected the Israelites from death. And now, Jesus ascends to the top of the mountain and is hung on a wooden cross for our sins. His blood stains the wooden cross just as it stained the doors on the Passover. The tree of life provides the wood which props up Jesus on the cross. The life of Jesus is expended on the tree of life for the sake of our life. Now, each time we rest underneath the branches of a tall tree and touch its trunk, we feel the wood of the cross which enables us to ascend the mountain and bask under the tree of life.

Jesus was nailed to the cross in agony and endured prolonged suffering, characterized by external bleeding and slow suffocation. As we are invited to see our sin in Jesus's trial and sentencing, we are invited to see ourselves standing at the foot of this tree. We are invited to behold the man upon the cross, bearing our sin in an extraordinary act of love and mercy. We are invited to picture Jesus on the tree with the pain of one who put him there. We cry tears for our savior and mourn our sin borne on his shoulders. Yet, these same tears are tears of joy, as we marvel at the enormous mercy of our God, who swallowed up the entirety of our sin on the mountain. Augustine superbly articulates this invitation:

> As they were "looking on," so we too gaze on his wounds as he hangs. We see his blood as he dies. We see the price offered by the redeemer, touch the scars of his

> resurrection. He bows his head, as if to kiss you. His heart is made bare open, as it were, in love to you. His arms are extended that he may embrace you. His whole body is displayed for your redemption. Ponder how great these things are. Let all this be rightly weighed in your mind: as he was once fixed to the cross in every part of his body for you, so he may now be fixed in every part of your soul.[2]

In his last moments, Jesus cries out "It is finished" (John 19:30). In so doing, he declares an end to tabernacle sacrifice. The finality of this sacrifice is made evident immediately when, at the moment of Jesus's death, the curtain in the temple—the screen which prevented the people from accessing the holy of holies—is ripped in two. Like the cloud, this curtain was a reminder that intimacy with God was impossible due to human sin. Jesus's death on the cross destroyed this barrier. Our sin is finished in Jesus, and we can now have a direct and personal relationship with God. This is why, in Christian churches, there is an altar in the back of the sanctuary, *but no curtain*! Any believer can encounter Jesus directly in the communion celebration of his body and blood.

As soon as the curtain was torn in two, Matthew states that "the earth shook, and the rocks were split" (27:50). Since Jesus has finished and fulfilled the temple sacrifices, the temple is no longer the exclusive place where one can encounter God. The stones of the temple—having been condemned by Jesus as the stones of Babel—began to shake and crack. This is a sign that the true temple, the true place of God's presence, will now be wherever Christians gather. As we will see, the church will be called the body of Christ and its members living stones. When assembled in his name, they become the true temple of Christ's body.

FALLING ON THE SWORD: JOHN 19:31–37

After Jesus cried out "it is finished," he exhaled his final breath, and John states that he "gave up his spirit." Right after this event, a solider stabbed Jesus in the ribs, and blood and water spilled out of his side. After they had sinned, Adam and Eve were banished from Mount Eden, and the entrance to the mountain was blocked by a flaming sword. The *sword* was a sign that entrance to God's mountain is forbidden. However, on the cross Jesus falls on this sword for us. He absorbs the blows of sin which prevent us from God's presence and restores access to God's presence on his mountain once again. Now, when our hands touch a sharp knife, we are reminded of the pain absorbed by Christ on Golgotha, but also of God's mercy for removing the barrier to Eden. This praise chorus sung by ancient Syrian Christians now becomes our joyful refrain: "Blessed is He who was pierced and so removed the sword from the entry to Paradise."[3]

Blood and water flow out of the side of Jesus as he falls on this sword, becoming two preeminent symbols of the church. Jesus's side is pierced so that "the Sacraments might flow,"[4] which are the waters of baptism and the wine of communion. Entrance into Christ's body, the church, now comes through this opening in his side, through these streams of blood and water. First, our entrance into Christ's body comes through the waters of baptism. Plunging into its waters is not only participation in Jesus's baptism but also participation in his death on the cross. The waters of baptism are nourished by the water pouring forth from his body at Calvary. Its streams lead us straight into the side of his body, which is the church.

While our entrance into the body of Christ comes through the water poured from Jesus's side, our life in this body is sustained by the blood mixed with this water. Blood is a sign of life, and blood poured out is a sign that life has been sacrificed for the sake of another. Jesus's blood is now the mark of eternal life—it is the blood of the eternal God poured out so that we may have eternal life. During communion we are nourished by this blood. The communion wine is not only a sign of our eternal banquet with Jesus, it is also the blood spilled which allows us to enter that banquet. Each time we approach the communion cup, we approach it as though we "are drinking from his very side."[5]

FULFILLING THE TABERNACLE: HEBREWS 9–12

Now that we have walked through the story of Mount Golgotha, it is imperative to step back and reflect on what Jesus accomplished on the cross, which the Letter to the Hebrews does superbly in chapters 9–12. Ever since the first sin on Mount Eden, human beings have experienced brokenness in the world and separation from God. We all feel the pangs of guilt when we sin and endure pain and hardship when others sin against us. Furthermore, we experience loneliness and isolation from God. The connection that we so desperately long for, to be close to our creator, is broken and frayed. In the book of Leviticus, God gave Israel the tabernacle as a way of addressing this issue of sin. However, as we saw, the tabernacle system of sacrifice was limited, temporary, and incomplete.

Hebrews chapter 9 summarizes this limited and imperfect system of tabernacle/temple sacrifice. According to the author, the perpetual sin of the people and of the priests meant that the sacrifices could only address sin on the bodily level but could not bring about a pure heart and a pure conscience. While the priest would bring blood into the holy of holies, this blood was only the blood of animals, incapable of fully covering human sin. These sacrifices were akin to giving Tylenol to a cancer patient. They provided a small amount of temporary relief but could never cure the internal disease.

Furthermore, the earthly tabernacle and the earthly temple were unable to bring us fully into God's presence, because they were only copies of the true temple in heaven. As we discovered, Moses received the plans to the tabernacle from Jesus on Mount Sinai, but these were only the blueprints of a replica, a model of the true location of God's full presence, the heavenly tabernacle. As such, the sacrifices conducted in the earthly temple were always incomplete, a kind of shadow sacrifice, bringing small scale relief of sin but never fully bridging the gap between God and humanity.

What Hebrews tells us, however, is that when Jesus physically climbed Mount Golgotha, he was also entering into the heavenly temple itself. His sacrifice on the cross occurred both on Golgotha and also within the Father's direct presence in heaven. The key passage for understanding this is Hebrews 9:24–26: "For Christ has entered not into holy places ... every year with blood not his own, for then he would have had to suffer repeatedly since the foundation of the world. But as it is, he has appeared once for all at the end of the ages to put away sin by the sacrifice of himself." The death of Jesus on the cross was not just an incident of capital punishment two thousand years ago in the Middle East, it was also a sacrifice that took place within the heavenly temple itself. Jesus climbs both the physical mountain of Golgotha and the spiritual mountain of God, and there offers his life as the perfect sacrifice for sin.

Jesus's death takes place in both heaven and earth at the same time. Another way of stating this is that the cross is in an event in both secular and sacred time. This is only possible because of the unique person of Jesus, who alone is fully human and fully God. He alone can be the only true and pure sacrifice for humanity because he alone is without sin. He alone can enter the Father's presence in heaven, since he is God. He is the only priest without sin, and hence the only one capable of entering the holy of holies.

The fact that Jesus's death takes place in sacred time allows us to enter into and experience it as if it were present to us. We can stack the notes of blood and wood from the cross together with the stories of Abraham and the Passover into one harmonious chord of everlasting mercy. We can then enter into these stories ourselves, experiencing the immediacy of forgiveness for our sins each time we confess to God in our hearts and each time we taste the cup of wine at church.

The Letter to the Hebrews reveals the significance of this sacrifice for us. First, Jesus's sacrifice is permanent. The early Jewish converts to Christianity abandoned the sacrificing of animals. There was no longer any need, since Jesus took upon himself the full weight of sin past, present, and future. This is possible because his sacrifice takes place in heaven. If we recall from Genesis 1, God exists before creation and above creation, and thus he is not limited by time like human beings. To enter into heaven is to enter a place that is outside of human time. Past, present, and future are one to God. And so, when Jesus enters into the heavenly temple to sacrifice himself, he is dying for all sin throughout all time.

The finality of Jesus's sacrifice, the "once for all" characteristic that is the refrain of the Letter to the Hebrews, is a source of enormous comfort for all those who believe in Jesus and believe in the truth of the cross, for it tells us that our relationship with God is secure in Christ. We don't have to worry about God refusing to forgive us if we mess up sometime down the road. Jesus stands ready to forgive our sins whenever we confess, because he has already sacrificed himself for all our sins: past, present, and future.

Our most secure relationships are those that are predicated on consistent love and mercy, and we need these relationships from the moment of our birth. Child development experts stress the need for caregivers to provide loving, consistent environments to enable children to grow into maturity. The child will, of course, make mistakes along the way and may even push away their caregiver. However, the consistency and predictability of the caregiver in the midst of the chaos of development ultimately allows the child to flourish and form secure attachments. As a foster parent, I saw firsthand how the lack of this stable environment stunted the growth of our foster daughter as she struggled with anxiety and unpredictability.

While the Old Testament tabernacle provided opportunities to experience God's love and mercy, the relationship established between God and Israel was still on tenuous footing. One had to sacrifice regularly to secure forgiveness, and one could not be sure that the priests would be there to intervene the next time they sinned. What if the sacrifices were not performed properly? What if one could not afford an animal? What if the temple was destroyed before one's sins were forgiven? Such anxious questions must have nagged at the Israelites as a result of the limitations of this sacrificial system.

But now, as Hebrews states, Christ has died to sin once for all. There are no more animal sacrifices and no more physical temples. Jesus has already died and does not need to be re-crucified. He stands eternally ready to forgive our sins, making it possible for us to enter into a relationship with God on the secure footing of his infinite mercy. Christ now acts as this loving, predictable, consistent caregiver for us. Even though we continue to sin, his sacrifice assures us that we can depend upon the consistency of our relationship with him. He is constant through our inconstancy and is an anchor for our wayward hearts.

This is why, when the church gathers in the name of Jesus, they no longer sacrifice animals, but instead celebrate the remembrance of his death in the Eucharist. As we come to this feast, we ascend into the heavenlies and experience Jesus's death on the cross, knowing for certain that our sins are forgiven through this once and final sacrifice. Furthermore, because Jesus's death is outside of time, we can remember this sacrifice as if it were present to us. Just as the remembrance of an important past event can bring up feelings and emotions in the present, when we remember the death of Jesus, we can experience it as if it occurred just yesterday.

In all these events leading up to and including Mount Golgotha, we see Jesus fulfilling the entirety of the Old Testament tabernacle and temple practices. All of the temple sacrifices find their fulfillment and true meaning in Jesus. All the limitations of the earthly tabernacle are erased as Jesus tears down the curtain and enters the holy of holies. Before the cross, there was distance. The curtain, the sword, the cloud, and the laws and regulations, were all reminders that the mountain of God was off limits. Now the curtains are torn, the clouds have departed, and the brunt of the sword is borne.

But this is not the end of the story. Jesus has brought about the forgiveness of sin on the cross, but death, the consequence of sin, still remains. We are now able to be at peace with God, but our relationship with him will still end at our death unless God intervenes. We have been freed from the guilt of sin, but evil and death still need to be dealt with. Fortunately for us, the same Son of God who died for our sins will also defeat death itself, rising from the grave so that we too might rise with him.

Lives again our glorious King, Alleluia!
Where, O death, is now thy sting? Alleluia!
Once he died our souls to save, Alleluia!
Where's thy victory, boasting grave? Alleluia

—Charles Wesley

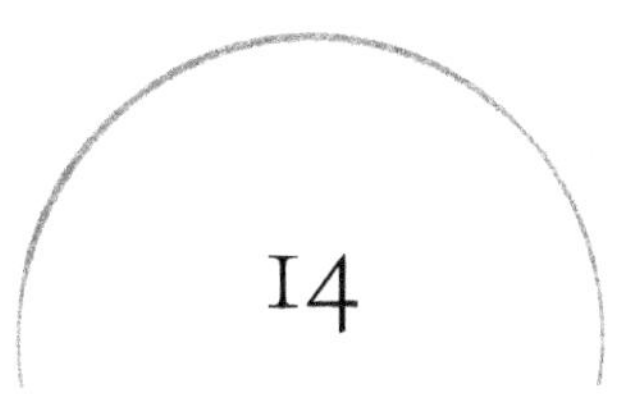

14

THE RESURRECTION

On John 19:38–42, John 20,
Luke 24:13–35, and Psalm 118:14–29

We long for more than the words and memories of our departed friends. We long for their physical presence: to be with them, to touch them, and to embrace them. When we converse on the phone with a faraway friend, it stokes in us a greater desire to see them face-to-face. We experience this longing most when we read letters from deceased loved ones which stimulate a bittersweet memory, simultaneously revealing their beautiful presence and their agonizing absence.

Sam and I became best friends during a year as roommates in Chicago. While I had previously known Sam, that particular year of living in close proximity and serving together in ministry strengthened our bonds of friendship. But, like so many other friendships in a highly mobile society, our time together was all too brief. After a year, Sam moved to Texas and I eventually moved to Pennsylvania. As the years apart turned into decades, we both married, had children, and embraced the manifold responsibilities of middle-aged men. Despite this physical separation, we have managed to keep our friendship going through fifteen years of regular phone calls. We talk, joke, counsel, and pray with each other through the miracle of long-distance communications, and this has allowed our friendship to continue to grow.

Every few years I'll have a work trip to Dallas and with it comes the opportunity to reunite in person. These precious moments are times where we can pick up where we left off, experiencing that fuller friendship that comes only with physical presence. Such times are both precious and difficult. We remember how much greater friendship is when it is experienced face-to-face, but also know that this fuller friendship is but a fleeting moment. We will not live in the same location ever again in this life.

I always weep when these visits come to an end, because they remind me that phone calls, texts, and video chats cannot ever fully satisfy my desire to be physically present with those I love. This should come as no surprise since God has created each and every one of us as physical beings. Human beings have physical bodies as well as souls, and these bodies are gifts from God. Our bodies and souls are, as Genesis 1 tells us, "very good" creations of God. However, one of the results of sin is that there is now a split between us and God, and this split effects us physically and spiritually. As a result of the fall, Adam and Eve no longer have their physical senses attuned to God—they no longer hear his voice clearly, they no longer feel his presence like a garment, and they no longer touch and taste from the trees in his garden. Furthermore, since God is the source of all life, this distance from God results in the deterioration of our physical bodies, culminating in death.

On the cross, Jesus began to heal our souls, enabling a connection to God once again. But if this were the end of the biblical story, we would never get to physically be in God's presence. Our relationship with God would remain as something akin to speaking with a close friend over the phone. It would be close and intimate, but not physical. Furthermore, since the damage caused by sin would still affect our physical bodies, we would still succumb to physical death, and this death would end our relationship with God forever.

For this reason, Jesus does not stop at the cross. After he took upon himself the burden of our sin, he entered fully into human death, complete with a proper burial: his body was wrapped in burial garments and placed in a tomb. Death is the separation of soul from body. In dying Jesus enters Sheol, the place of the dead, which is "that place that is to us formless and unseen and that receives the souls that travel there."[1] What this reveals to us is that the cross was not a kind of stage play. Jesus was not pretending to die, and he did not use his divinity to escape from pain and agony. Instead, he entered fully into human suffering and embraced suffering's end: the death of the body.

This is important to note, as we can sometimes be tempted to paper over our suffering in this world and put on a happy face through the miseries of life. We can falsely think that knowing Jesus protects us from suffering in this life, or we can even think that we should not acknowledge our hardship out of fear that it makes us less of a Christian. However, what we discover in the death of Jesus is the brutal fact that we *will* suffer in this life: none of us will escape the pains associated with our eventual bodily demise. But we also learn that Jesus has chosen to enter into our suffering and has chosen to suffer alongside us. As Jesus did not ignore his own pain, he does not ignore our pain. He continues to weep alongside us through the degradation of our own bodies, all the way down to our final breath.

And yet, Jesus does not stop there. This Jesus who entered fully into human death is the same Jesus who is fully God and the author of life. He is more powerful than death, since he has power over life and death. Jesus is stronger than the physical restrictions of his burial garments, and stronger than the chains that keep all other human beings imprisoned in death. And so, Jesus's descent to the dead is part of his mission: he enters into death to break free of its bonds and enable us to likewise escape death's clutches.

One of the ways early Christians envisioned this descent was as a twofold victory of Jesus over the twin adversaries of Satan and Death. Ephrem the Syrian imagines an argument between Satan and Death over the meaning of the cross. Satan comes to Death gloating over his perceived victory at convincing the world to crucify Jesus. He asks Death to open the gates of Sheol (the place of the dead) so that they can see the dead Jesus and boast over their conquest. In Ephrem's dialogue, Satan says to Death:

> "Open up so that we can see him and jeer at him,
> let us take up the refrain and say, 'Where is your power?'
> Three days are already passed;
> let us say to him, 'You, who are three days dead,
> raised up Lazarus, four days dead; raise up yourself now!' "
> In response to Satan:
>
> Death duly opened up the gates of Sheol,
> and out from it shone the radiance of our Lord's face!

Like the men of Sodom they were all smitten,
they groped around looking for Sheol's gate,
which had disappeared.[2]

We see in this poetic account that Jesus has the power to conquer death, to fling open the gates of Sheol so that those who know and trust in him will escape the clutches of the grim reaper. He entered fully into the snake pit and conquered Satan, ensuring that the serpent's venom will not bring about our permanent death.[3]

Jesus brings this defeat of death to completion three days after the cross as the Sabbath comes to a close. On that morning, Mary Magdalene went to the tomb to pay her respects and mourn the loss of her deceased friend. However, Mary is startled and troubled to find the stone rolled back from the tomb, and nothing in the tomb but empty funeral garments. These garments were the clothing of the dead, akin to the bloody, stained garments given to Adam and Eve after the fall. Jesus leaves these garments behind as a sign that he has defeated death. The time for covering oneself with dead animal skins is ending, and the time for covering oneself in the radiant glory of God is beginning.

As Mary beholds these garments in the empty tomb, she is visited by angels who inform her that Jesus is not there because he has risen from the dead. Death no longer has dominion over him. However, despite these instructions, Mary has not fully internalized what she has heard. As she departs the empty tomb, she begins conversing with someone who she believes is a gardener. She does not yet realize that it is Jesus. Why? Because people don't rise from dead! No one shows up to a funeral expecting to see the deceased alive. She is looking for the dead without realizing that she should be looking for the living. However, when this gardener shouts out her name "Mary!" the eyes of her body and the eyes of her heart see the risen Christ. She cries out "teacher" and embraces him.

This embrace communicates the world to us. It simultaneously reveals to us that Jesus is alive and that we should live our lives in expectation of his embrace. He wants to restore our souls and our bodies so that he can embrace us body and soul. As Jesus walks alongside of us through the pain and suffering of death, he continues to walk alongside of us *through* death and into eternal, physical life with him. We can now live in hope that after our death we will hear Jesus crying out our name and we will awaken. Like a loud trumpet blast, Jesus's voice will stir us to rise from our deep slumber and run to him. The eyes of our hearts and the eyes of our resurrected bodies will embrace Jesus just as Mary Magdalene did two thousand years ago.

The resurrection of Jesus Christ reveals to us that our eternal life with God will not be an ethereal and incorporeal swirl in the clouds. Our resurrection will be flesh and blood. It will involve embraces and kisses and eating and drinking. The resurrection story even begins to reveal to us what our eternal and physical home will look like. As Mary Magdalene struggled to grasp the meaning of the empty tomb, she sees the resurrected Jesus and identifies him first as the gardener of the cemetery. Mary was partially correct: Jesus is in fact the gardener, not of a cemetery, but of paradise. The garden referred to in John's gospel is an allusion to the Garden of Eden. It tells us that the gate to Mount Eden has been torn down, and that one day human beings will joyfully labor again when they arrive at Mount Zion, which is itself a kind of return to the paradise of the garden of Eden: "Our Lord was pleased to be likened to a gardener, for it is he who opened the gate to Paradise."[4]

THE FAITH OF THOMAS, THE FAITH OF ABRAHAM

The story of Mount Sinai began with an act of faith by Abraham. Over the course of his life, Abraham learned more about God's character, and even encountered God under the trees at Mamre. Abraham's faith began with the hearing and trusting of God's word, and over time his faith was filled out with a fuller and deeper picture of God.

When we got married, my wife and I engaged in an act of faith, promising to support each other through better and worse and through times of plenty and times of want. But we had only known each other for a year, and much of that time was spent hundreds of miles apart. The faith we had on our wedding day prompted us to get to know each other more and more. We both sought to fill out the object of our faith, getting a fuller picture of each other.

Our faith in God works in a similar way. None of us begin with a full understanding of God (indeed, we will *never* have a complete understanding of God, since we are not God!). However, our initial act of believing will spark in us a desire to learn as much as we can about God. St. Anselm calls this journey "faith seeking understanding." The story of Abraham proceeds along a similar set of lines. Abraham believes, and God reveals himself to Abraham through several encounters and events. But Abraham is only given bits and pieces of the puzzle. His faith is not yet filled out by understanding.

Jesus rises from the dead to fulfill the hopes of Abraham and reveal the object of his faith. This is one of the reasons why Jesus appeared to his disciples in a locked room following his resurrection. Despite the locked doors, Jesus appeared to them in resurrected flesh and invited them to touch his hands and side and to experience his physical, bodily presence. They see the wounds of the sword and they touch his nail-marked hands, yet they find no trace of blood. The signs of the victory of the cross are encoded on Jesus's body, yet the sign of blood is nowhere to be found. Blood has been spilt for sin, and there is no longer a need for further bloodshed. Now when we see blood today, we see a continued sign of the blood shed for us on the cross, but we also are reminded of the wounds of Christ which no longer bleed. This stokes in our hearts a longing for our life on Mount Zion, where there will be eternal peace and an end to all violence and bloodshed.

However, one of the disciples, Thomas, was absent on this occasion, and did not believe the testimony of his friends that Jesus had risen from the grave. So Jesus appeared again to his disciples and to Thomas. When Thomas is given the privilege of seeing and touching Jesus, he utters these simple words of belief: "My Lord and My God" (John 20:28).

It is in these words that the faith of Abraham is fulfilled. Abraham's faith has literally been fleshed out in the resurrected flesh of Jesus. We discover that God the Father had led Abraham up to Mount Moriah to teach him about God the Son. A son did need to be sacrificed for the sins of the world, but God himself provided his own Son to fall on the sword. And just as Abraham's son Isaac lived through the events of Mount Moriah, God's own son Jesus Christ would live again after his death on

Mount Golgotha. Abraham's proclamation that "God will provide" is fulfilled when Thomas beholds the risen Christ.

When Thomas utters the words "My Lord and My God" he reveals that the God of Abraham and Moses is Jesus of Nazareth. The ethereal voice that spoke to Abraham is united with the physical voice emanating from Jesus's mouth. The glory of God which radiated from the back of the tabernacle is united with the solid reality of Jesus's resurrected body.[5] This has a profound effect on our relationship with God. Before Jesus, we could not picture God in our hearts. But now as we see Jesus in his bodily and resurrected glory conversing with Thomas, we too can picture Jesus in our hearts and have a personal conversation with the God of the universe. As John of Damascus remarks: "In former times God, who is without form or body, could never be depicted. But now when God is seen in the flesh conversing with men, I make an image of the God whom I see."[6] When we think of God, we can now see in our mind's eye the risen Jesus Christ. We can now speak to this God as if to a person, knowing that one day we will see with our physical eyes what we already see in our mind's eye: the resurrected Jesus.

However, this is not the end of the biblical story. While Thomas is given the ability to see and touch Jesus, Jesus will soon ascend to heaven. Others will have to wait until Jesus returns to receive their embrace. In response to Thomas's profession, Jesus utters these words: "Blessed are those who have not seen and yet have believed" (John 20:29). While Thomas is given a unique opportunity to touch Jesus and so believe, all those that follow must first believe with the faith of Abraham. As Augustine puts it: "We touch Christ, you see, by faith, and it is better not to touch him with the hand and to touch him with faith than to feel him with the hand and not touch him with faith."[7] We must see Jesus first in our hearts before we see him with our physical eyes.

Soon after these events, Jesus will ascend to heaven, and it will be the duty and honor of his followers to proclaim his resurrection and invite unbelievers to profess Jesus as Lord and God. In many ways, the biblical story has now come full circle with the story of Abraham. Abraham's faith began with the hearing of God's words, and it was slowly filled out throughout the Old and New Testaments, culminating in the resurrection of Jesus. Now those who wish to have faith in God must also do so by hearing and believing God's word, this time with the words coming through the followers of Jesus and the New Testament books that they were inspired to write. Those who believe the testimony of Jesus's followers are given a promise that their faith will one day manifest itself in the physical sight and embrace of Jesus on Mount Zion.

While Jesus will soon ascend to the Father and turn over to his followers the responsibility of telling the world that he is risen, he does not leave them empty handed. As we will see in the ensuing chapters, he will send the Holy Spirit to work within them to complete the biblical story. But he also gives them a special *place*, the church, where they can gather to hear him and touch him.

THE ROAD TO EMMAUS

As a kid I got lost. A lot. Even at an early age, I would become so wrapped up in my thoughts that I would wander away from my parents in a crowded mall or airport. When I came to my senses and realized I was lost, I would frantically search for my parents in a sea of unfamiliar faces. Two things would always help me find my way back. The first was the sound of my mother's voice calling out my name. The distinct timbre of her voice coupled with the unique and familiar sound of "*Michael!*" was often enough for me to recognize her and be reunited. Second was the sight of my father's distinct walk. Even from far away, my father had the instantly recognizable walk of a man who spent a lifetime engaging in backbreaking manual labor. If I saw just a few of his steps, I would immediately recognize him and rush back to my parents to be reunited.

When we are lost in a sea of unknown, the sound of familiar words and the actions of close friends often alert us to their presence. A similar encounter took place between Jesus and two of his followers shortly after his resurrection from the dead. The disciple Cleopas and one other disciple were walking towards Emmaus, and naturally their conversation was fixated on the disturbing events of the cross just a few days earlier. As they were walking, Jesus began to walk alongside them and converse with them. However, the disciples did not recognize Jesus. They were lost in their own thoughts and downtrodden by the death of their teacher. But then Jesus begins to reveal to them that he is alive by speaking to them in familiar words: the words of the Bible. Jesus gives to them the greatest Old Testament teaching in the history of the world. He shows how every jot and tittle of the Old Testament, every story and every symbol, is fulfilled in him.[8] If only Cleopas would have put pen to paper and transcribed this teaching!

And yet, despite this greatest of Bible studies, Cleopas still had not fully recognized the risen Christ. But his heart was burning for more and more of this perfect and godly instruction, so he encouraged Jesus to stay with him and his friend through the evening. As they were sitting down to a meal Jesus engaged in a familiar act of blessing and breaking bread. Here the familiar words of Scripture were paired with a familiar action: The blessing of the Passover bread which has become the blessing of the bread at the Last Supper is now uttered over this ordinary piece of bread at the table. And it is at this precise moment that the scales fall from Cleopas's eyes. He and his friend finally see Jesus in his resurrected glory:

> When the disciple's eyes
>   were held closed,
> bread too was the key
>   whereby their eyes were opened
> to recognize the Omniscient:
>   saddened eyes beheld
> a vision of joy
>   and were instantly filled with happiness.[9]

The resurrected Jesus was made known through the unique words of the Bible and the unique action of breaking bread. In so doing, Jesus shows that the word and the sacramental bread are the key to opening our eyes as well. What Jesus is modeling for his followers is the pattern of church worship which will continue until the day he returns again in glory. Each Sunday, Christians enter church after a long week of trudging through the vicissitudes of life. Many walk through those doors having lost sight of Jesus in the busyness of the daily grind. As they enter church, they begin to hear the familiar words of the Bible read out loud. They hear the voice of Jesus speaking through these words and are reminded of the truth of the resurrection. And then they move from these unique words to the unique action of breaking bread at the eucharistic table. As they see the bread broken into pieces, as they taste the body of Christ broken for them, they experience physically the risen Jesus.

However, after this extraordinary moment, the church service ends, and the Christian departs in peace. Just when Cleopas recognized Jesus in the breaking of the bread, Jesus vanished from his sight. Like Mary Magdalene and Thomas, this physical experience of being with Jesus was only for a temporary moment. But Jesus's disciples leave those experiences with renewed, burning hearts of hope. They leave with a fiery expectation of Christ's return and a passion to tell the world that salvation has come through Jesus Christ.

So, too, for us. As we depart from church each Sunday, we return to a world still filled with hardships and brokenness. But we have heard the voice of our risen Lord and tasted his body, the manna of heaven, and can leave with hope restored and a longing to spread the good news of Jesus with all we meet. Each visit to church is like visiting a faraway friend. It is a time to delight in the physical presence of Jesus as we hear his words and receive his body. Yet it is a bittersweet time, as it is a reminder that we will not live fully with the physical, risen Jesus this side of Mount Zion. But the visit renews our hope that one day we will be with our best friend Jesus and dwell in his house forever (Psalm 23:6).

The story of Mount Tabor is finished. Sin has been forgiven, death has been conquered, and the object of our deepest desire has been revealed in resurrected glory. However, humanity has not yet been given the power to meet Jesus on Mount Zion. They need Jesus's power, the very power of the Holy Spirit, to be poured out among all flesh. The Holy Spirit is needed so that the bones of the dead may be risen to meet Jesus. So the story continues with Jesus's ascension and the sending of the Holy Spirit at Pentecost.

PART 4

THE STORY OF MOUNT ZION

When Christ went up to Heaven the Apostles stayed
Gazing at Heaven with souls and wills on fire,
Their hearts on flight along the track He made,
Winged by desire …
They do His Will, and doing it rejoice,
Patiently glad to spend and to be spent:
Still He speaks to them, still they hear His Voice
And are content.
For as a cloud received Him from their sight,
So with a cloud will He return ere long:
Therefore they stand on guard by day, by night,
Strenuous and strong.
They do, they dare, they beyond seven times seven
Forgive, they cry God's mighty word aloud:
Yet sometimes haply lift tired eyes to Heaven—
"Is that His cloud?"

—*Christina Rossetti*

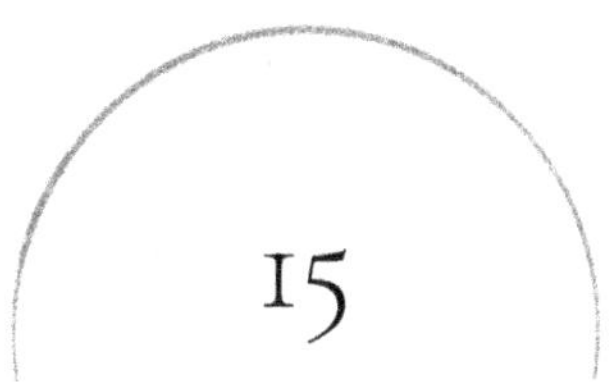

15

THE ASCENSION

On Luke 24:50–53, Acts 1:1–11, John 15:26–27, John 16, and Psalm 28

Life east of Eden involves a painful gaze heavenward. The sun in the sky reminds us of our lost glory on the mountain of God. The heat of the sun's rays remind us of the fiery holiness of a God we cannot approach in our sin. The clouds in the sky remind us that God is still present yet absent. We long for someone to help us ascend through these clouds, to pass through these fires, and take us into the very heart and presence of God.

Why didn't Jesus stick around after he rose from the dead? It certainly seems like life would be a lot easier right now if we could visit the resurrected Jesus whenever we wanted. We would not have to worry about misunderstanding his teachings and could rely on him to solve the latest problems in the world. But clearly this is not part of the plan. As Mary Magdalene embraced the resurrected Christ, Jesus said to her: "Do not cling to me, for I have not yet ascended to the Father; but go to my brothers and say to them, 'I am ascending to my Father and your Father, to my God and your God' " (John 20:17). The reason that Mary could not hold on to Jesus is that he had to ascend to the Father in order to complete his earthly mission. And sure enough, forty days after Easter, Jesus goes to another mountain, the Mount of Olives. There he is lifted into a cloud in the presence of his disciples, and angels announce that he has been taken up into heaven.

Jesus's ascension to heaven is not an add-on to his death and resurrection. It is not the denouement of his earthly life but is integral to his earthly mission. Why does Jesus ascend, and why is understanding this so important? As we will discover, Jesus ascends to give us access to the Father, to let us continue his work, and to send us the Holy Spirit.

JESUS ASCENDS TO GIVE US ACCESS TO THE FATHER

My wife once worked as a medical case worker for refugees, and a substantial part of her job was navigating complex medical bureaucracies in order to help refugees receive their basic healthcare needs. As you can imagine, this was not an easy task. It required hours on the phone with low level bureaucrats and customer service representatives. At times, she had to result to angry shouts and loud threats just to convince an agent to transfer her call to a high-ranking authority so that these refugees would get the care they were promised.

We have all experienced something similar. There is nothing more frustrating than contacting customer service, waiting for hours on the phone, only to discover that the person you contacted cannot help you. When we need help, we want an immediate connection to the person at the top, the person with the power and authority to address our problems.

Ever since the sin of Adam, human beings have been unable to be fully in the presence of God the Father. God cannot be diluted and will not tolerate any sin to exist within himself. Because of this, any human being who would come fully into God's presence would be consumed by God's pure fire. We have seen in Leviticus an elaborate system of sacrifices, curtains, and priests that were required so that *some* contact with God could be made without being consumed by this fire. However, the result of this system was that the worship of God was anything but immediate. To encounter God, rituals had to be performed, rites had to be followed, and priests had to be relied on as intermediaries. These were all signs that access to God was limited and remote. When these priests were corrupt or negligent, going to the tabernacle must have felt like going to the DMV.

On Mount Golgotha, we discovered that Jesus entered the heavenly temple to be the one, true, and final sacrifice for human sin, and as a result of this action, the temple curtains were torn in two. Immediacy with God is now possible through Jesus's death on the cross. And when Jesus ascended to the Father, he completed what he started on the cross by entering fully into the heavenly temple in his resurrected flesh. In his Ascension, Jesus becomes the first human being to enter heaven and the first human being to reach the top of the mountain of God. In Jesus, the human longing to be reunited with God the Father is first fulfilled.

It might be difficult for us to understand the magnitude of this reality because we did not grow up going to temple each week. Imagine instead that you went to church each Sunday, but inside the building you encountered persistent signs that you were distant from God—you saw the curtains and you saw the priests. You heard stories from the Bible about those who tried to approach God in their sin and perished. You heard that the most important person in the Bible, Moses, couldn't even get fully to God. The message would be clear—because of sin, human beings and God don't mix.

But now, the gap between heaven and earth has been scaled by Jesus Christ. A human being sits at the right hand of the Father in the true, heavenly temple. Humanity has finally been granted access to the heavens. Leo the Great articulates this joy:

> It was certainly a great and indescribable source of joy when, in the sight of the heavenly multitudes, the nature of our human race ascended over the dignity of all heavenly creatures. It passed the angelic orders and was raised beyond the heights of archangels. In its ascension, our human race did not stop at any other height until this same nature was received at the seat of the eternal Father. Our human nature, united with the divinity of the Son, was on the throne of his glory.[1]

As the first human in heaven, Jesus continues his mission of saving humankind. First, he prepares a place for us in heaven. Jesus is the forerunner who goes ahead of us to make heaven a dwelling place of humankind. Like a pioneer who enters a new territory to make it habitable for his family, Jesus ascends to heaven to prepare for us to join him there. As we will discover, this preparation will be complete when heaven descends upon

Mount Zion. At that time, Jesus will invite his family to meet him there.

Second, Jesus enters heaven in order to share our prayer requests with the Father. As the first human in heaven, Jesus hears our very human prayers. And since he is also fully divine, one with the Father, he is able to relay our prayers instantly to the Father (John 16:26–27). In a sense, he cuts through the red tape and the bureaucracy and goes to the source of all authority to share our requests. This means that when we pray there is a kind of Trinitarian conversation that happens—the Father, Son, and Holy Spirit discuss our prayers together. Because Jesus is human, he "intercedes with the Father on our behalf."[2] Because he is God, he answers our prayers together with the Father and Holy Spirit. While we can still ask others to pray for us and rely on others to intercede for us, we can also take our prayers straight to the top of the mountain. We do not need to shout or yell to get God's attention. As Paul says, we now "have access to God in boldness and confidence through faith" in Jesus (Ephesians 3:12 NRSV).

This is why Christians not only engage in formal prayer but can also engage in informal, conversational prayer with God. There is a human in heaven, and thus we can have a human to human, person to person conversation with Jesus, knowing that our prayers will be heard by the Father, Son, and Holy Spirit. When we pray, we can speak to Jesus just as Moses did, as a friend. And we trust that all our prayers and supplications will be handed over to our Father in heaven. We can share our deepest joys and fears, our deepest longings and desires, and trust that Jesus is listening as attentively as the closest of our friends.

JESUS ASCENDS TO ALLOW US TO FINISH THE JOB

I can still remember the first time I was given permission to mow our family's lawn. As a child, I could do little to substantially contribute to the life our household, and so that first day of sitting on the riding mower, pushing the gas pedal, and clutching the steering wheel marked a turning point. It was the moment when I moved from a passive recipient of my family's labors to an active participant in the life of our household.

We all long to be active agents in the world around us. This is one of the reasons why Jesus ascends to the Father: he wants *us* to participate in the completion of his mission to bring salvation to the world. He wants us to announce to the world the forgiveness of sins, he wants us to bring about healing in his name, and he wants us to invite our friends to enter the mountain of God by plunging into the waters of baptism. The ascension is the moment the baton is passed from Jesus to his followers. In so doing, Jesus is restoring to human beings their ability to joyfully work in his name. As he is ascending, Jesus blesses his disciples, conferring onto them the blessing of labor that Adam and Eve enjoyed on Mount Eden. Adam and Eve were able to cultivate the ground of Eden and nurture its wildlife. However, due to their sin, thistles, and thorns, boredom and burdens mark all work east of Eden. We continue to do these labors, not out of joy, but out of obligation to provide the food and necessities required for our daily existence. But now, with the blessing of the ascending Jesus, we can begin to labor like Adam and Eve in Eden. As Jesus is seated at the right hand of the Father, he looks down upon all our good work with delight. His blessings continue to flow down from the top of the mountain down to his disciples, and down to all those who have come to believe in him.

We can now experience this blessing of our labors and know that Jesus sits in heaven delighting in every single action done in his name. The simple act of nursing a child, of cultivating a garden, or mowing a field, are now activities that can be done in Jesus's name, and we can have confidence that God delights in these labors even if no one else on earth acknowledges our work. We no longer have to crave the recognition of others. We can joyfully labor knowing with deep confidence that the ascended Jesus sees our strivings and smiles. While this work is still marked with the thorns of a broken world, our burdens are now intermixed with joy and delight. This points us ever closer to our hope on Mount Zion, where all of our work will be free of hardship.

The ascension is the moment in which Jesus grants to his followers authority to carry on his mission. According to St. Paul, the Father seats Jesus at his right hand and makes him head over all things for the church, "which is his body, the fullness of him who fills all in all" (Ephesians 1:23). Jesus ascends as king in order to rule through his people, the church. Since the body of Christ is now located in heaven, the church now becomes the body of Christ on earth. It is the principal location through which we participate in the ongoing mission of Jesus Christ. And since Jesus is in heaven, the place that is outside of earthly time and space, he can be the king and leader of all of those who follow him. This is one of the principal reasons why Jesus ascends to heaven. If he were on earth, we would have to travel around the globe to seek his advice. Now, as he sits in heaven, he is above space and time itself. He thus stands ready to hear our requests and give us counsel *wherever* and *whenever* we ask. Since Jesus in heaven is above time, he always has time for us.

The ascension is thus our invitation to go from passive recipients of Jesus's work to active participants in what he is doing in the world through the church. While this opportunity should be received with joy, it will also challenge us in the ways we remain passive in our Christian lives. As the pastor of a church in a highly mobile community, I am accustomed to a steady stream of church shoppers and hoppers. Many people come through our doors with the hope of being entertained, of being recipients of the services and resources that our church has to offer. Unfortunately, a large portion of American churches are built on an entertainment model that fosters this shopper's mentality. What the ascension reveals to us is that the church is first and foremost a community of holy worship and joyful participation. The ancient word to describe the structure of church worship is liturgy, which means "the work of the people." When we enter into the church, we should enter with the expectation that God will work through us to continue his mission in the world and come ready to offer up our lives to this joyful labor. In light of the reality of the ascension, we should ask: "How can I contribute to the church?" before we ask: "What can the church give to me?"

JESUS ASCENDS TO SEND THE HOLY SPIRIT

Two questions rise to the surface when we ponder the awesome implications of Jesus's ascent into heaven. First, if Jesus has ascended to share our prayers with the Father, then how do we get our prayers to Jesus? Second, if Jesus has ascended to let us participate in his work, has he left us to do this work alone?

These questions bring us to the third reason why Jesus ascended: in order to send the Holy Spirit. As we will discover in the next chapter, the Holy Spirit will descend on Jesus's followers at Pentecost to empower and equip them to fulfill his mission on earth. Jesus ascends to the Father to send this Holy Spirit into the world. If he did not go away to the Father, the Holy Spirit would not come down upon his disciples (John 16:7).

As we have seen throughout the Bible, God desires to heal us from the inside out. While the prophets spoke about the Son of Man coming to take away the sins of the world, they also pointed to a time in which the Holy Spirit would be poured out on all people, that this Spirit would revive the dry bones of the dead. While Jesus has prepared a place for us in heaven, we must be made holy so that we can join him there. And so, Jesus ascends to give us the Holy Spirit, which is his Spirit, the Spirit of God. This Spirit will work inside of Christians to make them holy and to fashion them into people worthy of following Jesus into the Father's heavenly presence. The wind of the Spirit will work in the hearts of Christians to lift their souls into heaven, so that they might share their requests with Jesus and consequently with the Father. Furthermore, the Holy Spirit will be the fire inside of the hearts of Christians, the spiritual fuel that will enable them to participate in his salvific work in the world.

JESUS ASCENDS TO RETURN ONE DAY

While we can delight in our ability to take our prayers directly to Jesus, and joyfully receive his invitation to carry on his work, we must still acknowledge that these gains are bittersweet. We all, like the apostles, experience the "limitless deprivation" of his absence.[3] Jesus has ascended into heaven, and this means we cannot embrace him in this moment. Like Mary Magdalene, we cannot cling to the risen flesh of our Lord. The more the eyes of our heart see the ascended Christ in heaven, the more our physical eyes ache to behold his outstretched arms. The sadness of the ascension is shown in the reappearance of the clouds, which surrounded Jesus as he ascended. These clouds in turn remind us that his face remains hidden from us as well. But the angels gave to the disciples, and to us, hope when they declare that "This Jesus, who was taken up from you into heaven, will come in the same way as you saw him go into heaven" (Acts 1:11). As Jesus departed in clouds, he will return in those very same clouds to one day bring about the completion of his mission, to fulfill the story of Mount Zion and the story of the Bible. We are invited to ponder the words of these angels and to have our hopes rekindled for his return. As Philaret of Moscow explains:

> If your piercing gaze cannot plumb the depth of the heavens, which are closed by clouds, and the unattainable judgments of the Almighty seem to you nothing but uncertainty, then accept from the heavenly authorities this word, filled with power. It can fill your emptiness, soften your sorrow, put an end to your solitude, lighten your darkness, resolve your uncertainty, and give life to your spirit through a never-false and never-fading hope: This same Jesus, who was taken up from you into Heaven, will so come in like manner.[4]

God has given us clouds as a symbol of this sadness intermixed with hope. A cloudy day often evokes in us gloom even while we know that the water in those clouds will one day soak the earth and nourish its trees. The clouds that take Jesus up to heaven fill our souls with gloom, as we know that the sight of our savior still eludes us. But we also know that Jesus will return in those same clouds to nourish the tree of life and lead us on to Mount Zion. The Psalms declare that Jesus's return will be like rain pouring down on a mown field (Psalm 72:6). The rivers of life will saturate and nourish the earth, turning its grounds into the paradise of Mount Zion. The work that we now do, with the blessing of the ascended Jesus, is akin to mowing a lawn and caring for a field. We labor on this earth as part of God's household, the church, knowing one day he will complete these labors and saturate them with the rivers of paradise. Our labors prepare the earth as it awaits its heavenly nourishment when Jesus returns. While this labor can now be joyful, it is still at times painful and difficult. Fortunately, during those difficult times, we can look up to the clouds in the sky in hope, knowing that Jesus will descend from those clouds to wipe away all pain forever.

The ascension of Jesus is both an end and a beginning. It marks the end of the story of Mount Tabor, the story of the mountain of God coming down to us in Jesus Christ. Jesus has descended from the top of the mountain to take away the sins of the world and to conquer death. Now he has ascended back up the mountain in order to complete his earthly mission. But it also marks the beginning of the story of Mount Zion, the story of the descent of the Holy Spirit and his workings within the church to heal the world from the inside out. Now that Jesus has ascended to the Father, he can now send this Spirit in the extraordinary event of Pentecost.

Not gold and silver, jewels and fine linen, and skill of man to use them, make the House of God, but worshippers, the souls and bodies of men, whom He has redeemed.

—John Henry Newman

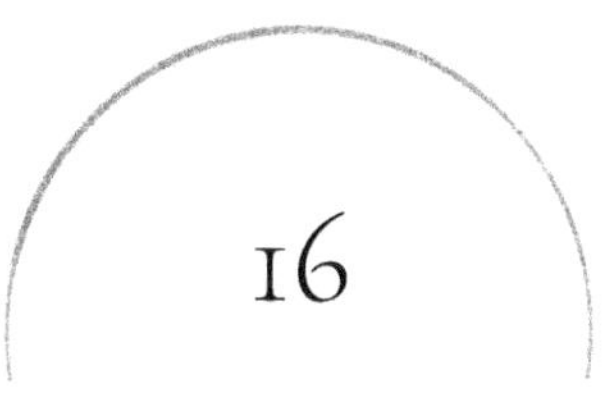

16

PENTECOST

On Acts 1–2, 2 Corinthians 5–7,
1 Peter 1–2, and Psalm 104:25–37

A climb up a mountain is aided by the wind in our lungs and the wind at our backs. The wind behind us pushes us upward, making our steps easier with each gust. Our climb up the mountain of God requires the wind of the Holy Spirit pumping through our spiritual lungs. It is our very spiritual breath, and without it we would die in God's presence. This very same wind surrounds us, pushing us higher and higher and guiding each step as we draw closer to God. Each time we feel a strong gust of wind at our side, it is a prescient reminder of this awesome power of the Holy Spirit.

Just before Jesus ascended, he instructed his disciples to wait in Jerusalem until they were "clothed with power from on high" (Luke 24:49). While the ascension marked the moment in which the baton was passed from Jesus to his disciples to continue his earthly mission, the disciples had not yet received the power necessary to carry forth this mission. They were like soldiers who had received their commission but had not yet received their swords and shields. As such, the disciples continued in their regular routines as they waited to be empowered by Jesus. Their waiting came to an end as they were celebrating the Israelite feast of Pentecost. It is at this moment that the wind and the fire of the Holy Spirit descend upon Jesus's followers.

PENTECOST AS THE REVERSAL OF BABEL

The tower of Babel was the apex of human sin and an awful sign of how far away from the mountain of God human beings had traveled. The man-made mountain was built to impress and challenge God. In response, God shattered this tower and separated human beings by language. Confusion, misunderstanding, animosity, and war now characterize the relationships between nations. The hope of Israel was that God would work through his chosen people to enable salvation for all peoples from every tribe and nation. As Babel scattered humanity, God would one day gather humanity back to him. The descent of the Holy Spirit is this moment of gathering meant to reverse the scattering at Babel. We see in the account of Pentecost three ways that it reverses the curse of Babel.

First, while human beings built Babel to *impress* God, God *impresses* humanity with the Holy Spirit at Pentecost. The construction of the tower of Babel was built in order to summon God to adulation. It was, in effect, one giant brag: an impressive achievement whose goal was the exaltation of its architects. At Pentecost, however, the disciples were quietly praying in obscurity, waiting for God to come down to them. It is in this moment of intense prayer that the Father and Son send the Holy Spirit to enliven the hearts of the disciples. The Holy Spirit was not earned as an award for some great accomplishment but is instead gifted to those who believed in Jesus and gathered to pray in his name. Those who wish to follow Jesus today are invited to continue in this Pentecostal way, forsaking their desire to impress God and prayerfully and quietly asking for God to send his Spirit into their hearts.

Second, what Babel *confused*, Pentecost *united*. The judgment and destruction of Babel led to the fragmentation of humankind and their descent into confusion and animosity. As sin fractures our relationships with each other, life after Babel is marked by large scale ethnic and cultural hostility. Thus, when God decided to reverse Babel he did so on the feast of Pentecost, a day when people from all around the world would gather in Jerusalem for celebration. The sending of the Holy Spirit at Pentecost resulted in a spectacular scene in which travelers to Jerusalem were able to understand each other's words despite speaking vastly different languages. What should have sounded like cacophony—hundreds of conversations in different languages taking place at the same time—became harmonized by the Holy Spirit. The Holy Spirit is like the conductor of the orchestra of the nations, bringing disparate sounds together in one beautiful polyphonic symphony. This was the first sign that the clash of civilizations would someday be no more.

Finally, the tower of Babel was the culmination of *domination* and *oppression*, while Pentecost was the inauguration of *healing* and *justice*. The false mountain of Babel was wrought with man-made stones: Bricks beaten together by the back breaking labor of bonded slaves. It is a monument to the pain and oppression that comes with the selfish desires of the rich and powerful. While

God pronounced his judgment on these oppressors by destroying their tower, injustice and oppression have remained a hallmark of human existence. Now, at Pentecost, we see the first inklings of reversal. The crowd gathered to wait upon the Spirit consisted of a wide variety of poor and working-class individuals. Shortly after this great event, they would disperse to heal others in Jesus's name and establish churches marked by the sharing of possessions rather than a fixation on material wealth.

THE FIRE AND WIND OF THE HOLY SPIRIT

From the very beginning of the Bible, we see the Holy Spirit at work giving form and life to God's creation. In Genesis 1, the *wind* of the Spirit hovers over the primordial waters, rushing through it to create land and life. That same wind of the Spirit is the very breath of God that inflated Adam's body, granting him the first gasps of human life. Later in the Bible, the wood of Moses's staff sent this wind blazing through the Red Sea to separate water from land and enable the Israelites to escape captivity in Egypt. The lifting up of wood enabled a pouring forth of the wind of the Spirit. And so, after Jesus is lifted up on the wood of the cross, he sends down his Spirit, the wind and breath of God, into the hearts of his followers.

In addition to wind, we have also seen the Holy Spirit manifested as *fire* throughout the Bible. In the Old Testament, this fire was received as a warning sign: God is perfectly holy, and as such cannot be in the presence of sin. Those who dared to enter God's pure presence saw their sin-soaked bodies consumed by his fiery holiness. But now, Jesus has dealt definitively with sin on the cross, giving us access to the mountain of God once again.

His broken body split the curtain that veiled the fire of the Holy Spirit. Through the sacrifice of Jesus, those who believe in him can now approach this fire with hearts cleansed of sin. There is, in effect, now a space in the human heart capable of receiving this fire without being burned. This is one of the most startling aspects of the story of Pentecost: the fire of the Spirit descends from heaven into the hearts of the disciples. And yet, the disciples live. The fire can reside within them without consuming them: "They partook of fire, not of burning but of saving fire. This is a fire that consumes the thorns of sins but gives luster to the soul."[1]

When we feel a strong east wind on a crisp autumn day, we are reminded how the Spirit of God passes through our souls. As that wind brought life to Adam and salvation to Moses, it continues to sustain our lives and carry us to salvation on Mount Zion. The sight of a single flame is no longer just a sign of danger, but also a reminder of the glory of God now accessible to us through the Holy Spirit.

THE WORK OF THE HOLY SPIRIT: LIFTING US UP

Through the death and resurrection of Jesus, his followers are now capable of being vessels of the Holy Spirit. The Spirit works within us to heal us from the inside out and draw us closer to Jesus. This is because he is the Spirit *of* Christ. Like attracts like. We are drawn to people when we have something in common with them. And so, when Christians receive the Holy Spirit, their desires are supernaturally drawn to Christ because they now have Christ's Spirit working inside of them.

How does the Holy Spirit draw us to Jesus? First, as the wind of God, the Holy Spirit lifts our souls into the heavenly temple so that we can have communion and intimacy with God. As we saw in the last chapter, Jesus has ascended to the Father and speaks to God on our behalf. Jesus sends us his Spirit to enter our hearts and lift us into the heavenly temple when we pray. Here we can talk with Jesus and have fellowship with the God of the universe. We can now, in a spiritual manner, enter God's presence. As Basil the Great explains: "Through the Holy Spirit comes the restoration to paradise, the ascent to the kingdom of heaven, the return to adopted sonship, the freedom to call God our Father and to become a companion of the grace of Christ."[2] According to St. Paul, the intimacy enabled through the Holy Spirit allows us to become adopted sons of God, and even to call God "Abba! Father!" (Romans 8:15). This term *Abba* is a term of close intimacy, akin to a child yelling out "*Daddy!*" To use this kind of personal address to God is virtually unheard of in the Old Testament but is now open to those who receive the Holy Spirit and are lifted by his wind into the heavenly temple.

Furthermore, as the fire of God burns in our hearts, the Holy Spirit enables us to be partakers of God's glory. The glory veiled in curtains in the tabernacle was a constant reminder that God's glory could only be experienced from afar. Now, since Christians receive the Holy Spirit, his fire acts as a light in our hearts, giving to us "knowledge of the glory of God in the face of Jesus Christ. (2 Corinthians 4:6). The Holy Spirit burns the veil that covers our hearts, allowing us to begin to see the face of Jesus in our mind's eye and hear his words with our inner ears.

As the Holy Spirit burns down the veil that covers our hearts, he opens and revives our spiritual senses. After the fall, Adam and Eve slowly lost their ability to see and hear God. As they were expelled from Mount Eden, they no longer experienced the sights, sounds, smells, and tastes of paradise. Not only were they physically far away from God and his mountain, but they grew spiritually distant as well. God's voice was no longer audibly present to humankind, and fewer and fewer human beings could even hear God whispering in their hearts.

The reception of the Holy Spirit into the hearts of Christians enables an awakening, a kind of rebirth, of these spiritual senses. Just as a newborn child physically sees and hears for the first time, those who receive the Holy Spirit are spiritually reborn, and can begin to see Jesus in their mind's eye and hear his voice in their hearts. First, they have their spiritual eyes opened. They can have visions of Jesus: the same fire that burns the veil now shines a light on Jesus, allowing them to see him more clearly in their mind's eye. Second, they can have their spiritual ears opened. The fire of the Spirit melts the wax that prevents them from hearing God's voice clearly, and so those who receive the Spirit receive the ability to hear and understand God's Word. As we saw, God's voice is difficult to hear because of sin, and when God audibly speaks in the Old Testament, it is often heard as a blaring trumpet blast. Now, in the Spirit, the sound of God's voice becomes clear to our spiritual ears. God's voice is no longer a fearful blast, but instead a pleasing, inviting melody. In chapter 2, I described how I fell in love with jazz music. At first, this music made no sense to me: it sounded like a loud jumble of notes and noises. However, during Lee Morgan's trumpet solo on the song *Blue Train*, I experienced a kind of musical awakening: the notes broadcast through my speakers seemed to transform from a clanging disruptive noise to a soulful melody. I had fallen in love with this music, and out of that love the music became intelligible to me. Something akin to this happens when we receive the Spirit. Before we receive the

Spirit, the words of the Bible usually gloss over us. They are nothing more than a jumble of ancient words written by long-dead authors. However, once we receive the Spirit, these words become intelligible and sweet to our inner ears. They become beautiful melodies: words of life meant to nourish our souls.

The work of the Spirit awakens both our inner sense of hearing and our inner sense of sight. When I was fifteen years old, I had an encounter with the Holy Spirit that forever changed my life. While laying down on the side of a mountain in western Virginia, I received a vision of Jesus on the cross, and felt his overwhelming mercy for the first time. Days later, I read the Bible and knew, for the first time, that Jesus himself was speaking to me through the words I read. I had seen thousands of pictures of Jesus in my life and had heard the Bible hundreds of times at church, but these were the first moments that I truly *saw* Jesus with spiritual eyes and *heard* Jesus with spiritual ears. As we will discover in chapter 18, the Christian life consists of the development and cultivation of all these spiritual senses as we learn to see and hear (and even taste, smell, and touch) more of Jesus and experience more of God's glory as we cooperate with the Holy Spirit working in our hearts.

THE HOLY SPIRIT BINDS CHRISTIANS TOGETHER

We bond together with those who share our same interests. We are capable of connecting with others who are vastly different from us if we have a common object of love. When I attended Northwestern University, the most diverse community on campus was the football team. Players came together across racial and cultural lines, from rich and poor families, and from urban and rural communities to form one team united around a common love of football. The simple common love of a sport was enough to unite these players and break down otherwise large barriers to fellowship.

At Pentecost, the Holy Spirit descended upon one of the most diverse group of persons ever assembled. At Pentecost, the Holy Spirit acted as a kind of bonding agent on this gathering, a glue that drew them together to each other and to Jesus. The Holy Spirit continues to glue Christians together whenever they profess Jesus as Lord and God. As we saw above, like attracts like, and so those who have the Spirit now share Jesus in common with each other. The symbols of wind and fire reveal to us this binding quality of the Holy Spirit. Wind, for instance, is immaterial and shareable. When I'm outside together with friends, we all experience the same gust of wind at the same time. Similarly, fire can spread without being diminished. In fact, the more one shares fire, the more it grows. If I use my torch to light my friend's torch, I am *increasing* the amount of fire in the world. The fire spreads while retaining its exact same qualities. Likewise, the fire of the Holy Spirit can spread while remaining the one and same Spirit of Christ.

Ever since Pentecost, Christians have continued to be knit together by the Holy Spirit when they gather as the church. When Christians assemble and profess Jesus as Lord and God, the wind of the Spirit pulls their hearts together, bonding them to each other as they are bonded to Jesus. The intimacy that the Holy Spirit builds between the church, its members, and Jesus is such that this gathering is now referred to as the body of Christ.

As the body of Christ, when the church gathers in the name of Jesus, it becomes the new tabernacle and the new temple, the portable mountain of God on earth. As we saw in chapters 8 and 9, God gave to Moses the blueprints for the tabernacle so that it would be a portable Sinai, a mountain-like gathering place as they continued their travels in the wilderness. While the tabernacle would become the permanent temple in Jerusalem, this temple eventually became corrupted by sin. In chapter 11 we saw that Jesus declared a judgment on this earthly temple and revealed something startling: the temple in Jerusalem was abrogated because *his body is the temple*. Jesus's very flesh is the tabernacle and mountain of God, and it is through his body that human beings can now encounter the living God. And so, when the church gathers, the Spirit binds them together as the body of Christ and, subsequently, the new temple on earth. As the Old Testament tabernacle was a portable Mount Sinai, the New Testament church is the portable Mount Tabor, the place where people encounter God's glory in the person of Jesus Christ.

The First Letter of Peter highlights this incredible reality of the church by calling Christians living stones. Each individual is a living stone that, when gathered together in the name of Jesus, builds the temple and mountain of God. When the church gathers, its members become the gold and onyx of Mount Eden, resting firmly on the solid foundation of Jesus Christ who is the rock of their salvation. The Holy Spirit binds these stones together with Jesus the cornerstone to form one spiritual building, one mountain through which God's presence is made known. The implications of this reality for the life of the Christian cannot be overstated. We do not attend church just because we want some advice on how to be a good Christian, or to sing songs, or because it makes us feel better. While all these things can and do happen at church, the primary reason Christians gather together for church is because it is our home with God on earth. We go to church because we want to *be* on the mountain with God and *become* the body of Christ on earth. We want to physically encounter Jesus Christ in the physical interactions that take place on this mountain. Each sturdy rock jutting out from the earth is a reminder of both the stones of Eden and our own invitation to become these stones each Sunday when we gather for church.

Because the church is the portable mountain of God, it becomes for Christians the primary location in which they experience *home, harmony, worship* and *work.* It is at this point in the story of the Bible that we can return to the four major themes that summarize life on the mountain of God. First, on Mount Eden, human beings were at home with God. The mountain was their physical as well as spiritual home on earth. Second, human beings experienced perfect harmony with each other and God's creation on Mount Eden. Third, the garden of Eden was the primary place in which human beings gave back to God in worship. Finally, there was work on Mount Eden, as Adam and Eve tilled the land and worked to expand the borders of Eden throughout the whole world.

We begin to see in the gathering of the church the first signs of a return to the mountain of God, a return that will reach its completion on Mount Zion. In fact, the first church gathering that is described in the Bible shows tracings of each of these marks (Acts 2:42–47). First, the church gathering is one in which people frequently shared meals together, with the culmination of these meals being "the breaking of the bread" which is a reference to communion. As we have seen, bread is a sign of the body of Christ, and those who eat of this communion bread come together with each other and with Jesus. As wheat is gathered to make bread, the church gathers to eat from one loaf of bread, becoming united to Jesus at his family dinner table.

Second, there is harmony amongst Christians who gather as the church. These first Christians shared all things in common and shared their possessions with all those who were in need (Acts 2:44–45). This is a sign of the kind of intimacy that is possible within the church: there is an erosion of the word *mine*. Time, money, energy, and possessions were viewed as opportunities to bless others in the church.

Third, there is constant worship of God in church. This first church was marked by the recitation of "the prayers." It was marked both by formal prayers of worship to God and by constant praise of God. As worship of God is the primary goal of all human beings, the encounter with Jesus in his portable mountain necessarily elicited praise and thanksgiving from all those gathered.

Finally, the work of expanding the borders of the mountain of God was occurring, as the "Lord added to their number day by day those who were being saved" (Acts 4:47). As more and more people joined this church, the number of stones in the temple increased, and thus the mountain of God expanded throughout the earth. This expansion of the church and the mountain of God continues throughout the book of Acts, which chronicles the ongoing mission of the Christians. The church gathering thus functioned to prepare and equip Christians for their work in the world, a work which culminates in proclamation and gathering. While the next section discusses this work in greater detail, we will discuss the active life of Christians in the church today in chapter 18.

THE HOLY SPIRIT SENDS CHRISTIANS OUT

On Mount Eden, Adam and Eve were invited to cultivate the ground and expand the borders of the mountain so that the whole world would be covered in God's presence. This mission was curtailed by their fall into sin. While God began to reverse the tide of sin through the formation of Israel, the goal was that salvation would be made accessible to all people from all nations. As the prophets foretold, it would be through the Son of Man that this mission of expanding God's presence and God's salvation to the ends of the earth would be inaugurated.

Pentecost marks the moment this prophecy begins its fulfillment. Now that Jesus has died for our sins, now that he has conquered death by his resurrection, and now that the ascended Christ has sent his Spirit into the hearts of those who believe in him, the church is empowered to go throughout the whole world and share this good news with everyone they encounter. As we see throughout the remainder of the book of Acts, the disciples proceed from Jerusalem and begin to scatter throughout the world. As they travel, they engage in two principal activities: *proclaiming* the good news of Jesus Christ and *gathering* all those who believe this good news into newly established churches.[3]

First, there is proclamation. As the disciples scattered throughout the world, they proclaimed to all the nations that Jesus took away the sins of the world on the cross, and that he conquered death in his resurrection. Then they invited their interlocutors to believe this good news, to profess Jesus as Lord and God, and to be plunged into the waters of baptism. Those who believed gained entrance onto the mountain of God through these waters and could encounter the divine fire of the Holy Spirit in their hearts. Christians are invited to continue proclaiming this good news today, praying for their neighbors and seeking opportunities to joyfully persuade them of the truth, goodness, and beauty of the resurrected Christ. In so doing they carry on the tradition begun by the disciples of spreading the fire of the Holy Spirit.

But the mission of the disciples did not stop at this proclamation. They did not proclaim a detached and individualistic faith. Instead, they gathered together all believers into newly formed churches. One of the more remarkable aspects of the working of the Holy Spirit is that it enables Christians to become the portable mountain wherever they meet in the world. As a temple built of living stones, the church is not limited to one location in the world. Instead, it exists wherever these stones assemble in Jesus's name. Because of this reality, the disciples did not have to transport new Christians back to Jerusalem whenever they were baptized. Instead, they were able to start new churches wherever these new believers resided.

The mission of Christians today continues in this act establishing new communities wherever individuals confess Jesus as Lord and God. Each one of these new gatherings is a manifestation of the mountain of God. This is incredible news, as it means that just a handful of Christians gathered together is as much the body of Christ as thousands. These Christians become the mountain and the visible temple, whether they meet in an opulent building or under a tree: "There needs no outward building to meet the eye, in order to make it more of a Temple than it already is in itself. God, and Christ, and Angels, and souls, are not these a heavenly court, all perfect, to which this world can add nothing? Though faithful Christians worship without splendour, without show, in a homely and rude way, still their worship is as acceptable to God, as excellent, as holy, as though they worshipped in the public view of men, and with all the glory and riches of the world."[4]

A large part of my life has been spent helping to start new churches in nursing homes. It is an opportunity to gather Christians who are unable to leave their care facilities and thus unable to attend any other local churches. What is amazing about these gatherings is that, according to Scripture, they are as important and as significant to God as the largest church in the world. When these residents assemble in their activities room, they become the living stones of the mountain of God, and this mountain is as strong and powerful as a thousand people gathered in St. Peter's Basilica.

The mission of Adam and Eve was to expand the borders of Mount Eden so that the whole world would be filled with God's presence. When Christians go out on mission and establish new congregations, they are participating in this primordial mission. Each new church covers a unique geographic location in the world and makes it a place where God's glory is made manifest. Each new member of the church is one more living stone, and the goal of the church is to expand these Edenic stones to cover every inch of the world.

UNFINISHED BUSINESS: THE HOLY SPIRIT AS A DEPOSIT

A turning point is an event that forever changes the course of history. For instance, the turning point of a war is usually an important battle. The victor of this key, turning point battle winds up winning the war. Many historians believe that the battle of Gettysburg was the decisive turning point of the American Civil War. After the South lost that battle, there was no way they could have won the war. Of course, this evaluation can only be done in hindsight. While the war was already won for the North at Gettysburg, hard and grueling fighting continued for several years. The road from the decisive battle of Gettysburg to the final victory at Appomattox was long and painful.

The story of Mount Tabor is the turning point of all human history. In his life, death, and resurrection, Jesus wins the decisive victory over the serpent and over death. We now can have confidence that the devil's days on earth are numbered and his defeat is inevitable. As we will see in the next chapter, this confidence is sedimented into our souls through the vision of Mount Zion given to John in the book of Revelation. When one confesses Jesus as Lord and God and receives the Holy Spirit, they begin to partake—right now—in God's glory and are given assurance that they will be surrounded by this glory completely on Mount Zion. While the decisive battle has been won by Jesus, there are plenty of battles still to be fought. Through the Holy Spirit, we celebrate the decisive victory of Jesus even as we continue to fight sin, evil, and death in the world today. As we continue to walk with Jesus we will experience this battle as a kind of tension, a struggle between old and new, taking place within our hearts, within the church, and within the world.

First, the battle continues to take place within our hearts. The Holy Spirit creates a space in the human heart that is holy, a space where God's glory can reside. But this is only a small space, and the rest of the Christian life is spent making room in the human heart to let more and more of the Holy Spirit in, "bringing holiness to completion in the fear of God" (2 Corinthians 7:1). But this is not always easy. As St. Paul puts it, the one who receives the Holy Spirit is a new person—a new self—in Christ. Yet, that old self, the one steeped in human sin, remains. While God has started a new work in us, there is still a battle with this old self. We still have part of Adam and Eve inside us, even as the Holy Spirit is bringing more of Jesus into our hearts. For instance, when I first became a Christian, I still had a wicked sense of humor that manifested itself in mean-spirited joking at the expense of others. For years after I became a Christian, I struggled to put an end to this part of my old self and let the Holy Spirit reform and make holy my sense of humor. The Christian life is filled with these kinds of internal, spiritual struggles as we make our way to Zion.

Second, the battle takes place within the church. Each individual Christian continues to struggle with sin, the "old Adam" at work in their bodies. They are still works in progress. Since the church is made up entirely of others who are also works in progress, the church is still a place where sin and evil exist. The harmony of the portable mountain of the church is constantly challenged by the remaining sin and brokenness of its members. As such, the church must be a place of forgiveness and reconciliation. Like the stones of a building, the living stones of the church are stuck together. They must learn to work through their differences, to repent of their sins, and to ask for and receive forgiveness from each other.

Third, because the world is still a sinful and broken place, Christians will face suffering and persecution. Life in the portable mountain of the church is still life in the wilderness. The serpent has been dealt a decisive blow, but still slithers. This is important to remember because, though our spiritual, internal life is transformed by the Holy Spirit through faith in Jesus Christ, our external, material circumstances might actually worsen as a result of this faith. We are all like the Israelites in the wilderness, happy to be free from our slavery to sin, yet aware that, in many ways, life has become more difficult as a result of our newfound freedom. The remainder of the book of Acts sees the disciples traveling around the world to proclaim the gospel and start new churches. But we also see that, more often than not, their mission is met with stiff resistance. The anger, jealously, and bitterness that led many to consign Jesus to death on the cross is now unleashed on those who bear witness to Jesus's death and resurrection. Eventually, all but one of the twelve disciples would be put to death for proclaiming the good news of Jesus Christ. Today, thousands of individuals are executed each year for believing in Jesus Christ. While most of us will not have to undergo such extreme suffering, many of us will endure hardship and experience loss for the sake of our faith, whether that be a loss of a job, of financial security, or even relationships.

Amanda, one of the college students in my church, once befriended an international student named Mei in the beginning of the fall semester. Amanda and Mei quickly became close, and delightful pictures of their budding friendship began popping up in my social media feed. Then one day, Mei abruptly ended their friendship without warning or explanation, refusing to even return Amanda's texts. We found out later that Mei's parents had ordered her not to be friends with any Christians, and she obeyed this demand. Christians should expect such hostility from time to time as they interact in the world, at times even accepting the loss of friendship for the sake of fidelity to Christ.

While some of us will experience financial or relational hardships because of this ongoing struggle with sin in the world, all of us will experience the results of this struggle in the suffering and degradation of our own bodies. Sin still exists in the world and still infects human DNA. Because of this lingering sin, our bodies are still susceptible to disease and death. While the Holy Spirit is at work renewing us from within, our physical bodies are continuing to break down because of this residual sin. This breakdown of our bodies will result in our eventual physical death.

The life of a Christian is thus one of experiencing more and more of God in our spiritual life even as our bodily life degrades. Our spiritual senses become more and more developed just as our physical senses become more and more dim. My own experience with hearing testifies to this reality. When I first became a Christian, I loved listening to and playing music, the louder the better. I would frequently blast loud music late at night, waking up my parents and my sister in the process. During these teenage years, my physical sense of hearing was strong, but my spiritual sense of hearing was still quite weak. I struggled at times to understand the Bible and found it difficult to hear God's quiet voice in my times of prayer.

Now, almost thirty years later, my situation is reversed. My spiritual sense of hearing is much more acute. I can hear God more clearly when I open my Bible and when I sit down to pray. His voice is louder and clearer in my heart. Yet, just as my spiritual sense of hearing has grown, my physical sense of hearing is in decline. I am experiencing the first signs of hearing loss, with voices in a crowded room becoming harder to distinguish, and the faint ring of tinnitus accompanying most of my alone moments. This hearing loss is an early warning sign that my body is deteriorating and that all my physical senses will fully deteriorate with the rest of my body at death.

Physical death is still the destiny of Christians. However, through the Holy Spirit, there is now hope. What God has started spiritually in our hearts will work itself to completion in the resurrection of our physical bodies. In our resurrection, we will be fully renewed, spirit and body, heart and soul, with all of our senses restored and perfected. This hope that we have, the hope of Mount Zion, is described by Paul as a kind of groaning:

> For we know that if the tent that is our earthly home is destroyed, we have a building from God, a house not made with hands, eternal in the heavens. For in this tent we groan, longing to put on our heavenly dwelling, if indeed by putting it on we may not be found naked. For while we are still in this tent, we groan, being burdened—not that we would be unclothed, but that we would be further clothed, so that what is mortal may be swallowed up by life. He who has prepared us for this very thing is God, who has given us the Spirit as a guarantee. (2 Corinthians 5:1–5)

Even though our bodies are withering away and dying, our hearts are being renewed by the Spirit. This Spirit functions as a kind of deposit, a guarantee that one day we will be completely surrounded by the Holy Spirit, our bodies clothed in the pure white garments of God's glory. We will one day wear the same radiant heavenly robe that Jesus wore on Mount Tabor. Our souls and our bodies will be fully clothed by the Holy Spirit, and we will thus be adorned in eternal life.

Through the Holy Spirit, Christians now receive a spiritual taste of paradise. They can begin to have their home in the portable mountain of the church, where they partake in heavenly worship and experience harmony with others. Furthermore, they are now equipped to expand the mountain of God as they tell others about Jesus and help to start new churches across the earth. But, as we have seen, these experiences are temporary, incomplete, and unfinished. The decisive victory accomplished through Jesus's death and resurrection must be brought to completion when Jesus returns. At that time, there will be a final banishment of the serpent and a return to the mountain of God, Mount Zion.

God has summoned me to His marriage feast,
says the Church to the invited guests,
to enter with Him into the Bridal Chamber.
O Peoples, rejoice with me for I have been saved.
With garments of glory am I clothed,
with raiment of light am I wrapped.
From the water I have become a virgin,
and behold, angels are rejoicing at me.
On my head has the Bridegroom placed His hand,
and look, his right arm embraces me.
Through the touch of His hand have I been reborn
from the baptismal womb.

—*Anonymous Hymn*

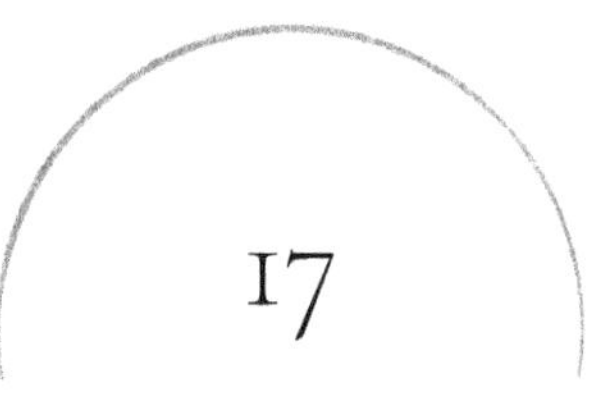

17

MOUNT ZION

On Revelation 19–22, Isaiah 2, 25–27, 60, and Psalm 87

The first fruits of paradise begin to blossom on earth in and through the body of Christ as the church carries on the mission of God in the world. Those who receive the Good News that Jesus is Lord and God experience relief from their sinful burdens and encounter the presence of God as their souls are lifted to heaven through the Holy Spirit. As they gather in the portable mountain of the church, Christians experience a foretaste of their eternal home, a place of harmony and worship.

But sin keeps sifting through. The serpent's venom is no longer deadly, but its bite still stings. The long history of the Christian church is one of advance and retreat, of faithfulness and failure. New churches spring up throughout the world just as others close their doors. The joys of following Jesus amidst the struggles of the world make us long for a time when trials will be no more.

As Jesus ascended in the clouds, the angels instructed his followers that he would one day return on those very same clouds.

This return would bring to completion his earthly work and the work of his church. What will this final end—this final victory—look like? We long for vivid pictures of our future to fuel our hope. We want a clear vision of our final destination to comfort us in our present sojourn. And it is for this reason that Jesus gives a vision to John concerning his second coming, which John writes down in the book of Revelation. Like the visions granted to the Old Testament prophets, this vision given to John is a collection of images and stories meant to captivate our imaginations. It gives us a robust picture of the goal of human life and challenges us to live with this final goal in mind.

The book of Revelation shares much in common with many of the visions of the prophets of old. In fact, many of the visions of the Old Testament prophets complement Revelation. The Old Testament prophecies are not only about Jesus's life, death, and resurrection, but also concern his return, what is often called "the second coming." This chapter will weave many of these prophecies into the picture given to us by John in the book of Revelation, first focusing on the final judgment of the world by Jesus, then describing life in our final home of Mount Zion, and ending with the depiction of our final end as a marriage of the church with Jesus.

JUDGMENT AND JUSTICE

There is no room for sin and evil on the mountain of God. To behold the pure brightness of a flame reminds us of the pure holiness of God. God cannot be polluted or diluted, and if human beings want perfect fellowship with God, then every minuscule molecule of sin must be eradicated and banished from His presence. And so, before human beings may come fully into God's presence on Mount Zion, Satan and his serpentine cohort of demons must be cast out of earth and all human sin must be eradicated in the pure fire of God's holiness. Isaiah prophesied that the Son of God, Jesus, would be the one person capable of accomplishing this task, and John tells us that Jesus's return will involve a final judgment of sin and evil and a restoration of complete and perfect justice on earth. As the ancient creed states, Jesus will "come again to judge the living and the dead." In John's vision, before this final judgment, angels initiate a series of plagues through the blasting of trumpets (Revelation 8–11). On Mount Sinai, the trumpet blast made the sinful Israelites quiver, reminding them that they could not approach God in their sin. Now, these same trumpet blasts resound throughout the earth, bringing destruction to those who refuse to turn to God and who oppress his people. In Revelation 19 we see Jesus descend from the clouds on a white horse with fiery eyes, and from his mouth comes a sharp sword by which he strikes down the evil, the wicked, and the demonic. The culmination of Jesus's victory comes in Revelation 20:7–15, where he casts Satan into hell, the lake of fire. We see in this vivid image the final manifestation of the fiery sword. After the fall, this sword guarded Mount Eden, preventing the sinful from entering. Later, Jesus falls on this sword to allow us back to the mountain of God. Now, in his second coming, Jesus goes on the offensive with this sword, wielding it to push back and destroy all sinful serpents from the face of the earth. The image of the *sword* stands as a warning to us of the consequences of sin. But for those who believe in Jesus, this sword becomes a sign of his great sacrifice on the cross, the pouring out of God's mercy as blood and water to nourish our souls. And now, in Jesus's return, this icon of compassion is transformed into a symbol of Jesus's triumph, a reminder that, however dark our days get here on earth, we have confidence that Satan will not ultimately prevail.

After this victory over Satan, Jesus sits on a great white throne to judge every single human being. The entirety of every person's thoughts, words, and deeds are laid bare before Jesus, and those who have turned away from Jesus are cast into the lake of fire prepared for the devil. The notion of hell and a final judgment cuts against the grain of our modern sensibilities. We live in a society that treats "judgment" as a four-letter word. One of the worst insults one can hurl at another is to call them judgmental. When I was in college, many of my peers perceived Christians as judgmental people, and there were plenty of anecdotes about harsh pastors and stern parochial school nuns to warrant this view. But judgmentalism is not limited to any particular people group. In fact, the one thing that seems to unite all of us today is our ability to judge. Many of us spend hours a day on social media, intaking and leveling judgments at others. We find it all too easy to judge our friend's political positions, their parenting styles, even their judgmental-ness!

While most of us can agree that judgmentalism isn't an attractive trait, the fact is, we need judgments in order to attain something that we all desire: justice. Judgment and justice go hand in hand. We all want to live in a world that celebrates the good that people do and diminishes the capacity of the wicked to prosper. No one wants to live in a world where murderers are celebrated as heroes. But, to obtain this justice, someone has to pronounce a judgment. For instance, in a courtroom, a judge weighs a collection of evidence that is often gray and murky, and from it renders a black and white judgment: guilty or innocent. This verdict provides justice if it is correct, fair, and accurate. Without this judgment, there could be no justice. The problem, however, is that human beings are not that great at rendering judgment. Each year, hundreds of people are sentenced to jail for crimes they did not commit, and the headlines are filled with criminals who get off scot-free. Furthermore, we see daily reminders of our unjust world. Wicked people grow rich off the backs of poor and honest laborers. Evil deeds are praised while good people go unnoticed. These daily injustices remind us of our inability as fallible humans to render perfect judgment.

For those of us who have grown weary of this unjust world, there is now hope with the revelation that Jesus will come again to judge the living and the dead, because Jesus *is* capable of rendering perfect judgment. Because Jesus is God, he is perfectly just, and thus capable of judging perfectly. He alone has the ability to see into the human heart and soul. He alone can see behind every action and every word in human history. And so, when Jesus returns, there will be a perfect separation of all that is good from all that is evil. All wrongs will come to light and be made right in the brightness of the resurrected Jesus.

This vision of Jesus's final judgment allows us to let go of our own desires to judge others. While a handful of people are given the responsibility for limited judgments—judges, rulers, and church leaders—we must remember the limits of our own ability to discern the hearts and motives of others. Our judgment is never as good as God's, but we can trust that Jesus's judgments are perfect and complete. We all have a mental list of people we think are probably on their way to heaven or whose crimes will send them straight to hell. But none of us can see the soul of another, and none of us have a perfect sense of justice. Jesus's perfect judgments free us from the burden of discerning the fates of others. We are not called to speculate about the eternal well-being of those who do not know Christ, but instead, to proclaim the good news that Jesus is risen and gift to them the opportunity to receive eternal joy and the certainty of salvation.

THE RESURRECTION OF THE DEAD

As a teenager, I stayed up late and slept in as long as humanly possible. But on Sunday mornings I was forced out of these deep slumbers by the booming voice of my father calling me to wake up for church. To this day, nothing can make me jump out of bed quite like this thunderous invocation of my name.

Ezekiel wrote that God would raise up a valley of dry bones through the Word of the Lord. Through this Word, the Spirit would descend like wind to stitch together bone and sinew and flesh in a glorious resurrection (Ezekiel 37). Once Jesus succeeds in casting out the serpent from the earth, this prophecy of Ezekiel can now be fulfilled. Jesus will shout out the names of the departed faithful, and their souls will awaken with their resurrected, eternal bodies to join Jesus on Mount Zion. The wind of the Holy Spirit will cascade out from the voice of Jesus, reviving each faithful soul and stitching soul and body together.

When Jesus comes again, all those who believed in his resurrection will follow him in their own resurrection. Those who die in Christ today are not dead, but only asleep. Throughout the New Testament, death is often referred to as a long slumber that will come to an end when Jesus returns. At that time, Jesus will call out each Christian by name, and they will leap up and enter their eternal home.

In one of the most powerful passages in the Bible, Jesus's close friend Lazarus dies and is buried in a tomb (John 11). Jesus, however, refers to Lazarus as only being asleep, much to the bewilderment of his disciples. When Jesus arrives at the tomb, he yells out "Lazarus, come out" and Lazarus wakes up and walks out of his grave. Jesus has the power to wake us up from death by the sheer sound of his voice. Those who confess Jesus as Lord and God can trust that, when they die, Jesus will see them as merely asleep. When Jesus returns, he will shout the names of the dead and they will rise like Lazarus. His voice will be a loud trumpet, but Christians will hear it as a pleasing sound and rise up to meet him.[1] The wind of Jesus's voice will descend on their dry bones, repairing both sinew and soul. In light of this glorious vision of our future resurrection, Christians no longer have to fear death. Death is merely a long and peaceful slumber. As we learn to hear Jesus's voice in our souls in this earthly life, we will hear his voice out loud in the afterlife, calling us to wake up and join him on Zion.

THE MERGING OF HEAVEN AND EARTH

Once Jesus fully banishes evil from the earth, earth becomes capable of being fully filled with God's presence. The book of Revelation describes this filling of the world with God's presence as a descent of heaven to earth upon Mount Zion. Heaven and earth merge upon Zion, and heaven, "the dwelling place of God" becomes fully accessible to humankind (Revelation 21:2). This has been the hope of humankind since the beginning. As we saw in Genesis 2, heaven and earth were united in the garden at the summit of Mount Eden. Adam and Eve's mission was to expand the borders of Eden, but this mission was thwarted by their own sin. From the moment of that first sin, heaven and earth split apart, and humanity's sense of God was greatly diminished. While the reception of the Holy Spirit awakens in Christians their heavenly ability to experience God, this ability remains largely interior and spiritual. As Christians sojourn on their way to Zion, they long for the spiritual and material, the heavenly and earthly, to be fully intertwined. They long not only to hear God in their heart, but also to hear God with their physical ears. They long not only to see God in their mind's eye but see Jesus with their physical eyes.

What we will see on Mount Zion is the fulfillment of this longing. The heavenly temple will descend, and God will dwell upon every inch of the earth. God's radiant glory will permeate every molecule of every living thing. His glory will be experienced in and through every thought, every word, and every action. One will feel God's glory in the river of life, taste God's glory in the fruit of the trees of Zion, and physically see God's glory in the radiant face of Jesus. As Ephrem puts it, in our resurrection our soul and spirit will be raised with our body, and we will in turn partake in God's glory with every fiber of our being:

> At the end
>   the body will put on
> the beauty of the soul,
>   the soul will put on that of the spirit,
> while the spirit shall put on
>   the very likeness of God's majesty.[2]

LIFE ON MOUNT ZION: HOME, HARMONY, WORK, AND WORSHIP

As the father of a three-year-old, I often wonder what my daughter will be like when she grows up. I see in her great empathy, intelligence, and beauty, and I pray that all these characteristics will reach their full maturity as she ages. We can see this kind of potential in all living things. For instance, as a gardener, my wife loves seeing the first sprouts that emerge from seed, dirt, and water. These sprouts conjure hope of full and bountiful tomato plants and multicolored tulips.

We long to see each living thing grow into its full potential and it is on Mount Zion that we see this longing come to fruition. Mount Zion is the fulfillment of the potential of Mount Eden and the hope of all of creation. While Eden was free from sin, its land and inhabitants had not matured. Adam and Eve were like young teenagers, and even the dirt, stone and soil were yet to live into their full potential. But when heaven descends upon Mount Zion there will be a kind of return to Eden, but an Eden that has reached its fulfillment: "Unspotted innocence was Eden's best; Great Paradise shows God's fulfilled behest."[3] On Mount Zion we see all of the stone, water, and trees of that primordial holy mountain, but all of these objects will now be vivified to their fullest potential. But more importantly, *we* will be brought to maturity. Human beings will be brought to full life on Zion where they will experience a deep and mature relationship with God and one another.

Since it is both a return to and fulfillment of Mount Eden, life on Mount Zion is also characterized by the four themes of *home*, *harmony*, *work* and *worship*. We will examine each of these themes, showing how Mount Zion brings to fulfillment the potential of Mount Eden.

HOME

We all long for home, a place where we are at ease and comfortable. Home is both a physical and relational term. It refers to a specific geographic location and a place where we reside with those that we love. Home in the Bible is the mountain, a physical place where we can have an intimate relationship with God and each other. The whole story of the Bible is, in a sense, a story about homecoming. It is about how humanity lost their mountain home on Eden and how, through Jesus Christ, they now have access to their eternal mountain home on Zion. As our eternal, physical home, Mount Zion has all the geographic features of Eden. It has *stones*, *water*, *trees*, *garments*, and *glory*. Each of these features are brought to fulfillment, to their fullest potential, on Zion.

Stones. Gold and onyx graced the glorious foundations of Mount Eden. These stones indicated the depth of beauty that characterized Adam and Eve's home: even the ground on which they walked was opulent. However, the depths of sin reached even these foundational stones, culminating in their destruction at Babel. Through his death and resurrection, Jesus has begun to heal even stones. He is the solid rock, the cornerstone of the church. Individual Christians can now, through Christ, become *living stones*, forming the portable mountain of God whenever they gather in Jesus's name. The foundation of our mountain home is now being laid through the church, and it is on Mount Zion where we see the complete fulfillment of this symbol of stone. On Mount Zion the stones of Eden and the living stones of the church reach their zenith.

First, the foundations of Zion will be adorned with twelve precious stones, more than the handful of stones on Eden. Every kind of jewel will exist on Mount Zion. As one walks its streets, views its buildings, and rests on its rocks, they will be immersed in a rich and radiant color palette the likes of which have never been seen. As we saw at the beginning of creation, God made the world out of nothing and graced it with an opulent and excessive beauty. God's creation is a bottomless well of glory. On Zion, we will see the fulfillment of this opulence. God fashions our home out of these materials because he is beautiful and wants to adorn even the ground that we walk with a beauty greater than the finest earthly palace.

Furthermore, as the living stones of the church, the stones on Mount Zion indicate the kinds of people we will be when we arrive at our forever home. Not only will the physical foundation of Zion shine with brilliance, *we* will shine with internal and external beauty. John describes the city of the new Jerusalem in Zion as being composed of gold which is clear as glass. Christians are the living stones of this city, the holy city of God, which will be free from all sin, all trials, and all temptations. These living stones have been purified with the fire of the Holy Spirit and are free of all impurity.

Just as a precious jewel has outer beauty, the human soul has inner beauty. But this inner beauty remains largely hidden from others. So much of who we are and what we do goes unnoticed. Few of our loved ones know how many hours we have spent praying for them. The care we provide to the very young and very old is rarely noted or reciprocated. But now, we have hope and assurance when we picture these translucent stones, because we know that the work that we do and the virtues we cultivate will not be lost or forgotten. We are all created in the image of God, yet this image is marred and damaged by the ugliness of the world. On Zion, all of this ugliness will be wiped away, our image will be restored, and our perfected beauty will shine through. Revelation states that these stones of Zion will be "pure as glass." This means that all our inner beauty, all our good qualities and virtues, all of those inner qualities that few see, will now be transparent and revealed to all.[4]

Waters. On Mount Eden, there was a river of life flowing down from the top to nourish and sustain all living creatures that tread on its sacred grounds. But we also saw that there were four rivers demarcating the bounds of Eden, indicating that the rest of creation was still largely unfinished and uncultivated. On Mount Zion, we discover that the "sea is no more," which means that there are no more waters separating the finished from the unfinished. Mount Zion is the mountain of God which now stretches throughout the entire world. All of creation is now brought to its fulfillment.

Despite the sea being no more, the river of life remains. The cooling waters of this river will bring a final and lasting healing to the human soul. Many of us carry with us a burden of physical or emotional pain. We have all experienced tragedy, loss, and heartbreak. Our physical sufferings leave marks on our bodies and our trauma leaves marks on our souls. The longer we live on this earth, the more wounded and torn apart our souls become, and we long to be mended. On Mount Zion, we will finally experience true healing. Our tears will be wiped away in the waters of the river of life. When our bodies and souls were plunged into the waters of baptism, we were given a foretaste of this eternal healing. Now, on Zion, we will drink fully of these waters and experience complete and everlasting healing. While we may still retain the memories of the challenges and hardships of our lives east of Eden, these memories will no longer carry their emotional sting: "In light of heaven, the worst suffering on earth ... will be seen to be no more serious than one night in an inconvenient hotel."[5]

Trees. An assortment of trees dotted the landscape of Mount Eden, providing nourishment to Adam and Eve as they continued to grow closer to God. The tree of life was to be consumed when they reached full maturity in their relationship with God. But in their sin Adam and Eve were cast down from Mount Eden, never to eat of this tree. However, God used this tree to help bring Adam and Eve back to him. Its fruit provided the oil to anoint Jesus as king and savior, and its branches provided the hardwood of the cross by which this King died to take away the sins of Adam, Eve, and all of their offspring.[6]

And now, on Mount Zion, we see the tree of life on the banks of the river. All those who have been healed by the wood of the cross can now bask under the tree of life just as Abraham rested under the tree at Mamre. The fruit of the tree of life, as well as every other tree in Zion, can now be consumed by its inhabitants. Furthermore, the fruit of these trees is like the fruit of the tree of knowledge, providing wisdom to all those who partake. The fruit of these trees contain the meaning of Scripture, and through this fruit, Christians on Zion will be able to partake in the deepest knowledge of God and his creation.[7] The picture of this heavenly fruit should stoke in Christians today a desire to read the Bible and probe the depths of its wisdom. To read and ponder Scripture today is to partake in a kind of spiritual chewing, an ingesting of heavenly knowledge that is a foretaste of these fruitful trees of Mount Zion.

Glory and Garments God's glory radiated from the summit of Mount Eden, and Adam and Eve were able to partake in this glory, their bodies clothed by it. But even then, God's glory did not fully cover the entire earth. Now on Mount Zion, we see God's glory permeating everything. In fact, the sun is no longer needed as a source of illumination. God's celestial brightness, which far exceeds all the stars in the galaxy, now encompasses the entire world. Today, as we walk outside, our vision of the world is made possible by the sun's brightness. In a sense, we see through the sun and see because of the sun. On Mount Zion, God's glory will be our sun. We will see everything *through* God's glory and see everything because of his glory. God's glory will be our atmosphere. We often speak of places in terms of the mood we feel while we are in them. For instance, we can speak of a restaurant as having a welcoming atmosphere or an office as having a gloomy one. Atmosphere describes both a physical place and the collective mood of the persons occupying it. On Mount Zion, everything will be pervaded by God's glory and God's goodness, and we will live creatively and joyfully within the atmosphere of God's pure brilliance.

In Isaiah's vision, he describes the extent of the glory of Zion even further: "The sun will no more be your light by day; by night you will not need the brightness of the moon. The Lord will be your everlasting light, and your God will be your glory" (Isaiah 60:19[8]). According to Isaiah, there is an almost direct equivalence between God's glory and our glory: we will *wear* God's glory as our heavenly garment. The brilliant white robe of Jesus on Mount Tabor will be our robe. Each time the sun in the sky fills the atmosphere and surrounds us with light and heat, we can long for the day when God's eternal brightness will surround us like the finest silk.

Figure 5: Mount Zion—Revelation 21–22

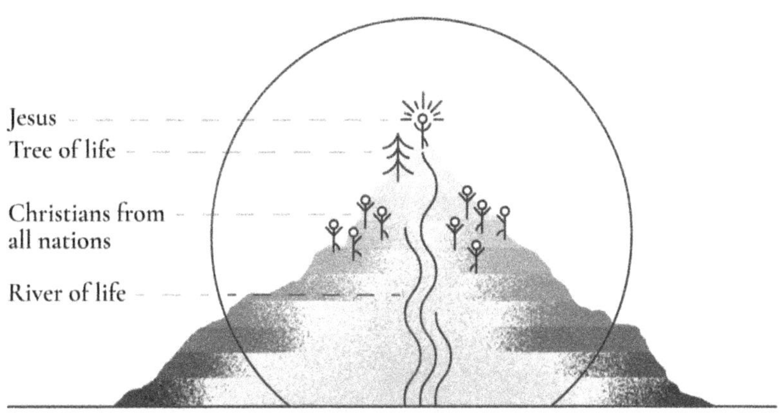

HARMONY

On Mount Eden, Adam and Eve were in harmony with God, each other, and with all of God's creation. But sin created disharmony and animosity between humanity and creation, and between Adam and Eve. Disharmony now reigns in our world, from minor quibbles between husband and wife to the large-scale wars fought between civilizations. The first inklings of peace have been made available within the portable mountain of the church, but this harmony is hard fought, forged through a never-ending process of forgiveness and reconciliation. Now on Zion, people from every nation stream to the mountain of God and experience perfect peace and harmony with each other.

While the fruit of the tree of life provides wisdom for the inhabitants of Zion, its leaves are provided for the healing of the nations. Bitter enemies lay down their weapons and embrace in the shade under these leaves. There will be no more prejudice, no more bigotry, no more hatred, no more animosity between those who are differentiated by race, language, or culture. Each person will retain their distinctives while still being able to perfectly relate to one other. Isaiah 2 paints a picture of the nations streaming to Mount Zion and Christ the perfect judge settling all lingering animosities. And yet, as members of these nations experience healing, they still retain many of their cultural distinctives. While the Bible speaks of universal healing and universal obedience to God on Zion, it does not ever speak of universal assimilation of differences.

WORK

One of greatest movies of all time, *It's a Wonderful Life*, chronicles the life of George Bailey, an intelligent and promising native son who dreams of one day leaving his hometown to travel the world and accomplish great deeds. But his responsibilities to his family and his community keep him stuck at home, working a tedious and frustrating job as a lender to provide quality housing for the lower classes of Bedford Falls, NY.

Growing up, I never understood the appeal of this movie. It was just another boring black and white film that lacked the frenetic explosions of a modern action movie. But as I entered my forties, I became overwhelmed with the burdens of middle-age life. I was hit with a range of responsibilities—I had to care for a young child during a global pandemic, and began to care for my aging parents. The stress of increased responsibilities at work was multiplied by the financial burden of providing for my family and our future. The demands on my time brought with it the realization that many of the things I had wanted to accomplish in life would simply not happen; I would not be able to accomplish all I wanted in life before I died.

Work east of Eden involves a mix of frustration and loss. Our labors are often boring, burdensome, and tedious, and most of us dream of being able to have the time and freedom to pursue other more joyful ventures. When Jesus died on the cross and conquered sin and death by his resurrection, he began to reverse all the effects of human sin, including the curse of painful labor. While work remains difficult and challenging, Christians are now given the opportunity to offer up all their actions, however small, to God. When they do, they know that the ascended Jesus delights in them amidst the tedium of sweeping floors and clicking keyboards.

But we all long for an end to this tedium and the freedom to engage in other pursuits. When Jesus banishes all sin and evil from the earth, he will also eradicate the tedium of toil. As heaven descends upon earth on Mount Zion, all the land will be covered in God's goodness and glory. Isaiah depicts what labor will be like once the nations gather together on Mount Zion, where individuals will "beat their swords into plowshares, and their spears into pruning hooks" (Isaiah 2:4). Weapons of war will be transformed into gardening tools. The labor expended on the machinery of war will be swallowed up. In its place will be peaceful cooperative labor exercised for the cultivation God's creation. This labor will be done not out of necessity, but out of joy. We will continue to nurture God's creation and continue to discover the manifold ways we can flourish on this mountain. Gardening, music, dancing, painting, husbandry, engineering, and reading will all be waiting for us on Mount Zion.

Because life on Mount Zion is infinite, we will be able to continue to explore these jobs and these hobbies for eternity. We will no longer have to fear missing out on anything good in this present life. Those of us who, like George Bailey, have had to sacrifice promising careers or let their skills and talents lay fallow for the sake of duty and responsibility will be rewarded in Zion with the time needed to pursue all the beautiful things God has created.

WORSHIP

When we encounter something beautiful or miraculous, it elicits from us an ecstatic response. One of the most noteworthy events that triggered this kind of ecstatic response was Duke Ellington's performance of the song "Diminuendo in Blue" at the Newport Jazz Festival in 1956. At the time, Ellington's big band had fallen on difficult times and their popularity was waning. But during this song, Ellington's saxophonist Paul Gonsalves delivered an epic, twenty-seven-chorus solo which led the audience to break out in uproarious spontaneous dancing. The event triggered a revival in Ellington's music, as thousands rediscovered the beauty of his compositions.

When we encounter the magnificent, we are overcome with awe and wonder, and will often respond with cheers, laughter, singing, and dancing. We are designed by God to respond in this way to that which is good, true, and beautiful. The pinnacle of our response comes when we encounter the *source* of *all* that is good, true, and beautiful: God. We call this ecstatic response worship, and this special response of worship is meant to be reserved for God alone. On Mount Eden, the culmination of Adam and Eve's active life came in their worship of God in the garden. But after the fall, worship of God became more difficult and disordered. Even as Jesus has lifted the spiritual veil that separates us from God, our worship is still frustrated by our old sinful selves and muted by the brokenness of a still sinful world.

But when Jesus returns to banish all sin and wickedness from the earth, human beings will be completely free to worship God, unencumbered and unhindered. Isaiah 25 describes how God will lift the veil that is covering all the earth. When heaven comes down upon Mount Zion, all barricades and curtains, anything that prevents us from joyfully praising God, will be removed. In response, the people of God will lift their voices in a song of thanksgiving. Revelation 19 goes one step further, revealing that our voices will be joined with the intonations of angels in praise of God.

God's beauty is deeper and richer than all the finest works of art ever created, and as such, an encounter with this beauty will draw out of us never ending praise. The pinnacle of this pure and unhindered worship will come at the pinnacle of Mount Zion, when all those gathered to praise God will see Jesus face-to-face.

THE BRIDE OF THE LAMB

The culmination of Mount Zion, the culmination of the book of Revelation, and the culmination of the whole Bible, comes with the vision of Jesus's face next to the tree of life: "They will see his face, and his name will be on their foreheads" (Revelation 22:4). The name of Jesus written on our foreheads is a sign of the permanency of this intimacy: "These words symbolize the abiding memory they have of God and their union with him. For just as God rests upon them and is imprinted on them, so he is always present with the saints."[9] We will remain united with God in a permanent state of intimacy for eternity. This is our final, deepest, and truest desire. We long to see Jesus in all his radiant glory, just as Moses beheld him on Mount Sinai. We also long, like Peter, to build a permanent home on Tabor. We want to gaze into the eyes of Jesus, bask in his glory, and know for certain that the lights will never go dim.

The preeminent image used to describe this joyous day is that of a wedding. We have already seen that the tree of life was meant to be a sign of full intimacy with God. We have also seen that faith in God, the faith of Abraham and Thomas, was akin to a kind of wedding commitment: it was not just an assent to factual knowledge, but a wholehearted relational commitment of trust in God with all of one's mind, body, strength, and soul. So, it should come as no surprise that the book of Revelation describes our eternal union with Jesus on Mount Zion as a wedding. Jesus is the Lamb and bridegroom, and the church, the entire collection of faithful men and women, is his bride. The story of the Bible is a rescue story about how God descends the mountain to rescue his sinful creation. But it is more than that. It is a love story. God descends the mountain to save his creation so that we can be eternally united with him.

The symbols in the Bible can be viewed from the vantage point of the peak of Mount Zion. As it turns out, many of the symbols that God has woven throughout scripture are meant for us to appropriate so that we might climb the mountain of God and prepare for our wedding with Jesus.

Our entrance back onto the mountain is made possible through Jesus's death on the cross. As our loving bridegroom, he descended to rescue us by sacrificing his own life, falling on the sword for our sins. While on the cross, he was pierced in the side, and blood and water flowed out. These symbols reveal the entrance to the mountain. We enter the mountain of the Lord through the blood of Christ and the waters of baptism. From the vantage point of Zion, we now see that the church was pulled out of Jesus's side at Calvary. Just as Eve was taken from the rib of Adam to be his bride, the church is taken from the side of Jesus to one day be his bride. It is for this reason that the church is now called the bride of the Lamb:

> And fittingly does he call the bride the "wife" of the Lamb. For when Christ was slaughtered as a lamb, he at that time betrothed [the church] with his own blood. For just as when Adam was sleeping, the woman was formed through the taking of the rib, so also the church, formed through the shedding of blood from the side of Christ as he was sleeping voluntarily on the cross through death, was united with him who suffered for us.[10]

The climb up the mountain of God now becomes an ascent to the marriage altar, and the symbols in Scripture now reveal to us how the church is being prepared to be the bride of Christ. The fire of the Holy Spirit kindles in the heart a burning desire for Jesus the bridegroom, allowing our souls to be lifted up the mountain like flickering sparks. The waters of baptism cleanse the church of its sin, making the bride of Christ pure as gold and perfectly holy for her wedding day. The oil of healing which is pressed from the tree of life flows down from the anointed king and bridegroom Jesus, and it becomes for his bride a fragrant oil, a sweet perfume that beautifies. The heavenly garments of God's glory become for the church her wedding dress; the ineffable light of the risen Christ is woven around her like the finest linen.

And finally, once the church has been anointed with oil and has put on its wedding garments, it can ascend to the top of Zion, walking the aisle to meet Jesus at the top. Here, the church will look into the eyes of Jesus, will behold his glory face-to-face, and will be with him forever.

The altars built on the top of the mountain and the back of the tabernacle are now revealed to be banquet tables crafted for this wedding feast. The manna that nourishes the body and the communion bread that nourishes the soul are revealed to be the bread of heaven, a sign of the eternal satiation waiting for the church on Mount Zion. The wine of celebration and praise, the cup shared by Abraham and Melchizedek, the cup which Jesus instructed his church to receive when gathered, is now revealed to be the wine of the church's eternal wedding feast. The church will lift its glass in endless praise of Jesus, and there will be celebration and delight forever and ever. Amen!

THE END AND THE BEGINNING

The best things in life never get old. Caravaggio paintings elicit endless praise and commentary. Literary scholars continue to discuss, debate, and dissect *The Brothers Karamazov* as the greatest novel ever written. *Blue Train* by John Coltrane, that song that sparked my love of jazz music, is still spun regularly on my turntable. After thousands of listens, I have barely begun to scratch the surface of its beauty.

While these works of art continue to challenge and inspire thousands, none of them compare to the depth and beauty of a human being. As creatures made in the image of God, human beings are more complex and intricate than any man-made creation. And so, our relationships with each other carry with them the possibility of even more depth and richness.

Consequently, marriage is both an end and a beginning. On the one hand, marriage is the culmination of a courtship between bride and groom. A man and a woman have spent months or years getting to know each other, growing closer together with every passing minute. This courtship culminates in a lifelong commitment to each other that is celebrated and consecrated at the church altar. While the wedding ends the courtship, it is also the beginning of a new life together. Husband and wife get to know each other more and more as they grow old and continue to delight in each other in often surprising ways. The best marriages have the constancy of commitment punctuated with moments of newness and surprise.

My parents, for instance, have had the exact same daily routine for fifty years. My father goes to work early in the morning while my mom cleans and manages household affairs. My father comes home from work at a predictable time, and they share a meal and conversation. This routine provides daily stability and joy. My mother once remarked that she still looks forward to my dad coming home from work every single day. And yet there are still moments of surprise. At my grandfather's funeral, for instance, my stoic father broke down and wept while giving the eulogy. My mother had never seen such an outpouring of emotion from my father. It was an incredible and surprising moment where more of my father's inner beauty was revealed to my mother.

If there are elements of both constancy and newness in the best of human marriages, how much more faithfulness and joy will exist in the marriage of the church with Christ? When we are united to Jesus, we are united to God himself, the one who is infinitely good and infinitely beautiful. This means that there will always be more and more of God to know and love: "There is no limit to the operation of love, since the beautiful has no limit."[11]

Whatever words we might articulate to describe our eternal life with Jesus, one word that will never be uttered is "boring." There will always be more to do and explore on Mount Zion, and more friendships to cultivate. As Gregory of Nyssa puts it, the human heart will have the capacity for more and more goodness. Each new experience of love, joy, and wisdom will spark an even greater desire and greater capacity for all that is good, true, and beautiful. We will always grow and never cease to grow.[1] The pinnacle of this never-ending growth in goodness will be the cultivation of our relationship with Jesus Christ. Our relationship with him will continue to surprise and delight us for eternity. It is this vision of Jesus standing at the top of the mountain with us that should motivate every single one of our actions in the present. It compels us to rid of ourselves of anything in our hearts that is unfit for Zion. It prompts us to begin this ascent up the mountain today by living lives of holiness and faithfulness. And it sparks in us a desire to experience a taste of Mount Zion today in the portable mountain of the church.

Through the vision of the prophets and the revelation of John, we now have a detailed picture of our final goal in life. We can now begin to understand how our lives *must* be lived in accordance with our infinitely beautiful and glorious final destination.

What then are we taught through what has been said? To have but one purpose in life: to be called servants of God by virtue of the lives we live. For when you conquer all enemies ... cross the water, are enlightened by the cloud, are sweetened by the wood, drink from the rock, taste of the food from above, make your ascent up the mountain through purity and sanctity; and when you arrive there, you are instructed in the divine mystery by the sound of the trumpets, and in the impenetrable darkness draw near to God by your faith, and there are taught the mysteries of the tabernacle and the dignity of the priesthood.

—Gregory of Nyssa

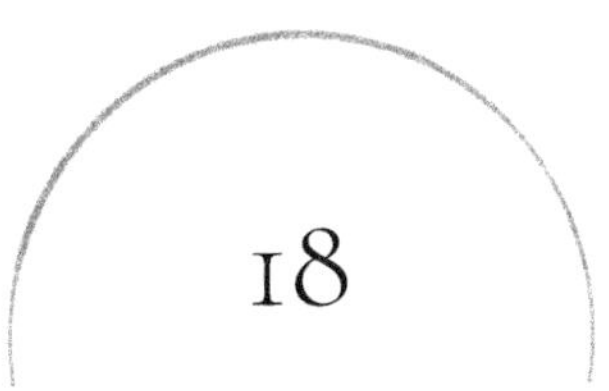

18

CLIMBING THE SPIRITUAL MOUNTAIN

On Hebrews 12 and Psalm 40, 146

When I fell in love with jazz music, I picked up an instrument and started to play. This love of music prompted me to practice regularly and to form a band with my friends. As inspiration, I hung up photographs of famous musicians on my walls: one of Dexter Gordon resting a cigarette on his tenor sax, the other of a sunglasses-clad Miles Davis cooly blowing his trumpet. My dream was to be as famous as these musicians, to one day have a black and white photo of myself next to Dexter and Miles. What I longed for, in a sense, was to join the *story* of jazz music, to become one of the legendary figures within this musical tradition. I wanted my name to be written in its history books.

When we fall in love with something, we want to join its story, to be a part of it and make it our own. The Bible invites us to fall in love with God through Jesus Christ and take our place within its story. But the Bible is not merely one story among millions of tales that line bookshelves. It is *the one true* story of the world. God is inviting each and every person alive to fall in love with him and enter into this one true story. We are invited to see ourselves as key players in this story as it progresses from Mount Tabor to Mount Zion. Our story is being written by God after the book of Acts and before the book of Revelation.

Near the end of the book of Revelation, John sees a vision of the book of life (Revelation 20:11–15). In it are written all the names of those who have been faithful to God. At the final judgment, this book will be opened and read out loud, with the persons named in it rising to join Jesus on Mount Zion. When we fall in love with God and enter into his story, he is writing, reading, and remembering our story. God is writing our individual stories and placing them next to the book of Acts in this great history of the world. The incredible news is that when we accept this invitation and join this story, we can trust that we will not be forgotten. In every other venture in life, our names will eventually be forgotten. In just a few years no one will remember that I played jazz music or wrote this book. But when we join the story of the Bible, our names will be written and remembered by God, etched in the eternal book of life, the one true history book.

How do we enter into the biblical story, and what we should do once we enter? These final chapters are meant to help answer these questions, showing how we enter this story through belief and baptism, and how we live in this story through our prayer and church life.

ENTERING THE STORY: BELIEF AND BAPTISM

As we have seen throughout the story of the Bible, God has enabled us to get back to him by sending his Son Jesus Christ to die for our sins and conquer death in his resurrection. God has *already* done this for us: it is a free gift. In order to become a Christian and take our place in the biblical story, all one must do is receive this gift. We do this through two activities: *belief* and *baptism*.

Our entrance into the story of God comes by believing in God and what the Father has done in sending his Son to rescue us. As we have already seen, faith is the word used to describe this act of believing. Faith is the starting point of our spiritual commitment to believe in Jesus and follow him as our Lord. However, since humans are spiritual *and* physical beings, this spiritual assent to faith is meant to be consummated in a physical act of faith: a plunge into the waters of baptism. In baptism, heaven and earth come together in water. As one enters the water, they are taken up into the same waters that surrounded Moses in the Red Sea and the same waters in which Jesus was baptized. Baptism becomes for Christians their first experience of Mount Zion, a moment in which the heavenly and the earthly are joined together: it is our first dip in the eternal waters of the river of life.

Belief and baptism allow us to fully enter into God's story, but they do not take place simultaneously. For some people, belief comes to them like a bolt of lightning. I have met many individuals who have come to faith through an unexpected vision of Jesus, similar to the one experienced by Paul on the road to Damascus (Acts 9). For others, belief comes slowly over years or decades.

Many are baptized as infants and grow up in Christian households. Like those Israelites who carried their children through the Red Sea, parents who have their children baptized believe on behalf of their child, raising them to accept and confirm their baptism as they grow to maturity. For instance, I was baptized and raised in a Christian home, learning bits and pieces of the gospel throughout my early life. However, my faith was cemented by a vision of Jesus on the side of a mountain as a teenager.

God brings people to faith in a number of different ways, and Christians have required that this faith be cemented in the physical act of baptism. We enter fully into the story of the Bible through this inner, spiritual faith commitment to Jesus Christ, and through this physical act in which a bit of heaven comes down to earth in the waters of baptism. Once we do, we take our place amongst God's people journeying towards Mount Zion. Just as the Israelites passed through the waters of the Red Sea and journeyed to the promised land, we too pass through the waters of baptism and journey with the church to our eternal promised land.

GROWING IN CHRIST: THE TWO MOUNTAINS

What do we do once we have entered into this story? What does our journey toward Mount Zion encompass? As belief and baptism show us, the Christian life is both spiritual and physical. As we continue our sojourn to Zion, we are called to continue to grow in Christian maturity both spiritually and physically.

Since the beginning of the church, Christians have continued to grow in their relationship with God through two key activities. First, they cultivated their inner, spiritual lives by having daily prayer time. This time, which was known in some circles as performing the daily office or hours, is what many Christians today call "having a quiet time." Each day, Christians take time by themselves to be with God and perform some combination of prayer, confession, and reading scripture. Second, Christians cultivated their communal, physical lives by going to church each Sunday. Just as Christians took an hour or two a day in quiet before God, they also took a day a week to join with other Christians to worship together in church.

Our life in Christ unfolds along these two trajectories, and we can use the biblical symbols as a guide and help. The symbols in the Bible are meant to be used to deepen both our quiet inner times with God, as well as enhance our time together with other Christians in church. As we have seen, God speaks to us in images as well as words, and has designed human beings to learn in this way. When I teach my daughter how to read, I don't just draw the letters c-a-t on paper, but instead place a picture of a cat next to those words, so that she associates those three letters with a furry feline friend. Likewise, God wants us to draw closer to him in prayer, confession, and communion, and so he uses biblical symbols as well as words to help us. He invites us to associate confession with fire, bread with communion, and to make other connections in order to deepen our experience with him.

In fact, we can use the preeminent symbol in the Bible, the mountain, to guide and enhance our entire quiet time with God and our entire time in church. We can picture these two activities (quiet time and church time) as two interrelated mountain climbs: a climb up the *spiritual mountain* develops our interior life in God, and our climb up the *physical mountain* of the church

Figure 5: Ascending and Descending the Spiritual Mountain—*Symbols* and Actions

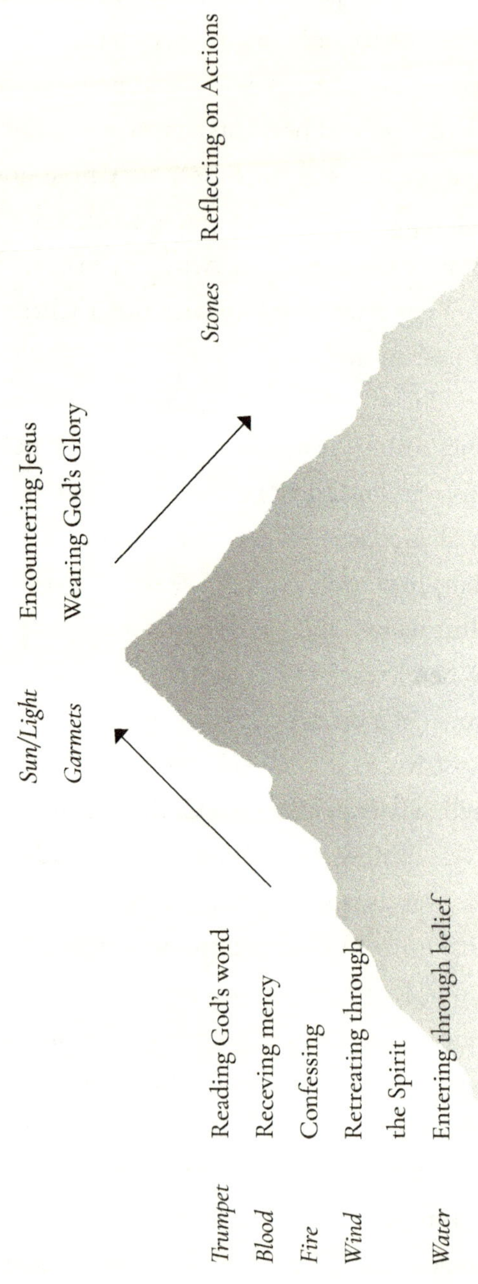

cultivates our physical life with God. This chapter describes our ascent up the spiritual mountain, while the ensuing chapter will discuss our ascent into the physical mountain of the church.

CLIMBING THE SPIRITUAL MOUNTAIN: CULTIVATING OUR SPIRITUAL LIFE

Jesus has already scaled the mountain in his ascension, reaching heaven and making a place for us in God's very presence. He has also sent the Holy Spirit into the hearts of his followers to allow them to be lifted into this spiritual dwelling place. Those who have received the Holy Spirit can now enter this heavenly temple, the spiritual mountain of God, whenever they retreat from their interactions in the world and enter into their inner life.

How do we cultivate this inner spiritual life? In Hebrews 12:22, we read that through Christ's blood we can now enter the spiritual Mount Zion, the heavenly temple as we wait for the moment when this heavenly mountain will descend upon earth. The various symbols—water, wind, fire, sword, etc.—can be our guides to help us climb up this spiritual mountain. They are like rungs on a spiritual ladder, helping us to draw nearer and nearer to God and getting us closer and closer to his glory.

ENTERING THE MOUNTAIN

To enter the mountain of God, we have to leave behind the world and spend as much quality time with God as possible. We all crave quality, uninterrupted time with the ones we love. We all need that time to intentionally remove ourselves from distractions and responsibilities and cultivate intimate relationships. The same is true for our spiritual life with God. Throughout each day, Christians are invited to hit the pause button on our earthly activities and retreat to a quiet place. We are invited to close our physical eyes and open our spiritual eyes.[2] We are called to quiet our physical ears so that our spiritual ears might hear from God. When we do, we allow our souls to be lifted up by the wind of the Holy Spirit to the spiritual mountain and into God's presence. Wind surrounds us every moment of our lives, but most of the time we do not even notice it, since we are caught up in other tasks of the day. Likewise, the wind of the Holy Spirit is constantly at work around us, all we need to do is create space for our hearts to acknowledge it, and it will elevate us up to the mountain and into God's presence. In a sense, when we withdraw from the material world and quiet our senses, we open up a spiritual sail in our hearts, ready to catch the wind of the Spirit that pushes us further and further towards God.

ENCOUNTERING THE FIRE, BEHOLDING THE WOOD

Once we arrive on the spiritual mountain, we are immediately confronted by the awesome and wondrous holiness of God, and, in turn, our own *lack* of holiness. The fire of the Holy Spirit confronts our souls, demanding that we confront our own sin in front of the holy and powerful God. Therefore, to allow this fire to purify our hearts, we engage in an act of confession. When we confess, we allow this fire to light up the dark recesses of our soul.[3] We recall the Ten Commandments and the Sermon on the Mount, allowing them to perform a kind of sin diagnostic on our hearts. Just as a doctor performs a diagnostic to discover what is ailing their patient, the Ten Commandments help us unearth the sick areas of our soul. We ask God to reveal the ways we have turned against him with our inner and outer senses: the ways we have viewed explicit material with our physical eyes and the explicit images we worship in our mind's eye. The words spoken out loud that belittle a neighbor, and the hateful words we mutter under our breath.

Like the poking and prodding of medical equipment, this sin diagnostic is painful and difficult, but we have confidence that it will lead to our healing. After we confess our sins to God, we recall Mount Golgotha and the blood pouring out of Jesus's side for our sake. We see the blood of Jesus pouring out of his hands, feet, and side. And we let that blood wash us clean of our sins. This blood covers our hearts, our minds, our lips, and our ears, and we hear that the almighty God has had mercy upon us and has forgiven us all our sins. We hear those words of forgiveness and are grateful at the outpouring of God's mercy on the cross: "Ah Jesus, your mercy! Jesus, hung on the cross for my sins. For those same five wounds from which you bled on it, heal my bloody soul from all the sins by which she is wounded through my five senses."[4]

HEARING GOD'S WORD

Now that our sins are forgiven, we can begin to climb the mountain and hear God's voice speak to us once again. The trumpet-like sound of God's voice no longer makes us tremble in our sin. Through the forgiveness of the blood of Jesus, it now invites us up the mountain, to climb up to Jesus and receive his divine teaching. As Gregory of Nyssa states, we are invited to "make your ascent up the mountain through purity and sanctity; and when you arrive there, you are instructed in the divine mystery by the sound of the trumpets."[5]

As we climb the spiritual mountain, we open up the Bible to hear the words of Jesus ring out from Zion. Like those who flocked to hear the Sermon on the Mount, our spiritual climb is an ascent to meet the author of the Bible, Jesus. It is a moment to cultivate our spiritual sense of hearing. As we read the Bible over the days, months, and years, we discover that the noisiest, most difficult passages to read will slowly begin to make sense to us. What was once an inarticulate trumpet blast will become, to our spiritual ears, a pleasing melody.

Not only are we invited to open up our spiritual ears to hear God's word, but we are also invited to open up our spiritual sense of taste to savor God's word. We have seen throughout the story of the Bible how knowledge of God is correlated with our sense of taste. For instance, eating the fruit of Mount Zion will be the means by which human beings acquire knowledge of God and wisdom concerning God's creation. The smell and taste of these fruits are meant for the nourishment of our souls, just as one might pluck, peel, and savor a tangerine on a hot day to refresh the body. As we climb this mountain, we are invited to come with a spiritual hunger to know more about God. We are called to ingest and savor the words of the Bible, to allow them to assimilate into our body and course through our veins.

REACHING THE TOP: PRAISE AND WORSHIP

As we feast on these heavenly words of God, our mind's eye lifts upward in search of their source. We look to the summit of paradise in search of the person whose voice has emanated down to us. At the peak we see the source of these words, the Word of God, Jesus, standing in his brilliant, transfigured glory. Just as Moses saw with his physical eyes the radiant face of Jesus on Tabor, we are now invited to see the face of Jesus in our mind's eye on the top of the spiritual mountain. We use these image making portions of our brain, our mind's eye, daily. For instance, if I am going to meet a friend at a restaurant, I might prepare for our conversation by picturing the two of us speaking over a meal.

Now, through the Holy Spirit, we can use these faculties to directly speak with Jesus in heaven. We picture in our mind and in our heart Jesus's clothes turning an iridescent white, we see his glorious face, and we are invited to converse with him just as Moses did on Tabor. Our response to this incredible invitation must be to praise God the Father, Son, and Holy Spirit. This encounter with God's glory necessarily draws out from us an offering of mental and emotional energy in worship of God. Now that we have ingested his word in our gut and seen his glory in our mind, we are invited to open up our mouths, to let out words from the recesses of our stomach that praise God for who he is and what he has done for us.

My wife is an expert at writing cards and thank you notes. She is able to quickly and beautifully scroll a handwritten note to a friend that perfectly encapsulates their virtues and their inner beauty. As one who is not particularly great at writing notes, I once asked her to divulge her letter writing secrets. First, she pictures her friend in her mind and begins to contemplate their good qualities. She then begins to describe specific actions that they have done that exemplify their goodness: perhaps it was a time they visited her in the hospital, or a time they went out of their way to help someone in need. Then she recounts their goodness and their character, the specific virtues that they exude in their very being. Finally, she ends by talking about her specific feelings and emotions towards them.

Praise and worship of God follows along a similar line. It begins by picturing Jesus at the top of Mount Tabor, and proceeds to a contemplation of God's good works and God's perfect character. We start by praising God for what he has done for us—for creating us, for redeeming us, and for allowing us to ascend to him. Then, we praise God for his character, for who he is. We praise him for all his divine attributes: his eternal goodness, his constant mercy, his radiant beauty. And finally, we sing hymns and recite poetry declaring our love of him.

I often feel tongue-tied in these moments of worship, in the same way I find it difficult to write a birthday card to a friend. Fortunately, God has given to us the language of praise within the Bible itself by giving to us the Psalms. The Psalms contain songs of praise and thanksgiving, describing in detail what God has done and will do for his people. They reveal God's divine attributes and are overflowing with effusive expressions of human love for God. When we read the Bible, we are invited to ingest the words of the Psalms, to chew on them, memorize them, and allow them to course through our veins. Then, we are invited to stand on top of the mountain next to the transfigured Christ and shout out these very same words in worship of God. This is why Christians throughout the centuries have made the memorization of the Psalms a top priority. If we need words to thank God, we recite "Great things are they that you have done, O Lord my God! How great your wonders and your plans for us!" (Psalm 40:5) If we need help worshiping God, we memorize "Hallelujah! Praise the Lord, O My soul! I will praise the Lord as long as I live" (Psalm 146:1). For those who do not know where to start, memorizing the entirety of Psalms 1, 23, 95, 100, and 121 will provide a solid grammar of praise.

When we open our mouths and hearts in praise of God, we draw nearer to Jesus at the top of the mountain. Expressions of love move us closer to the object of our love. This is why a note written to a friend will usually end in a hug. Similarly, as we praise Jesus, our hearts will reach out and embrace him. In so doing, his glory will surround us and cover us, and we will begin to be clothed in his glory just as Adam and Eve were clothed on Mount Eden. As Ephrem declares:

> Among the saints none is naked,
> for they have put on glory,
> nor is any clad in those leaves
> or standing in shame,
> for they have found, through our Lord,
> the robe that belongs to Adam and Eve.[6]

PRAYER: CONVERSING WITH GOD

After we hear God's word, see Jesus in our hearts, and praise him, we can then begin to converse with God in prayer. Prayer is both communication and communion with the God of the universe. We can think here of a quiet night of conversation with a close friend. Here, there are long periods of silence punctuated by an exchange of words. One offers up words, and one receives words in return. Questions are asked, requests are made, and counsel is offered. Over the course of this evening, two individuals draw closer to each other and are more fully known by each other.

The purpose of prayer, much like the purpose of friendly conversation, is connection and intimacy with God. One of the great misunderstandings surrounding prayer is that it is principally about asking for and getting things from God. While this is certainly a part of prayer, the main purpose is simply to be with God. If we view prayer as only about asking for things, our relationship with God will be purely transactional. It will be like a business relationship. I do not have a personal relationship with *Amazon*. I give them money, and they send me stuff in return. Our relationship will end if they no longer send me the things I order on time. There is a danger of turning prayer into this kind of transactional relationship: we send prayers to God and then expect him to answer them on our schedule. If we do not receive what we want, we end the relationship in frustration.

Instead, we are asked to see prayer in the context of this personal, spiritual encounter with Jesus on top of the mountain. When Moses beheld the glory of Jesus, he had a conversation with him, as he would a close friend (Exodus 33:11). Similarly, we are invited to converse with God in prayer. We share our joys and fears, we ask for advice on how to live, parent, and work. We spend moments in silence as we listen for God to respond.

While our prayers to God can resemble the conversations we have with our friends, there are, of course, significant differences. Our friends are finite, God is infinite. Our friends are fallible, God is perfect. We can physically see and talk to our friends, but we must speak to God spiritually in prayer. Because of these differences, it can be difficult for us to find the right words to pray. Fortunately for us, Jesus has given us instructions on how to pray by giving us the Lord's Prayer (or Our Father). In this prayer, we do ask God to provide the basic needs of life, "our daily bread," but we spend most of our prayer time centered on God and the needs of the world. For instance, we are invited to pray that God's will be done "on earth as it is in heaven," for more of heaven to come down to earth. We are also invited to pray for protection from temptation, asking Jesus to use his sword to slay the serpents and demons that tempt us to turn away from God.

DESCENDING THE MOUNTAIN: REFLECTING AS STONES

However incredible this mountaintop experience is, it must eventually end. In these deep moments of prayer and praise on top of the spiritual mountain, we long—like Peter—to build dwellings to remain there forever. But heaven has not yet descended upon Mount Zion. The demands of the world still beckon us to descend down the spiritual mountain and prepare to enter back into the wilderness to continue battling on mission for Jesus. When we descend, we must open our physical eyes and look out upon the labor that God has put in front of us. We must open our physical ears to receive the words of friends and family. We must use our physical hands to work and struggle through the demands of the day.

As our time alone with God comes to a close, we are called to reflect upon the encounter. As we climb down the mountain and view our earthly life below, we are invited to consider how we are going to live out this earthly life in light of what we have learned and experienced on top of the spiritual mountain. What changes do we need to make to keep God's commandments? How can we bring more of heaven down to earth? How might we have more patience, more love, and more joy at work and in our relationships?

These moments of reflection help to instill in us Christian virtue, or character. As we consider how we should treat our neighbor, we will become people that exude more and more justice in our lives. As we consider how we might need to change our eating, drinking, and leisure habits as a result of our time on the mountain, we will exude more temperance in our lives. As we ponder the love of God poured out onto us in these quiet times, our hearts will exude more and more love toward others.

As we continue this process of ascending and descending the spiritual mountain, we will slowly grow in Christian virtue. God will unearth entrenched areas of sin in our heart, and we will experience more of his mercy. God will pour out more of his wisdom upon us as we taste his word. In reflection, we will learn how to translate these spiritual words into physical actions in the world, becoming more and more the living stones of Mount Zion. On Mount Zion there are twelve types of stone, twelve precious jewels that shine in a multitude of colors. The unique colors of each are signs of the multitude of virtues that are imbued on the heart of Christians as they continue their climb up the spiritual mountain. As we continue to trek up and down the spiritual mountain, our lives will begin to reflect these precious stones. In *reflecting* on God, we will *reflect* the stones of Zion.

Hence these moments of reflection enable us to discern how to live differently in the future, but they also give us a glimpse of our past progress. While the Holy Spirit is at work forging us into a brilliant jewel of Zion, it is sometimes hard for us to see our growing luster. We can become frustrated by our present failures, and the burdens of the day are like moss which conceals the progress that we have made. In these moments of reflection, God grants to us glimpses of the bright spots on our soul, those parts of us that shine with more love, more peace, and more justice than before. These moments can provide great comfort as we climb down the mountain, as they remind us that these virtues will be forged to perfection when we reach Mount Zion. There, God will fully hone our souls into precious sapphire (Isaiah 54:12).

THE RESULTS: CULTIVATING THE SPIRITUAL SENSES

The Christian life is punctuated by frequent ascents and descents of the spiritual mountain. Throughout the history of Christianity, many individuals and churches have developed methods and resources to help structure these ascents up the mountain. My own Anglican tradition has the *Book of Common Prayer* that helps readers ascend this mountain four times a day. It contains four daily prayer routines that include formal confession of sin, collects of prayers, antiphons of praise, and a guide for reading the Bible. Other traditions have similar books. Some also find that taking full days away for retreats to be a more intense and important part of their spiritual lives. As we have shown, the biblical symbols can map onto these various activities and can help us visualize our spiritual ascent. However, we do not have to view these symbols as a kind of rigid hierarchy. We are free to expand and adapt as we learn how to enter God's presence more fully. Psalms, for instance, move back and forth through confession, lament, prayer, and praise, and weave together a host of biblical symbols in an endless variety of combinations.

Whatever routines we develop, we should expect that over time we will experience more of the Holy Spirit at work in our lives. As we have seen in the story of the Bible, God desires to heal us from the inside out. When we profess faith in Jesus Christ, the Holy Spirit is poured into our hearts and we begin to experience new life in our soul. The Christian life is one of cooperation with the Spirit, allowing more of our new self to emerge and more of our old, sinful self to fade away. One of the ways we will discover this growth into our new life in Christ is through the development of our spiritual senses. When we first believe in Jesus, our ears begin to hear his word in our heart, and our mind's eye begins to picture Jesus on Tabor for the first time. But at first these are still faint whispers and fuzzy pictures. However, if we continue ascending the mountain, we will be able to hear God more clearly in our times of prayer, and our picture of Jesus in our mind's eye will become clearer. We will feel more of God's presence in our hearts and will savor more of God's word in our mouths. We will even be able to smell the hidden sweetness of the anointed Jesus as we become more alert to his presence.

As we partake more and more of God's glory through our spiritual senses, we will desire more of this time with God and more of his glory. Because God is infinitely good and infinitely beautiful, there will always be more of him to desire, more ways to see, hear, and feel him. The more we experience God's glory, the more our hearts will burn for him. As Augustine remarks: "You called and shouted and shattered my deafness. You flashed, you shone, and you put my blindness to flight. You smelled sweet, and I drew breath, and now I pant for you. I tasted you, and now I'm starving and parched; you touched me, and I burst into flame with desire for your peace."[7]

As we desire to experience more of God's glory in our spiritual senses, we will naturally yearn for these spiritual realities to burst forth into the material world. While we have both inner and outer senses, they are both interrelated and intertwined. As God begins to heal us on the inside, we will begin to experience more of this healing on the outside. We long for the day in which there will be a full healing of the spiritual and material when our inner vision of Jesus is fulfilled in a physical vision of Jesus on top of Mount Zion. Our cultivation of the spiritual senses only increases this longing for our heavenly home on earth, but we know that we are not there yet. We are on our way to paradise, but our life is still a sojourn in the wilderness. Fortunately, God gives us time each week to get a glimpse of our final home; time when heaven and earth come together for a few hours; time when we can begin to see with our physical senses what God is cultivating in our inner senses. This God does by inviting us each week to the physical mountain of the church.

For we offer to Him His own, announcing consistently the fellowship and union of the flesh and Spirit. For as the bread, which is produced from the earth, when it receives the invocation of God, is no longer common bread, but the Eucharist, consisting of two realities, earthly and heavenly; so also our bodies, when they receive the Eucharist, are no longer corruptible, having the hope of the resurrection to eternity.

—*Irenaeus*

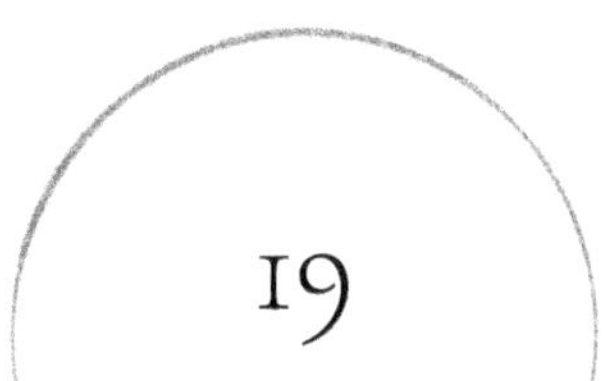

CLIMBING THE PHYSICAL MOUNTAIN

On 1 Corinthians 11:17–34 and Psalm 48, 84

I remember the first time I visited the ocean. I had read about saltwater, seen drawings of waves, and even pictured what it would be like for me to build sandcastles on a beach. But living in landlocked central Pennsylvania meant that I could only experience the ocean in my mind. Until one day, our family took a vacation to the Jersey shore, and the words and images in my mind suddenly came to life. My hands touched the sand grains, my tongue tasted the salty waters, and my body was tossed around by the crashing waves. What I had experienced previously in my mind, I now experienced in my body.

We all long to unite the inner and outer, the spiritual and the physical. I want to think about my friend and speak to my friend. I want to feel the love of my wife in my heart and embrace her with my arms. The same is true for our relationship with God. We long for both our spiritual and physical senses to be united with God. We long for our eternal paradise on Mount Zion, when heaven and earth will be united and our physical and spiritual senses will be fully attuned to God.

However, our lives are marked by a disparity between these senses. As we continue to cultivate our inner, spiritual life with God, we will experience a disjunction between our inner heavenly times alone with God and our physical experiences in a still sinful world. This disparity makes us long for the day when heaven and earth will be united, and for the day in which our bodies will be resurrected with Christ for eternity. Fortunately for us, God provides us a taste of paradise each and every Sunday, when we enter into the portable mountain of the church. The church is the unique space in which heaven and earth, the physical and the spiritual, come together to strengthen our faith, unite us together with other Christians, and give us a preview of our eternal life with Jesus on Mount Zion.

Just as the symbols have helped us climb the spiritual mountain, they also help us to enter the portable mountain more fully. The symbols that have woven together the mountains in the Bible reach out of its pages, pervading the church space and inviting us to be lifted up to God each Sunday. Church is the place where the symbols that we picture in our mind spring to life in three dimensions. Just as I had to travel to the Jersey shore to physically experience the beach, Christians go to church to physically *see, taste, touch, hear,* and *smell* the symbols that they read in the Bible. In so doing, they become to us more than symbols. They become gifts given to us by God.

A gift is a physical object that is meant to draw two people together. My daughter, for instance, loves drawing me pictures and giving them to me as gifts. When she finishes a somewhat abstract portrait of our day at the park, she rushes into my office to interrupt my workday shouting, "I made this for *you*." While these frequent outbursts certainly diminish my productivity, I am always overjoyed to receive these gifts. When I receive these pictures, I hang them up in my office, and we both share a moment admiring her handiwork. In this process, a simple piece of paper and crayon is transformed into a shared object of love. The drawing itself becomes both a material extension of her love for me and a kind of glue that draws us closer together.

The symbols in the Bible have the capacity to become in the church (and as we will see in the next chapter, in nature) these kinds of gifts from God. When we see the altar, hear the Bible, taste the bread, and smell the wine, we can experience these as God-given gifts. In receiving these things in faith, they become a shared object of love between us and God, allowing us to draw closer to him.

Our experience with these symbols in church can be envisioned as a kind of ascent up and descent down from the physical mountain of God. As the figure below depicts, our climb up the physical mountain begins when we enter the physical space of the church, proceeds through confession, prayer, and praise, and culminates in the reception of communion as our heavenly meal. I will use as the model for a church service the structure of worship found in the Anglican *Book of Common Prayer*. The general shape of this service is similar to that found in Catholic, Orthodox, Lutheran, and other Protestant churches. However, my account of life in the physical mountain is meant to be encouraging and challenging for all Christians, whether their particular forms of church worship are more or less structured than the one I describe.

Figure 7: Ascending the Physical Mountain of the Church—*Symbols* and Actions

Bread, Wine, Altar Receiving communion

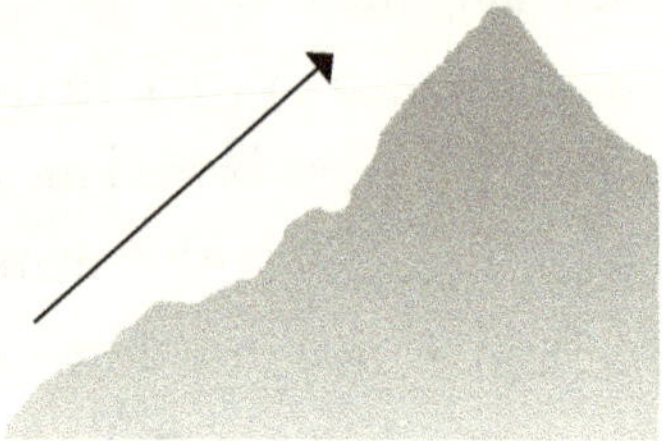

Trumpet Hearing God's word

Fire Confessing sin

Stone Joining the fellowship

Water Entering through baptism

LEAVING THE WORLD AND CROSSING THE WATERS, BECOMING A STONE

In order to enter the mountain of God we first must leave behind the cares and concerns of our daily lives and physically relocate to gather with other Christians at a specific time and place. For many of us this is the most difficult part of entering into the mountain. In college I frequently stayed up until 4 a.m. and woke up at noon. I did not want anything to disturb this schedule, so eventually I stopped enrolling in courses that met in the morning. I even dropped a potential major because it had a required course at 8:30 a.m. Needless to say, I was not a frequent church attender in college. My academic and church life revolved around my sleep and social schedule, not the other way around.

In our busy society, we all face the temptation to squeeze church in here and there, to make it conform to our schedule. But fully entering God's presence in the church requires the opposite. It demands that we sacrifice some part of our schedule to regularly and actively engage in corporate worship. In the Old Testament tabernacle, the Israelites were asked to bring their best animals into God's presence as a sacrifice to show that this physical time with God was the most valuable part of their week. Likewise, we are called to sacrifice the most valuable time in our week to physically go to church and pour out our energy in worshiping God there. We should secure and safeguard our worship schedule before we make our work, travel, and leisure schedule.

We enter church by crossing the threshold of the building and entering a specific space set aside for Christian worship. In many churches, there is a basin of water at the entrance, inviting people to dip their hands in the baptismal stream and swim with Jesus across the river and onto the mountain of God. As soon as we enter, we take our seat with others, gathered together, stone joining together with stone, creating a sacred space to physically and spiritually encounter the presence of God.

As the physical mountain of God, we encounter God's presence with our physical senses when we gather in this sacred space. A cross, an altar, special tapestries or garments may be visible, reminding us that we are in a special place unlike any other space that we encounter in the world. The smoke of candles or incense fills our nostrils, as we begin to smell the aroma of Christ in this sacred space. As we shake hands and embrace our friends, we feel the physical presence of the body of Christ. In these small moments, we see the symbols of the Bible spring out of its pages and into the physical world. That which we read about in the pages of the Bible and picture in our minds is suddenly presented to us in three-dimensional space. We are being invited to experience God through our senses by seeing, hearing, smelling, touching, and tasting the symbols of the Bible.

CONFESSION

Just as our ascension into the spiritual mountain immediately brought us into the holiness of God, when the church service begins, one should be instantly confronted with the holy presence of God, and in response, consider the accumulation of their sins from the past week. As the candles on the altar are lit, one is reminded of the all-consuming fire of the Holy Spirit, which prompts in the congregation a desire to confess their sin. One unique aspect of this corporate confession is that we can confess together the sins of our community, and our sins against others in the church. Later in the service, the church engages in the *passing of the peace*, a time where we are called to go and seek forgiveness from anyone in the church that we have wronged. The point of this exchange is to physically enact forgiveness. Just as we receive spiritual forgiveness through Jesus Christ, we ask for and extend this forgiveness to others in the church. We physically feel the forgiveness of Jesus as our brother or sister embraces us in an act of reconciliation.

HEARING GOD'S WORD

After we confess our sins, a reader goes to the back of the sanctuary and reads out loud from the Bible. After the reading, a pastor or other leader in the church gives teaching and instruction related to the biblical passages read aloud. One of the purposes of reading and teaching God's word aloud is to ensure that God's people are hearing his word correctly. We all experience times when we misunderstand or are misunderstood by someone else. Think about the popular children's game called "telephone," in which one person whispers a sentence to someone else, who then whispers this message through a few other people. At the end of this line, the last person repeats the sentence out loud. Children are amused to discover that the original sentence has mutated into something totally different.

When we read God's word alone, we hear it with our still-developing spiritual ear. Difficult passages of the Bible are still hard to comprehend, and there will even be times that we hear what we want to hear from the Bible, mistaking our words for God's. For this reason, we must gather with other faithful Christians in the portable mountain to hear God's word read aloud. Teachers in the church are then charged with helping us unpack the significance of the Bible and to help clear up any misunderstandings we may have. These teachers have learned to take the complex and complicated passages of scripture, those parts that sound like harsh trumpets, and discern how God is speaking words of life through them. The sound of sweet, melodic, heavenly teaching has the power to dispel any of our readings "that still bow towards the earth."[1] As we hear the word of God read aloud, we are given a glimpse of what it will be like to hear the very words of Jesus with our physical ears on Mount Zion. It gives us hope for the day in which there will be no more confusion and misunderstanding.

COMING TO THE ALTAR

As we confess our sins and hear God's word, our hearts are moved higher and higher up the mountain. We hear the words of Jesus, our bridegroom, calling out to the church, his bride, to come closer to him, to meet him at the top. And so, the church service proceeds with us drawing both spiritually and physically higher, to the top of the mountain, which is the altar at the back of the sanctuary. As the pastor ascends this altar, they invite the congregation to join with angels and archangels to sing praises to God. In this great invitation, the gates of heaven open, and the voices of humanity are joined with the voices of angels in praise to God. The words that we sing during this time (called *the Sanctus*) are nearly identical to those uttered by Abraham and Melchizedek at that ancient altar: We praise and bless our holy God in the highest. In these moments of praise, we get one of our clearest pictures of life on Mount Zion, where there will be endless praise by human and angel alike.

Just as Abraham and Melchizedek sang this hymn in front of bread and wine on an altar, we too behold a loaf of bread and a chalice of wine on the church altar as we life up our voices to God. Soon after our voices die down, the pastor takes this food and utters over them the same words that Jesus spoke over the bread and wine at the Last Supper. Of the bread: "take, eat, this is my body." Of the wine: "take, drink, this is my blood." Then the Holy Spirit is called upon to come down from heaven and make holy this bread and wine. The church responds in words of praise and by praying the *Our Father* together. Finally, they begin their physical ascent up the mountain, approaching the altar to eat this bread and drink this wine.

Through this whole process of entering heaven, of hearing the words of Jesus spoken over the bread and wine, of the Holy Spirit descending upon the elements, and finally of chewing the bread and drinking the wine, faithful Christians truly participate in Jesus Christ.[2] In this one complete action, the bread becomes our manna from heaven, a gift from God as we sojourn in the wilderness. We receive it just as Moses did in the desert, with souls desperate for sustenance in a sinful and broken world. The bread becomes the body of Christ broken for us, and as we chew this bread our souls are nourished by Christ's body. Similarly, when we taste the wine it becomes for us the blood of Christ, the blood that poured out of Jesus's side on the cross, the blood that was shed so that we might be healed of our sin.

In this great act, God takes the physical stuff of the world and brings heaven down upon it, so that through it we might get a taste of our eternal life on Mount Zion. In communion, we see the fulfillment of all symbols in the Bible, since it is here that the bread and wine, when consumed in faith, actually become that which they symbolize. In this act we are taken up into sacred time, experiencing both past and future in the present. We eat this bread next to Moses in the wilderness, we drink this cup next to the side of Christ on calvary, and we share this heavenly wedding banquet with Jesus upon Mount Zion. The altar becomes for us our banquet table, and the bread and wine the food that we will share with Jesus and with all other Christians for eternity.

When we participate in this feast, God works through the physical means of bread and wine to strengthen us spiritually. While we can envision our life in Christ as both a spiritual and physical climb up the mountain, they are not completely separate journeys. I am one person, with a body and a soul, not two separate persons. Because of this reality, our physical ascent into the portable mountain of the church is also a time in which we are drawn spiritually closer to Christ. Communion is thus an opportunity to attune our spiritual senses to Christ through our physical senses. As Thomas Cranmer puts it, "The eating and drinking of this sacramental bread and wine is, as it were, a showing of Christ before our eyes, a smelling of him with our noses, a feeling and groping of him with our hands, and an eating, chewing, digesting and feeding upon him to our spiritual strength and perfection."[3]

Just before the pastor distributes the bread and wine, they say "the gifts of God for the people of God." Just as my daughter changed paper and crayon into a physical, shared object of love, God takes bread and wine and changes it into a physical gift of love to share with us. When we receive and eat in faith, we participate in Jesus. Jesus gives us his body and blood as a free gift, and we receive the bread and wine not as those who have accomplished great deeds for God, but as people who joyfully receive gifts we cannot produce on our own. The one word that we give to this celebration of bread and wine, "eucharist," sums it up best, as it simply means "thanksgiving."

DESCENDING THE MOUNTAIN

After we receive the bread and wine, we return to our seats and reflect on this experience on top of the mountain. As our stomachs ingest our heavenly meal, we contemplate with great joy these heavenly gifts and consider the ways our earthly lives will be different because of what we have seen, heard, and tasted that day. This moment of reflection prepares us for our descent from the mountain and departure out of the church.

When Jesus appeared to his downtrodden disciples on the road to Emmaus, he began to lift their hearts and spirits with holy teaching from the Old Testament. Later, when he took bread and broke it, his followers were finally able to see him in all his resurrected glory. But, just at that moment, Jesus vanished before their eyes. His disciples left this encounter with conflicting emotions:

joyful, having physically encountered Jesus, but sad that they could not stay in his physical presence forever. They had to return to the world with all its problems, but now they could return with hearts on fire with the Holy Spirit, prepared to tell the world the good news that salvation has come through the risen Christ.

We experience something similar when we break bread in the portable mountain of the church. As our stomachs finish digesting the bread and wine, our feet pass through the threshold of the church, and the living stones assembled scatter back to their homes. Just as Jesus appears to us in this heavenly communal feast, so he vanishes from us. The lights go dim as we enter back into the humdrum world of labor, finances, and hardships. There are diapers to change, dishes to clean, grandparents to care for, and budgets to balance. Like Moses, we must trudge on through the wilderness of life as we patiently wait for our arrival in paradise.

But now we enter back into the world with burning hearts rekindled with the fire of the Holy Spirit. We enter back into the world with our minds renewed by the word of God. We enter back into the world with stomachs satiated with the body and blood of Christ. We are reminded that the hardships of this life will one day come to an end, that the glorious presence of God that we experience on the mountain will one day be the norm rather than the exception.

LIFE OFF OF THE MOUNTAIN: VOCATION AND MISSION

When we descend and depart from church, we return to the world with renewed hearts and a renewed sense of purpose. Our experience in the portable mountain not only makes us long to get to Mount Zion, it also makes us long to bring Mount Zion to the world and to bring all of our friends up to Mount Zion with us. The purpose of our journey through the wilderness is thus to bring the mountain down to the world and bring the world up the mountain, to bring heaven down to earth and bring earth up to heaven. The first of these we accomplish by living into our *vocations*: our responsibilities as workers, as parents, as friends, and as citizens of a community. The second of these we do by engaging in *mission*: telling our friends about Jesus and inviting them into the church.

First, we bring heaven down to earth in our vocations. We all wear many hats. Many of us are workers, spouses, children, parents, friends, and citizens. Each of these vocations require that we interact with the world around us, a world that is still sinful and broken. As such, each of these vocations carry with it joys as well as struggles. Often, we enter church on Sunday tired and exhausted from the responsibilities inherent in these vocations. But our experience in the portable mountain is meant to be a time of renewal, of refreshment by the cool wind of the Holy Spirit. The Spirit empowers us to descend from this mountain with renewed energy and with a renewed sense of purpose: to bring the love, joy, peace, and goodness experienced on the mountain into our places of work, into our homes, and into our communities. We descend with renewed eyes capable of seeing God's purpose for us in the world, and the strength to do the work put before us. This short stanza sums up our vocational life:

> Teach me, my God and King,
> In all things thee to see,
> And what I do in anything,
> To do it as for thee.[4]

We bring the joy of Christ into our homes when we love our young children and care for our aging parents. We bring the peace of Christ into our relationships by practicing forgiveness in our friendships. We bring the justice of Christ into our communities when we serve the poor and outcast. When we live in this way, we become what St. Paul calls "the aroma of Christ," spreading the fragrance of the knowledge of Christ into every corner of the world (2 Corinthians 2:15). Over time, these spaces of life will be imbued with more of God's glory, and more of God's heavenly goodness will emerge in the world through our labors.

Second, our purpose is to bring our friends up to the mountain through mission. As we labor through these various vocations in life, we will encounter numerous people who have not come to believe in Jesus as Lord and God. Our hope for each of these persons is to have them join us on the mountain of God. As we work and live in the world, we pray for the well-being of our friends, and we know that their eternal well-being can only be secured through a profession of faith in Christ. And so, the culmination of our mission in the world comes when we open our mouths to tell those around us that Jesus Christ is risen, and then invite them to profess faith in him as Lord and God.

Jesus wants us to be active participants in his mission on earth. He wants us to have a part in bringing the good news of his resurrection to all the ends of the earth. When we open our mouths and begin to explain the gospel to a friend, a worker, or a neighbor, we are fulfilling this heavenly invitation from Jesus. Sometimes this invitation is met with acceptance and we get to witness our friends pass through the waters of baptism and share with them the same cup of Christ at church. But other times, this invitation will be met with rejection, even animosity. However, God delights in us for simply sharing Jesus, no matter the results. The act of proclaiming Jesus to our friends is itself an act of praise that glorifies God and strengthens our faith, regardless of the response.

How do we go about proclaiming the Gospel and gathering our friends into the church? There are many books that help spell out this process, but a key element is directly related to our sojourn up the spiritual mountain: prayer.[5] In our times in prayer on the spiritual mountain of God, we should envision not only ourselves standing next to Jesus on Mount Zion, but also our friends that do not know Jesus. The key to Christian mission comes in this vision in prayer: we see our friends praising Jesus with us on Mount Zion, we see in our mind's eye a picture of them standing next to us in church, and these images stoke in us loving hearts, compelling us to go and share with them the way up the mountain. I have been a pastor for decades and have tried various methods and strategies to help my churches live into this missional calling. While some of these methods have been marginally helpful, I have found that nothing is as important as prayer. If my congregation and I are earnestly lifting our friends in prayer, if our hearts are burning for them to know Jesus, if we weep over the fact that they do not know him, then the right words and right actions will follow.

As we continue living in the world through our vocations and proclaiming the good news of Jesus to those around us, we will undoubtedly grow weary. We will need a break from our godly labors in the wilderness. We all know the value of taking a break when we have been working hard. One summer day, as part of my job, I had to shovel hot asphalt for a paving project. There are few things more tiresome than scooping 300-degree tar and gravel on a 95 degree, humid day. When the clock struck noon,

I had finally earned a break. I nearly collapsed on the sidewalk, cracked open a soda and tore into a sandwich. Nothing has ever been as refreshing as that can of Pepsi was that day. Nothing was more nourishing than that simple slice of bread and meat on that scorching July afternoon. Our godly work in the world can be spiritually and emotionally exhausting. Life in the world is still a life of battle with the serpent. Although we know that our final victory is secure in Christ, we know that struggles and hardship will continue until this victory is made complete on Zion. Fortunately for us, God provides space and time for us every seven days for a reprieve. At church we are given rest from these battles and restored for the future struggles ahead. The bread that we receive in communion becomes for us our missionary food, our spiritual sustenance, and divine energy to strengthen us for these ensuing battles. The wine that we receive nourishes our souls, reminding us that eternal rest and heavenly riches await us on Mount Zion.

LONGING FOR MOUNT ZION

The cultivation of our life in God comes through these frequent visits to the spiritual and physical mountain. These two mountains push us further to that third and final mountain, Zion, which is the merging and fulfillment of these two. On Zion, heaven and earth will be fully intertwined, and that which we experience in our inner senses will emerge in our physical senses.

Our journey to Mount Zion is one of immense joy and continuing struggles. As we grow closer and closer to Christ, we see with greater clarity the disparity between this world and the world to come. As Paul puts it, we live as aliens, strangers in a foreign land. We are, in a very real sense, in the wilderness with

Moses: excited to be with God, but aware that we are not fully home with God. We experience this disparity not only in the world around us, but also in our own bodies. As our spiritual senses become more aware of God's presence, our physical senses slowly degrade with the passing of time.

Those of us who have entered middle age, experience this disparity between our growing spiritual selves and our declining physical bodies acutely. On the one hand, the passing of time has given the blessing of hindsight. We can reflect on our lives and see how the Holy Spirit has slowly been at work in our hearts. We see less anger and more gentleness, less bitterness and more joy, less selfishness and more other centeredness. Our souls have become more like the precious jewels of Zion. But this advancement in our souls is paired with the degradation of our bodies. Each morning, we are confronted with minor aches and pains. We no longer hop out of bed with pep in our step. Indigestion and cholesterol become regular words in our vocabulary, reminding us that our bodies are no longer functioning as intended. These are the first signs of our physical breakdown. While our heavenly self is growing, our earthly self is deteriorating.

But these trips up the mountain give us renewed hope. Our ascent up the spiritual mountain strengthens our inner senses. We see Jesus more clearly on top of Tabor, and we learn to hear his voice more clearly in our hearts. Our ascent up the physical mountain of the church gives us assurance that these inward realities will become outward ones. When we hear the word of God read out loud at church, we are assured that we will hear Jesus call out our name like a trumpet blast after our long slumber, shouting for us to wake up just as he called Lazarus to come out of the tomb. When we rise from our chairs and approach the church altar, we are given confidence that we will climb to the altar of Zion, where we will be united with Jesus forever. When the bread touches our lips and the wine our tongues, we know that our eternal wedding banquet is waiting for us in paradise. While this present world stumbles along and our bodies slowly wither, we gain in these trips a clearer picture of our eternal destination and a renewed confidence that we will rise to meet Jesus there.

Who is capable of comprehending the extent of what is to be discovered in a single utterance of Yours? For we leave behind in it far more than we take from it, like thirsty people drinking from a fountain.

—*Ephrem the Syrian*

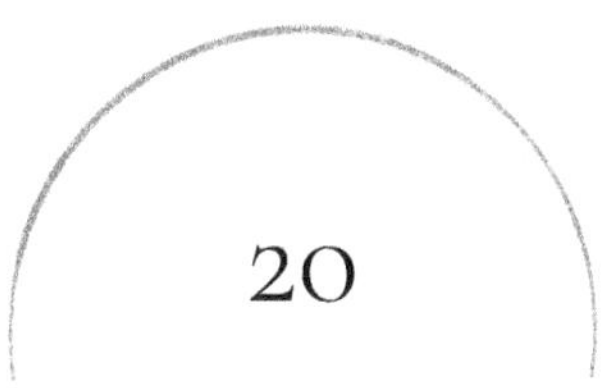

20

THE BIBLE AND OUR CLIMB

On Isaiah 55:6–11 and Psalm 90, 119:105–12

This book has presented the story and symbols of the Bible to help Christians cultivate a deeper life in God as they journey to Mount Zion. My hope is that, by using these mountains and symbols as a guide, more of the Bible's hidden treasures have been unearthed and a fresh way of reading the Bible has been uncovered. The various quotes and poems that began each chapter highlight the immense diversity of Christians throughout history that have seen these symbols as joyful gifts meant to help us connect the various books of the Bible to each other and draw us up into the very life of God.

But this book has only scratched the surface of the enormous depth and endless riches of the Bible. There are hundreds of stories and countless mountains that have not been discussed: I have said little about David, Elijah, Ruth, Enoch, and Ezra. I have not had the time to talk about Mount Horeb and Mount Carmel. In addition, there are thousands of other symbols and connections to be drawn between these symbols: gold, incense, leaves, fruit, and other signs are waiting for us in the pages of the Bible, ready to provide insight into God's story and draw us into God's life.

Once you have finished reading this book, you will notice these symbols *everywhere* in the Bible. This final chapter seeks to provide the tools for readers to enter every story of the Bible and continue to discover new symbols, new connections, and new ways to draw closer to God. In so doing, I hope you will continue to drink from the endless fount of Scripture as you sojourn to Mount Zion.

How can we continue to read the Bible this way? There are three key aspects of this approach to reading scripture. First, there are prerequisites: commitments we must make before God unlocks the stories and symbols of the Bible for us. Second, there is the actual process of entering into the Bible, inhabiting its stories, and drawing connections between its symbols. Third, there is an invitation to discover the ways the symbols of the Bible spill out into our world and into nature.

PREREQUISITES: BELIEVING, BELONGING, AND OBEYING

When we receive the light of the Holy Spirit in our hearts, it enables a burst of God's glory to shine through the pages of the Bible. Our spiritual ears are opened, and our mind's eye can now see the words of the Bible for what they truly are: the word of God. But when we see the Bible with our mind's eye, we still look at it as through a cloudy window. As Paul says, we see through a glass darkly as we long to see Jesus's face clearly (1 Corinthians 13:12). How can we learn to read the Bible more clearly, and allow more of its brightness to shine in our hearts? To do so we must make three commitments: to *believe* in the Bible as God's word, to *belong* to a faithful church, and to *obey* Godly instruction.

BELIEVING

To experience the glory of God through the pages of the Bible, we need to learn how to read it clearly. If I pick up a book and read some random page without knowing anything about the author or the plot, chances are I will only be confused by the words I read. For instance, if I read the words "The boy had, with the additional softening claim of a lingering illness of his mother's, been the means of a sort of reconciliation" without any context, it would sound like gibberish. However, if I know the author (Jane Austen) and the title and plot of the book (*Emma*) I will be able to place these words in the context of the story. One of the ways that one gets to know the author and basic plot of a book is by reading its front and back covers. The purpose of a cover is to provide all the essential details one needs to read the book well: its essential plot, what type of book it is, and a brief biography of its author.

To read the Bible clearly, we cannot just pick a random page and start reading. If we did, chances are we would be confused. What we all need is some basic information about the Bible before we read it on our own: we need to believe in the author (God) and understand its central storyline. From almost the very beginning of the church, Christians have summarized the essential beliefs about God and the Bible in the Apostles' Creed.[1]

The Apostles' Creed is like the book cover of the Bible. It tells us what kind of book the Bible is—that it is the word of God and the story of God's interactions in the world. It also tells us more about the author of this book: God the Father, Son, and Holy Spirit. In this way, the creed is like the "about the author" section of a book cover. In addition, just as a summary of a book is usually written on the back of its cover, the Apostles' Creed gives us a summary of the basic plot of the Bible: it begins by telling us that God created heaven and earth and continues to describe the life, death, resurrection, ascension, and return of Jesus Christ. It then tells us about the Holy Spirit and ends by affirming everlasting life in God. When we profess the faith of the Apostles' Creed, we affirm our belief in God and our belief in the central message of the Bible. These beliefs then guide our reading of the Bible, helping us find the bright spots in otherwise confusing passages, as well as protecting us from false readings that pull us away from the brightness of God's Word.

BELONGING

In addition to believing in the creed, we must also belong to a church community and learn from its teachers. As we have already seen in the previous chapter, we need to hear the Bible with our physical ears, lest we misunderstand God with our still developing inner ears. Part of living our life within the ongoing portable mountain of the church requires us to read and discuss the Bible together with others and allow ourselves to be guided by teachers within our church.[2] This requires us to develop the posture of a lifelong learner, admitting that we do not have all the answers, and acknowledging that other faithful Christians are needed to help point us in the right direction. This does not mean that we have no voice—we are welcome to bring our insights and wisdom to the community—however, we are one voice among not only those in our local church, but also among all faithful Christians who have ever lived. While there may be some differences of opinion regarding relatively minor matters of Christianity, there is a strong overwhelming agreement amongst most Christians throughout time and space regarding the core beliefs of the Bible. This means that our understanding of the Bible must be qualified and challenged by the billions of other faithful Christians in the world, starting with those in our local congregation.

Our reliance on others is not meant to stymie our journey with the Bible, but to enrich it. Other people have the ability to help illuminate passages of scripture that we could not discover on our own. For instance, my friend Jon has an acute awareness of the presence of the Holy Spirit and frequently receives dreams and visions from God. This friendship has allowed me to more fully understand the workings of the Holy Spirit and the dreams and visions imparted to the disciples in the book of Acts. My wife Allison has a profound sense of justice and the need to care for the poor and oppressed. When I read scripture with her, I notice more fully the multitude of ways the Old Testament prophets point to the perfect justice of God. Reading other faithful Christians from other times and places can also have this effect. I discovered the enormous significance of mountains in the Bible by reading Ephrem the Syrian's *Hymns on Paradise* and have had similar experiences while reading other ancient authors.

Reading the Bible within this great tradition of faithful Christians begins within the church and requires us to come under the teaching and guidance of pastors and other leaders. Sadly, there are some churches whose leaders do not believe in the core teachings of the Bible, so a challenge for those currently not committed to a church will be to find one whose teachings are consistent with the message of the Bible. While some denominations require all their pastors to uphold core points of the Christian faith such as the Apostles' Creed, others are not as firm. My friend Bobby joined my church in college because he noticed an oddity at the church he was attending: the pastor never spoke about sin in his sermons. This perplexed him since sin was obviously an important issue in the Bible! So, he asked to have a conversation with his pastor to discuss. To his surprise, he discovered that this pastor did not believe in sin. Bobby rightfully concluded after this conversation that he could not come under the guidance of this church and promptly left.

While life in the portable mountain of the church will be difficult for us at times, most of the time we are called to stick it out, to live and learn from others who are different from us. There are, however, a few times in which leaving a church is appropriate. One of those is when a church comes under the guidance of a false teacher. Another is when a leader refuses to obey the very teachings that they are entrusted to uphold. Unfortunately, there are abusive pastors who refuse to repent of their own sin. Such persons have abandoned their fidelity to the Bible through their conduct and should not be followed.

OBEYING

When we come under the guidance of the creed and the teaching of the church, it helps us encounter more of the brilliant insights in the Bible. But this brightness will also make visible the lingering sin in our hearts. For this reason, our climb up the mountain requires regular confession and obedience to the teachings of the Bible, notably the Ten Commandments and the Sermon on the Mount. This routine of confession and obedience helps to scrape the dirt off our souls, allowing us to experience even more of Scripture's riches. Thus, obedience to the Bible's teachings goes hand in hand with our ability to allow the Bible to lift us up in greater love and knowledge of God. Obedience is intertwined with wisdom, love, and joy, as Psalm 119 declares:

> Your word is a lantern to my feet
>   and a light upon my path.
> I have sworn and am determined
>   to keep your righteous judgments.
> Your decrees are my inheritance for ever;
>   truly, they are the joy of my heart.
> I have applied my heart to fulfill your statutes
>   for ever and to the end. (Psalm 119:105–106, 111–112)

Believing, belonging, and obeying are prerequisites to fully and properly reading the Bible. Without them, our readings of scripture will fall into error, and we will begin to hear what we want to hear, twisting and contorting the Bible to conform to our desires. For many of us, though, the idea of having our reading limited in these ways can seem harsh. Most of us do not like obeying rules, and we are accustomed to thinking of any limits placed on us as burdensome and unnecessary. These limits feel like the walls of a prison, restricting our freedom and preventing us from flourishing.

It is true that believing in the creed, belonging to a church, and obeying the teachings of the Bible set borders that limit our readings of the Bible, but these borders are more like the fencing of a playground rather than the walls of a prison.[3] In elementary school I would rush out into the playground for recess. The playground was lined with fencing meant to keep me from wandering off the school grounds, but I never really considered climbing over that fence. Why would I? Inside that fence were swings and slides and opportunities to play games with friends. Outside that fence was the world of adults, a boring world of taxes and timecards and adjustable-rate mortgages. The fence was not an oppressive barrier to a freer existence, but a helpful demarcation of the space where I could delight in joyful play.

Together, believing, belonging, and obeying function as this kind of playground fence for the Bible. They help us identify the fun spaces in which we can playfully delight in the very words of God. They are meant to separate this fun space from the boring heretical readings that lie outside of the playground. While we might think we will have more freedom if we go outside of that fence, we will soon discover that those false readings of the Bible will lead us to some ugly places.

ENTERING SACRED TIME, SACRED WORLD, AND SACRED LIFE

Once we commit to a life of believing, belonging, and obeying, we can enter the Bible like we are entering into God's playground. We are free to joyfully and creatively inhabit the Bible, drawing connections between its symbols and placing ourselves within its stories. In the process, we will discover a deeper and more intimate relationship with God. What does it look like to inhabit the Bible, to make it our home and our playground? In order to inhabit the stories and symbols of the Bible, we are invited to enter into the *sacred time* of the Bible, enter into the *sacred world* of the Bible, and into the *sacred life* of God.

ENTERING THE SACRED TIME OF THE BIBLE

I remember November 26, 2015, more clearly than I remember yesterday. On that day, my wife had major surgery to deal with complications from a chronic illness. In the months prior, her health had been deteriorating, and there was a good chance that she would die if she did not consent to surgery. The surgery, however, presented its own risks, and the possibility of her dying that day or in the following days was not insignificant. I held Allison's hand all the way from the hospital bed to the surgery room, putting on an air of stability and confidence to comfort her. Our eyes were fixed together as the doctors moved her into the operating room, and the automatic doors soon closed on me. I could not bear to sit in the waiting room amidst all the other nervous people waiting for their loved ones. So I escaped and searched desperately for a private room. Once I found an unoccupied lounge, I took out my phone and began to compose a text to my friend Jon. I began to type "Can you pray for me? Allison just went into surgery, and I am scared that …" But I could not finish the text. I broke down and wept bitterly for what seemed like hours.

I can remember the finer details of that day better than I can remember the details from this past Wednesday. When I recall that day in November, I experience some of the same feelings and emotions that I felt eight years ago. I sometimes even weep just as I wept on that day when I think of Allison on that hospital bed. In a sense, when I think about it, I feel like I am reliving the past. My heart rate, my nerves, and my tear ducts react as though I am still in that hospital lounge. I have an experience of being in two places at once—the past catches me in the present.

Fortunately, the surgery was successful and, after several challenging months of recovery, my wife's health stabilized. However, her illness and the effects of that surgery have permanently changed her life, and my life as a result. I am relieved and grateful that she is alive, but I also long for the day when she will be fully healed, when she is lifted by Jesus onto Mount Zion. Therefore, when I remember that day in November, the pain and anxiety of the past are mingled with the relief of the present, and the hope of full healing in the future. Past, present, and future are intertwined in my mind and in my heart.

The reason I can experience the past, present, and future is because God designed human beings with these capabilities, and he wants to use them to help us enter into his world and his life. We have already seen throughout this book the significance of sacred time. On the one hand, we can think of time as strictly chronological, with one thing happening after the next. But God is not limited to this chronological, secular time because God stands outside of time. God is above time because he created time.

When we enter into life with God, we too have the opportunity to be lifted up to heaven and experience this sacred time. In the previous chapter, we saw how the reception of the communion bread and wine gathers together the past sacrifice of Jesus on the cross and our future heavenly banquet on Zion into a present act of eating bread and drinking wine. God uses the bread and wine to bring past, present, and future together.

Similarly, since the Bible is sacred Scripture, it invites us to enter sacred time. Since it is a heavenly book, it is capable of lifting us to heaven, harmonizing past and future with our present. We see this most visibly in the books of the prophets, whose visions are meant to simultaneously remind Israel of their past, exhort them to change their behavior in the present, and describe events that will happen at different points in the future. In the first chapter I described this phenomenon as akin to a harmonious musical chord. A chord takes several notes and stacks them on top of one another, creating one pleasing sound.

These harmonious connections give us a richer understanding of the God we encounter in Scripture. We experience God's mercy more vividly when we see it manifested in the blood of the tabernacle and the blood on the cross. We understand the rescuing power of baptism more fully when we encounter it simultaneously in the waters of the Red Sea and the waters of the Jordan. We see this kind of harmonizing happening within the Bible itself: Hebrews 11 invites us to explore the beautiful dynamics of faith in Jesus Christ through the stories of Abraham, Jacob, and Moses.

We are invited to continually make connections between the stories and symbols of Scripture as we encounter God in its pages. We are invited to allow these connections to overlap and combine, providing greater insight and depth into each page of the Bible. The connections to be made are endless, inviting countless readings and a lifetime of insight. This book itself is meant to be a kind of primer, helping to start us on a lifelong journey of drawing these connections through books such as 1 Kings and 2 Corinthians and symbols such as crowns and candles.

While these connections are endless, this does not mean that we can make any kind of connection we would like. As we have seen above, we cannot make a connection that goes against the clear story of the Bible as summarized in the creed and the clear teachings of the Bible as we see in the Ten Commandments, the Sermon on the Mount, and elsewhere. We may need to hear a voice of correction from someone in our church when we are unknowingly going out of bounds. In making these connections, we cannot make one part of the Bible repugnant to another part.[4] The goal is harmony, not cacophony.

However, if we stay within the borders of the playground, there is never-ending joy available to us. There will always be more and more insights, greater moments of awe and wonder as the infinite depth of the Bible is revealed to us. The poet George Herbert likens this adventure of stacking the stories and the symbols of the Bible to the combining of the stars in the sky to make constellations. One can endlessly combine the various lights of the stars to form the shapes of animals and heroes and objects. But the lights of the Bible, the twinkle in each page and each symbol, have even greater potential than this:

> Oh that I knew how all thy lights combine,
> And the configurations of their glory!
> Seeing not only how each verse doth shine,
> But all the constellations of the story.
> This verse marks that, and both do make a motion
> Unto a third, that ten leaves off doth lie:
> Then as dispersed herbs do watch a potion,
> These three make up some Christian's destiny.
> Such are thy secrets, which my life makes good,
> And comments on thee: for in ev'ry thing
> Thy words do find me out, and parallels bring,
> And in another make me understood.
> Stars are poor books, and oftentimes do miss:
> This book of stars lights to eternal bliss.[5]

ENTERING INTO THE SACRED WORLD OF THE BIBLE

When we confess Jesus as Lord and God and are baptized in the name of the Father, Son, and Holy Spirit, we take our place amongst the millions of other Christians journeying from Mount Tabor to Mount Zion. God's story becomes our story. Our names are written in the book of life, and we have an important part to play in the sacred history that takes place after the events of the book of Acts and before the events of Revelation. God is, in a sense, writing our story into the story of the Bible.

When we read the Bible, we are invited to dive headfirst into its story, to inhabit its world and make it our own. As we enter its sacred time, as we see how past, present, and future come together like a beautiful constellation, we are invited to take the next step and place ourselves *into* its stories. We are a part of a shared history along with Abraham, Moses and Peter. We encounter the same symbols as our forebearers, and we use these symbols to draw connections between our story and their stories. We are invited to stack our own climbs up the spiritual mountain and the mountain of the church onto the mountains of Eden, Sinai, Tabor, and Zion. Each climb up one of these mountains is an ascent up all of them.

ENTERING INTO SACRED LIFE

We enter into the sacred time and sacred world of the Bible so that, ultimately, we might draw closer to God. We engage in horizontal readings of the Bible so that we might be fully lifted vertically into the presence of God. It is in these vertical encounters that we better understand the full potential of the various symbols in the Bible. We must believe in Jesus as Lord and God. We must believe in Scripture as the word of God. We must belong to Christ's church and live our lives in obedience to the teachings of Jesus. Once we do these things, we will discover that the symbols have the potential to lift us up to God. They will become like arrows or vectors, pushing us up into heaven to experience more of the love, joy, peace, and mercy of God the Father, Son, and Holy Spirit. The words, characters, and symbols of the Bible enable us to scale heaven and drink from the sacred life of God. God has "revealed all this to us in the sacred pictures of the scriptures so that he might lift us in spirit up through the perceptible to the conceptual, from sacred shapes and symbols to the simple peaks of the hierarchies of heaven."[6]

In encountering God through these symbols, our hearts will in turn long more deeply for our eternal goal: to see the face of Jesus on Mount Zion. As we are pulled closer to Jesus through these encounters with the Bible, we will also discover that Jesus is at work in our hearts through this process. We will be formed and shaped by the words of the Bible even when we are not fully aware of its effects. God himself declares through the prophet of Isaiah that his word, when it descends the mountain, will not return empty handed. Instead, God says "it shall accomplish that which I purpose, and succeed in the thing for which I sent it" (Isaiah 55:11). This means that we do not need to read the Bible with any purpose other than to draw close to God. God will work on our hearts and will shape us into a precious, living stone simply through our encounter with his words.

The poet John Donne remarks on this incredible influence of God's word and the enormous power of its signs and symbols to mold, shape, and comfort us. For Donne, none of the words of the Bible are frivolous. Instead, God makes "thy signs seals, and thy seals effects, and thy effects consolation and restitution, wheresoever thou mayst receive glory by that way."[7] For whoever approaches the Bible with awe and wonder, ready to receive God's glory, the signs and the symbols of the Bible will have their effects, providing us comfort, strength, and consolation.

EXAMPLE: READING LEVITICUS

To better understand how we can continue to read the Bible by entering into its sacred time, sacred world, and sacred life, I will share my own experience reading the following passage from the book of Leviticus, which tells of how one should perform a sacrifice in the portable mountain of the tabernacle:

> If he brings a lamb as his offering for a sin offering, he shall bring a female without blemish and lay his hand on the head of the sin offering and kill it for a sin offering in the place where they kill the burnt offering. Then the priest shall take some of the blood of the sin offering with his finger and put it on the horns of the altar of burnt offering and pour out all the rest of its blood at the base of the altar. And all its fat he shall remove as the fat of the lamb is removed from the sacrifice of peace offerings, and the priest shall burn it on the altar, on top of the Lord's food offerings. And the priest shall make atonement for him for the sin which he has committed, and he shall be forgiven. (Leviticus 4:32–35)

While I had read this passage sporadically over the past twenty-five years, I usually wrote it off as a description of an obsolete event in the past. I thought that, since Jesus was the true sacrifice for sin, this passage no longer had much meaning. However, as I began to understand that the Bible was inviting me into its sacred time and history, I began to notice all the connections between the various symbols in this passage. I noticed that Jesus is called the lamb of God and that he takes away our sins just as the lamb in this passage took away the sins of the owner. I saw the blood pouring out and was reminded of the blood pouring out of Jesus's side on the cross. I saw the altar and was reminded of the altar upon which Abraham placed Isaac, and the altar at church set with bread and wine. I saw that this passage was not just about one anonymous Israelite and one priest thousands of years ago. It was also a story about Abraham and Isaac, and about Jesus on the Cross, and about *me.*

This led me to enter the sacred world of this passage, and I began to see myself in the Old Testament tabernacle. I particularly noticed the hands of the Israelite being placed on the lamb. These were my hands. I was placing my hands on this innocent lamb, and I in turn was placing my hands upon Jesus on the cross. I saw, I felt, I knew, in that moment, that it was my hands and my sin that were put on Jesus. The blood in the tabernacle was his blood, shed for me out of the abundance of his mercy. I heard in my inner ear Jesus speak to me the last five words of this passage, "And he shall be forgiven." I felt the immense pain that my sin caused, saw how it was pressed into the body of Jesus through my hands, and understood how Jesus's blood had fully forgiven me.

In encountering this passage through the symbols of lamb, altar, and blood, and by seeing the stories of Abraham and the cross merge upon the story of the tabernacle, I learned more about God's love and mercy than any textbook could ever teach. Experiences such as these are waiting for all of us who wish to drink from the endless fountain of sacred Scripture.

DISCOVERING THE SYMBOLS IN OUR WORLD AND IN NATURE

From time to time this book has sought to describe the ways that the symbols in the Bible show up in the world around us, particularly in our interactions with nature. This final section details how we might see the symbols of the Bible spill out into our experiences in the world beyond Scripture and church.

When I first began dating my wife, I began to see signs of my love for her everywhere. A bright day was a reminder of her ebullience and a cloudy day was a reminder that I missed her. To this day, simple objects around me remind me of our love. When I see an old *Volvo* station wagon driving down the street, I instantly recall, and even re-experience, the day when I drove her to our first date in my rusty, old car. In these moments, the world around me is interpreted *through* the lens of my love for her. When we become deeply embedded in a relationship or deeply invested in a story, it has the power to have this kind of spillover effect. Objects we see in our day-to-day lives become reminders of that story or that relationship. These objects might even become opportunities to relive key moments in that relationship. In these instances, there are no longer clear-cut boundaries between time with someone and time apart from someone. A sunny day allows us to feel their warmth, and the blossoming of a flower an opportunity to experience their beauty.

As we inhabit the world of the Bible and cultivate a deeper relationship with God, we will soon discover its world spilling out into all areas of our lives. Experiences will remind us of our relationship with God, and objects that we see, touch, and taste will remind us of the symbols in the Bible. As we put on a shirt in the morning, we will be invited to contemplate our heavenly garments of glory. As we sit at the family dinner table, we will be reminded of the communion altar and our banquet table upon Mount Zion. In the same way that seeing a robe in the Bible takes us up to the white robe of Jesus on Tabor, the simple act of putting on a shirt can function as a kind of vertical symbol, extending to us an opportunity to draw near to Jesus.

This opportunity to see the symbols of the Bible spill over into the world is most acute in our experiences in nature. It is no coincidence that most of the major symbols in the Bible are drawn from nature—sunlight, water, stones, wind, trees, and fire. This is because each of these things are creations of God, and thus carry with them a trace of his beauty. The same God that created nature spoke the words of the Bible. In fact, all of nature was created *through* the Word of God, Jesus, as we saw in Genesis 1. Because nature is created through God's word, it bears the trace of God. Creation can now point us to God, just as a painting can tell us something about the artist who painted it.

Nature, as it turns out, is itself a book. It can be read much like the Bible: we can inhabit the symbols of nature and be lifted into God's presence. As Ephrem describes it, there are two books, the book of nature and the book of the Bible:

> In his book [Genesis] Moses
> described the creation of the natural world,
> so that both Nature and Scripture
> might bear witness to the Creator.[8]

While there are two books, the Bible takes primacy over the book of nature. As we saw above, nature is actually the product of God's word. We can tend to think of the Bible as one book that exists in a world full of other objects. But it is the opposite.

Nature is actually contained within the Bible! In order to see God at work in the world, and in order to allow God's creation to lift us to God, we have to first understand it *through* the stories and symbols of the Bible. Ephrem pushes this point even further, stating that doctrine, the teaching of the Bible that comes to us in the creed, is a key that helps to unlock both the Bible and nature:

> The keys of doctrine
> which unlock all of Scripture's books,
> have opened up before my eyes
> the book of creation,
> the treasure house of the Ark,
> the crown of the Law.
> This is a book which, above its companions,
> has in its narrative
> made the Creator perceptible
> and transmitted His actions;
> it has envisioned all His craftsmanship,
> made manifest His works of art.[9]

As we continue our journey to Zion, the Bible invites us to enter its story and to be lifted up to God through its symbols. It then invites us to see our world *through* this story, to let its pages spill out into our everyday experience of nature. When we do, we will experience the symbols in the world around us as gifts from God, just like our experience with them in the physical mountain of the church. These symbols become more than reminders of God. They become physical bridges allowing us to *experience* God and participate in his goodness and love through our physical senses.

Before I became a Christian, when I looked at an apple tree, I thought of it principally as an object made up of wood, bark, fruit, and leaves. But a tree is much more than that. In the Bible, I discovered that trees are symbols of the tree of life. Its wood is a symbol of the cross, its fruit a symbol of wisdom, and its leaves a symbol of healing. As I begin to inhabit the world of the Bible, I can now "read" that apple tree in a new, sacramental way. God has given me this apple tree as a gift, an opportunity to experience the cross of Christ when I touch its trunk and an opportunity to get a taste of heaven when I eat its fruit. The apple tree is still beautiful on its own—there is still a native beauty to its leaves, fruit, and trunk. But now, it also carries with it an ability to draw me up into God.

When we read the world through the Bible, a sunny day becomes not just a reminder of God's glory, but a gift from God allowing us to *experience* more of his glory as we soak up the sun's rays. A strong east wind at our backs is not only a reminder of the winds parting the Red Sea, but also a gift from God allowing us to experience the power of the Holy Spirit. As we begin to draw out these connections, the barriers that separate word from world, heaven from earth, physical from spiritual, will begin to erode. In so doing, we will move one step closer to Mount Zion, where there will be no separation between word and world—the Word of God will be physically present in our world. Jesus will be our world. Heaven and earth will no longer be distinct, as each physical molecule will fully radiate with God's presence. The physical and the spiritual will come together in one glorious gaze at the beautiful face of Jesus our bridegroom.

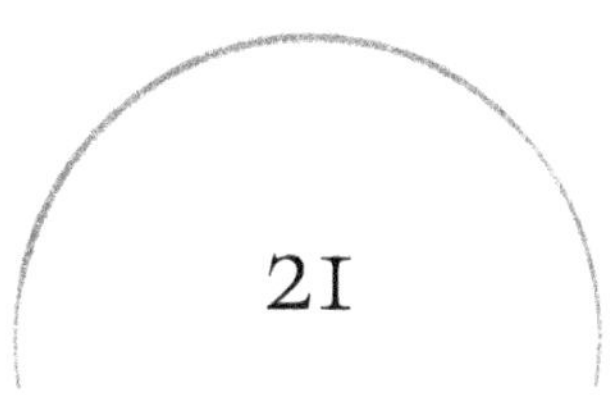

21

OUR FINAL CLIMB UP MOUNT NEBO

On Deuteronomy 31–34

In conclusion, we will consider Deuteronomy 31–34 as an example of how we can enter into the stories and symbols of the Bible every time we pick it up. We will see how this story summarizes our entire journey up the mountains as we await our final home on Mount Zion.

Deuteronomy 31–34 is a story about dying well. For those of us who are given the blessing of old age, the final days and months of life can be an extended time of reflection on our past life with God and a preparation for our future life to come on Mount Zion. It is a time to celebrate the good gifts God has given us, the ways God has worked through us, and the ways that God has had mercy on us despite our failings. A great example of this kind of reflection is found in the novel, *Death Comes for the Archbishop*.[1] The book tells the story of Jean Marie Latour, a bishop sent to New Mexico to grow the church and minister to its population. As Latour lies bedridden in his final months alive, he searches in his mind's eye through the stories and pictures of his past. He notices how he has grown in wisdom, how "he judged conduct differently now; his own and that of others." He reflects on the good things that he has seen in his lifetime, particularly having witnessed the Navajo people, who had been banished from their native lands in a great act of injustice, finally restored to their home country. He also recalls the many mistakes in his life. But in recalling these mistakes, he is granted the grace of God to put them in perspective. They are less important to him as his earthly life wanes and his eternal life approaches.

The approach of death provides an opportunity to reflect upon our lives. We allow God to reveal how our stories have aligned with his story, and we can see how the fire of the Holy Spirit has been at work forging our souls into brilliant jewels. It is a time in which God can weave the disparate events of our past into one tapestry of a life well-lived. It is also a time to acknowledge how the blood of Jesus has forgiven all our past sins. Despite our manifold sins, our lives as a whole are defined by the lamb, not the serpent. These reflections on the past help to cement our faith in the future hope of our resurrection and entrance into eternal life.

Deuteronomy 31–34 is an account of Moses's final days on earth. Moses pronounces a blessing on Israel, recounting all the things God has done through him and through others to build God's people. He also comes to grips with the fact that, because of his past mistakes, he will not be able to enter the promised land. However, God's mercy still shines down upon Moses. God prompts Moses to hand over his mantle of leadership to Joshua, and then invites Moses up one final mountain, Mount Nebo, to get a glimpse of the promised land from afar. Though Moses is weak, God has preserved his vision so that he might look upon this land. His eyes behold this beautiful land, but his feet never enter it. Another leader, Joshua, will take God's people across the finish line and into this promised land. After Moses dies, the Bible bestows upon him the title, "servant of Yahweh." Moses has been a faithful servant to God and can die in peace knowing that God will continue on with his people through Joshua.

While Moses does not witness it in his lifetime, Joshua will lead God's people into the promised land. In one dramatic story, Joshua commands a loud trumpet blast to destroy the walls of Jericho so that Israel might enter this land as free people. Through the trumpet blast, God fulfilled his pledge to Moses that his people would enter the promised land.

We are called as Christians to live like Moses and die like Moses. By faith, we trust that the blood of the lamb will save us from death. By faith we pass through the Red Sea in our baptism, and by faith we eat the heavenly bread to nourish us through the wilderness of life. By faith we ascend the mountain to behold God's glory, and by faith we ascend the mountain of the tabernacle at church. By faith we lift high the wooden cross to bind the evil serpent. By faith we journey through this life in hopes of reaching the promised land of Zion.

However, unless Christ's return is immanent, we will, like Moses, die without gaining our heart's true desires. Moses knows God intimately, and it even states in Deuteronomy 34:10 that Yahweh knew Moses face-to-face. However, Moses never sees God with his physical eyes. We too, like Moses, have that intimacy with God through the death and resurrection of Jesus Christ. With the wind of the Holy Spirit at our backs, we too can ascend the mountain and know God as a friend. But just like Moses, we are denied a physical vision of Jesus and will die without receiving our heavenly reward.

Not only does Moses not get his wish to see God face-to-face, he also never makes it to his destination. Moses leads his people all the way through the wilderness, but his health begins to fail him just as he is approaching the promised land of Israel. Instead, he is called up to Mount Nebo to see the promised land from afar and to prepare for his death.

We, too, are like Moses. We carry on a long journey through this life, knowing full well that we will not enter our promised land, Mount Zion, in this lifetime. As we continue to climb the spiritual mountain and the mountain of the church, God gives to us a clearer picture of Mount Zion. Though our health slowly deteriorates, God allows our inner eye to develop and see more clearly this final destination. At the end of our life, we too must make one final climb up to the top of Mount Nebo and embrace our own death. As scenes from our bygone days pass before us, we recall the immense mercy of God in granting us forgiveness for our manifold sins, and the immense joys that have come through our simple faithfulness. Our goal in this life is to be a servant of Yahweh, following Jesus as Lord and God as we journey to a destination that is beyond our death. While this climb up Mount Nebo will be one of pain and suffering, we can climb it with the same hope of Moses, the hope that Joshua will carry God's people through to the promised land.

The Old Testament name "Joshua," when translated into the Greek of the New Testament, is pronounced "Jesus." Like all things in the Bible, this is no coincidence. Jesus is our Joshua. Jesus is the one who will take us over the finish line after we die. Those who walk in the wilderness as faithful servants of Jesus can die with the assurance that death will not be their final destination. When Jesus returns, there will be a loud trumpet blast, and he will call each of them by name to awake and arise. He will carry them into the promised land and up to the mountain of Zion, where they will be with him forever and ever. *Amen.*

NOTES

Chapter 1: Story and Symbol

1. An exquisite example of this approach is found in Craig Bartholomew and Michael Goheen's *The Drama of Scripture*, which portrays the biblical drama as a six act play with covenant and kingdom as the major themes. See Craig Bartholomew and Michael Gothenburg, *The Drama of Scripture: Finding our Place in the Biblical Story* (Grand Rapids: Baker Academic, 2014).
2. There are numerous other mountains in the Bible. One could go through nearly every book of the Bible and see mountains, or poems or visions related to mountains. In the interest of telling a more focused story, I have concentrated on these four mountains.

Chapter 2: God Creates

1. Throughout this chapter there will be a number of metaphors and analogies that help us understand God and the ways God went about creating the world. We must remember that all metaphors are limited. None of us could ever fully understand the depth of God's being, and none of us could ever fully grasp the intricacies of his creative process.
2. Thomas Aquinas, *Summa Theologiae*, 1.20.2, trans. by Alfred Freddoso, https://www3.nd.edu/~afreddos/summa-translation/TOC.htm.
3. Though, unlike human beings, God created the water that he used to form creation. God alone is capable of creating everything out of nothing.
4. Isaac Newton, "Fragments from a Treatise on Revelation," in Frank Manuel, *The Religion of Isaac Newton* (Oxford: Clarendon Press, 1974), 120.
5. Andrew Louth, ed., *Ancient Christian Commentary on Scripture: Genesis 1–11* (Downers Grove, IL: InterVarsity Press, 2001), 28.

Chapter 3: Mount Eden

1. Sebastian Brock, "Introduction," in *St Ephrem the Syrian, Hymns on Paradise*, ed. and trans. Sebastian Brock (Crestwood, NY: St Vladimir's Seminary Press, 1990), 52.
2. Irenaeus, *Against Heresies* 4.38.
3. Ephrem the Syrian, in *Ancient Christian Commentary on Scripture: Genesis 1–11*, ed. Andrew Louth (Downers Grove, IL: InterVarsity Press, 2001), 62. Theophilus Antiochenus likewise states: "But Adam, being yet an infant in age, was on this account as yet unable to receive knowledge worthily." From Theophilus Antiochenus, "Letter to Autolycus," Christian Classics Ethereal Library, https://ccel.org/ccel/theophilus/autolycus_i/anf02.iv.html.
4. G.K. Beale, *The Temple and the Church's Mission: A Biblical Theology of the Dwelling Place of God* (Downers Grove, IL: InterVarsity Press, 2004), 67.
5. Augustine, "Two Books on Genesis Against the Manichaeans," in *Ancient Christian Commentary on Scripture: Genesis 1–11*, ed. Andrew Louth (Downers Grove, IL: InterVarsity Press, 2001), 60.
6. St Ephrem the Syrian, *Hymns on Paradise*, trans. and ed. Sebastian Brock (Crestwood, NY: St Vladimir's Seminary Press, 1990), 206.
7. Syriac translations of Psalm 8:6, for instance, read: "You created man a little less than angels: in honor and glory did you clothe them."

Chapter 4: The Fall from Mount Eden

1. "The tree was, according to my theory, contemplation, which is safe only for those who have reached maturity of habit to enter upon, but which is not good for those who are still somewhat simple and greedy, just as neither is solid food good for those who are yet tender and have need of milk." Gregory of Nazianzus, "Second Oration on Easter," in *Ancient Christian Commentary on Scripture: Genesis 1–11*, ed. Andrew Louth (Downers Grove, IL: InterVarsity Press, 2001), 62.
2. According to Augustine, evil is not a thing or a nature. We do not desire to commit evil and turn to evil as an object, rather it is the *turning away* from the good which is itself evil. The failure of human beings "does not

consist in defection to things which are evil in themselves; it is the defection in itself that is evil. That is, it is not a falling away to evil natures' the defection is evil in itself." Augustine, *City of God* 12.8, trans. Henry Bettenson (London: Penguin, 2003) 403.

3. St. John Chrysostom, *Homilies on Genesis* 16.14 in *Ancient Christian Commentary on Scripture: Genesis 1–11*, ed. Andrew Louth (Downers Grove, IL: InterVarsity Press, 2001), 79–80.

Chapter 6: Abraham

1. Caesarius of Arles in *Ancient Christian Commentary on Scripture: Genesis 12–50*, ed. Mark Sheridan (Downers Grove, IL: InterVarsity Press, 2002), 66.
2. Bogdan Bucur, *Scripture Re-Envisioned: Christophanic Exegesis and the Making of a Christian Bible* (Leiden/ Boston: Brill, 2019), 47.
3. L. Michael Morales, *Who Shall Ascend the Mountain of the Lord* (Downers Grove, IL: InterVarsity Press, 2015), 227.
4. Caesarius of Arles in *Ancient Christian Commentary on Scripture: Genesis 12–50*, ed. Mark Sheridan (Downers Grove, IL: InterVarsity Press, 2002), 104.
5. Anonymous, "Abraham and Isaac: Anonymous Dialogue Poem," *Treasure-House of Mysteries: Exploration of the Sacred Text through Poetry in the Syriac Tradition*, trans. and ed. Sebastian Brock(Yonkers, NY: St Vladimir's Seminary Press, 2012), 74.

Chapter 7: Out of Slavery and into the Wilderness

1. W. E. B. Dubois, *Darkwater: Voices from Within the Veil* (New York: Harcourt, Brace and Howe, 1920), 207.
2. Tertullian, "The Resurrection of the Flesh," in *Ancient Christian Commentary on Scripture: Exodus, Leviticus, Numbers, Deuteronomy*, ed. Joseph T. Lienhard and Ronnie J. Rombs (Downers Grove, IL: InterVarsity Press, 2001), 25.
3. Martin of Braga in *Ancient Christian Commentary on Scripture Exodus, Leviticus, Numbers, Deuteronomy*, ed. Joseph T. Lienhard and Ronnie J. Rombs (Downers Grove, IL: InterVarsity Press, 2001), 60.

4. Cyprian in *Ancient Christian Commentary on Scripture: Exodus, Leviticus, Numbers, Deuteronomy*, ed. Joseph T. Lienhard and Ronnie J. Rombs (Downers Grove, IL: InterVarsity Press, 2001), 87.

Chapter 8: Life and Law on Mount Sinai

1. Theodore of Heraclea in *Ancient Christian Commentary on Scripture: Matthew 1–13*, ed. Manlio Simonetti (Downers Grove, IL: InterVarsity Press, 2001), 48.
2. For a detailed examination of each of the Ten Commandments, see season 2 of the podcast *This We Believe*. Michael Niebauer, *This We Believe*, https://thiswebelieve.buzzsprout.com.
3. Saint Athanasius, *On the Incarnation*, trans. and ed. John Behr (Yonkers, NY: St Vladimir's Seminary Press, 2011), 77.
4. Origen in *Ancient Christian Commentary on Scripture: Exodus, Leviticus, Numbers, Deuteronomy*, ed. Joseph T. Lienhard and Ronnie J. Rombs (Downers Grove, IL: InterVarsity Press, 2001), 125.
5. Augustine in *Ancient Christian Commentary on Scripture: Exodus, Leviticus, Numbers, Deuteronomy*, ed. Joseph T. Lienhard and Ronnie J. Rombs (Downers Grove, IL: InterVarsity Press, 2001), 148.
6. This desire to see both the face and glory of God helps to explain the apparent oddity of Exodus 33:11, where it states that Moses spoke to God face-to-face. Here, Moses sees God's face, but is not beholding his glory. It is akin to the kinds of face-to-face interactions we have with casual friends, but not our closest loved ones.
7. The appearance of Jesus will become apparent only after the events of Mount Tabor. John of the Damascus draws the connection thusly: "In ancient times, on Mount Sinai, smoke and darkness and a windstorm and terrifying fire covered that peak, and proclaimed the lawgiver as inaccessible; he revealed his back parts in a shadowy way, and showed through his own creatures that he was the best of creators. But now all is filled with light and radiance! For the lawgiver himself, the creator and Lord of the universe, comes down from his Father's breast, without leaving his own rightful identity, or even his place near the Father's heart; he has lowered

himself to the level of his servants and made the servants' form his own, becoming human in nature and form, so that the uncontainable God might be available to men and women, revealing through himself and in himself the brilliance of the divine nature." John of Damascus, "Oration on the Transfiguration of Our Lord and Savior Jesus Christ," *Light on the Mountain: Greek Patristic and Byzantine Homilies on the Transfiguration of the Lord*, trans. Brian E. Daley (Yonkers, NY: St Vladimir's Seminary Press, 2013), 210.

8. Christina Rosetti, "Ascension Day," in *The Complete Poems of Christina Rossetti, Volume II* (Baton Rouge: Louisiana State University Press, 1979), 232.

Chapter 9: The Tablenacle

1. This section draws from L. Michael Morales, *Tabernacle Pre-figured: Cosmic Mountain Ideology in Genesis and Exodus* (Leuven: Peeters, 2012), pages 300–310.
2. Solomon's Temple further highlights how the entrance further into the tabernacle/temple corresponded to a further climb up the mountain of God: there are two doors with cherubim and tree carvings which hide the entrance into the nave and inner sanctuary. So as one entered further into the temple, they were climbing further up through the trees on Mount Eden. See 1 Kings 6:21–36.
3. The cherubim on the curtain also recall the angelic being standing next to the flaming sword at the base of Eden. The cherub blocks the entrance to Eden—it is a sign that full entrance into God's presence is forbidden due to the sin of Adam and Eve.
4. "The weakness, rather than the goodness, of God is made known by neglect, if, after creating, he abandoned his own work to be corrupted, rather than if he had not created the human being in the beginning." Saint Athanasius, *On the Incarnation*, trans. and ed. John Behr (Yonkers, NY: St Vladimir's Seminary Press, 2011), 63.
5. L. Michael Morales, *Who Shall Ascend the Mountain of the Lord* (Downers Grove, IL: InterVarsity Press, 2015), 127.

Chapter 10: The Prophets Prepare

1. See Daniel Hays, *The Temple and the Tabernacle: A Study of God's Dwelling Places from Genesis to Revelation* (Grand Rapids: Baker Academic, 2016), 68–78.
2. Justin Martyr in *Ancient Christian Commentary on Scripture: Ezekiel, Daniel*, ed. Kenneth Stevenson and Michael Glerup (Downers Grove, IL: InterVarsity Press, 2008), 237.
3. Melito of Sardis, *On Pascha*, ed. and trans. Alistair C. Stewart, 2nd ed. (Yonkers, NY: St Vladimir's Seminary Press, 2016), 66.
4. Sahdona of Halmon in *Ancient Christian Commentary on Scripture: Ezekiel, Daniel*, ed. Kenneth Stevenson and Michael Gluerup (Downers Grove, IL: InterVarsity Press, 2008), 119.

Chapter 11: Jesus Descends

1. Timothy Keller, *Encounters with Jesus: Unexpected Answers to Life's Biggest Questions* (New York: Dutton, 2013), 56.
2. Hugh of St. Victor, "De arca Noe," quoted in *The Catechism of the Catholic Church* (Mahwah, NJ: Paulist Press, 1994), 37.
3. Theodore of Mopsuesta, "Fragment 14," in *Ancient Christian Commentary on Scripture: Matthew 1–13*, ed. Manlio Simonetti, (Downers Grove, IL: InterVarsity Press, 2001), 51.
4. https://www.scribophile.com/academy/what-is-chekhovs-gun.
5. "He had no need for baptism. Rather, through him the cleansing act was sanctified to become the waters of our immersion." Hilary of Poitiers in *Ancient Christian Commentary on Scripture: Matthew 1–13*, ed. Manlio Simonetti (Downers Grove, IL: InterVarsity Press, 2001), 50.
6. John Chrysostom, "Homily XIII," in *Saint Chrysostom: Homilies on the Gospel of Saint Matthew*, ed. Philip Schaff, trans. George Prevost and M. B. Riddle, vol. 10, A Select Library of the Nicene and Post-Nicene Fathers of the Christian Church, First Series (New York: Christian Literature Company, 1888), 83.

Chapter 12: Jesus Ascends

1. Chromatius in *Ancient Christian Commentary on Scripture: Matthew 1–13*, ed. Manlio Simonetti (Downers Grove, IL: InterVarsity Press, 2001), 78.
2. John of Damascus "Oration on the Transfiguration of Our Lord and Savior Jesus Christ," in *Light on the Mountain*, 207.
3. "he who with great power led the sun on its way, who formed the light before the sun, and later crafted the sun, as a vessel of light, to be its lamp. For he himself is the true light, eternally generated from true and immaterial light—the hypostatic Word of the Father, the shining forth of his glory, the natural stamp formed from the individuality of God his Father. This was the one whose face shone like the sun!" John of Damascus, "Oration on the Transfiguration of Our Lord and Savior Jesus Christ," in *Light on the Mountain*, 221.
4. Emperor Leo IV, "Homily 39," in *Light on the Mountain*, 255.
5. "But my Jesus went up Mount Thabor in the way we have said, leading with him his disciples Peter and James and John. And he placed Moses and Elijah beside him—Moses, for whom he once also wrote the tablets of the law and handed them to him on Sinai. He leads him once again even to Thabor, in order that he [Moses] might be able—not there but here—to see the one who wrote them. There, [Moses] sought and desired to see him, but did not, and heard that he would be protected by the rock and could see his back parts. Entering that protection, and the shadow it provided, he did not see God's face but his back, because of the shadow—although one must also realize that even the "back parts" of God are his face! But everything that then was shadows and types of what would later be revealed in Christ, Moses is now led to understand by vision itself. Now, apart from anything that might hide him or conceal him or shade him over, Moses gazes on Christ as God, shining forth and glowing in flesh—flesh belonging to him and not at all consumed by the flames, as once he saw him burning in the bush and not in the least burning it away." Nikephoros Choumnos, "On the Holy Transfiguration of Christ," *Light on the Mountain*, 298–99.

6. Thomas Aquinas, *Summa Theologiae* 3.45.4.
7. Gregory of Nyssa, *The Life of Moses*, ed. Richard J. Payne, trans. Abraham J. Malherbe and Everett Ferguson (Mahwah, NJ: Paulist Press, 1978), 98.
8. See Beale, *Temple*, 183–84.
9. Anonymous in *Ancient Christian Commentary on Scripture: Matthew 14–28*, ed. Manlio Simonetti (Downers Grove, IL: InterVarsity Press, 2002), 142.

Chapter 13: The Crucifixion

1. Severus of Antioch in *Ancient Christian Commentary on Scripture: Matthew 14–28*, ed. Manlio Simonetti (Downers Grove, IL: InterVarsity Press, 2002), 125.
2. Augustine, *On Virginity*, in *Ancient Christian Commentary on Scripture: Mark*, ed. Thomas C. Oden and Christopher Hall, 2nd ed. (Downers Grove, IL: InterVarsity Press, 1998), 224.
3. St Ephrem, *Hymns on Paradise*, 85.
4. George Herbert, "The Sacrifice," in *The Country Parson, The Temple* (New York: Paulist Press, 1981), 148.
5. John Chrysostom, *Homilies on John*, in *Ancient Christian Commentary on Scripture: John 11–21*, ed. Joel C. Elowsky (Downers Grove, IL: InterVarsity Press, 2007), 329.

Chapter 14: The Resurrection

1. Andrew of Caesarea, *Commentary on the Apocalypse*, in *Ancient Christian Commentary on Scripture: Revelation*, ed. William C. Weinrich (Downers Grove, IL: InterVarsity Press, 2005), 349.
2. Ephrem the Syrian, in *Treasure-House of Mysteries*, 236–37.
3. Ambrose, *Explanation of the Twelve Psalms* in *Ancient Christian Commentary on Scripture: Isaiah 1–39*, ed. Steven A. McKinion (Downers Grove, IL: InterVarsity Press, 2004), 108.
4. Jacob of Serugh, "Resurrection hymn," in *Treasure-House of Mysteries*, 264.
5. Hans Urs Von Balthasar pg. 121 in *The Glory of the Lord: A Theological Aesthetics, Volume I: Seeing the Form (San Francisco: Ignatius Press, 1982), 121.*
6. John of Damascus, *On Divine Images*, trans. David Anderson. (Crestwood, NY: St. Vladimir's Seminary, 2000), 23.

7. Augustine, in *Ancient Christian Commentary on Scripture: John 11–21*, ed. Joel C. Elowsky (Downers Grove, IL: InterVarsity Press, 2007), 350.
8. "Everything in those Scriptures speaks of Christ, but only to him who has ears. He opened their minds to understand the Scriptures. And so let us pray that he will open our own." Augustine, in *Ancient Christian Commentary on Scripture: Luke*, ed. Arthur A. Just (Downers Grove, IL: InterVarsity Press, 2005), 381.
9. St Ephrem, *Hymns on Paradise*, 183.

Chapter 15: The Ascension

1. Leo the Great, *Sermon 77:3–4* in *Ancient Christian Commentary on Scripture: Luke*, ed. Arthur A. Just (Downers Grove, IL: InterVarsity Press, 2005), 393.
2. Augustine, *Tractates 102.3–4* in *Ancient Christian Commentary on Scripture: John 11–21*, ed. Joel C. Elowsky (Downers Grove, IL: InterVarsity Press, 2007), 219. This gives us assurance that our prayers are heard by God.
3. Philaret of Moscow, "Homily on the Ascension," in *Sermons on the Great Feasts of the Lord* (Riverside, CA: Patristic Nectar Publications, 2021). Retrieved from https://www.everand.com/read/569946629/Sermons-on-the-Great-Feasts-of-the-Lord#.
4. Philaret of Moscow, "Homily on the Ascension," in *Sermons on the Great Feasts of the Lord* (Riverside, CA: Patristic Nectar Publications, 2021). Retrieved from https://www.everand.com/read/569946629/Sermons-on-the-Great-Feasts-of-the-Lord#.

Chapter 16: Pentecost

1. Cyril of Jerusalem *Catechetical Lecture 17.15* in *Ancient Christian Commentary on Scripture: Acts*, ed. Francis Martin and Evan Smith (Downers Grove, IL: InterVarsity Press, 2006), 22–23.
2. St Basil the Great, *On the Holy Spirit*, trans. Stephen Hildebrand (Yonkers, NY: St Vladimir's Seminary Press, 2011), 68.
3. For a more detailed account of the practices of proclamation and gathering, see Michael Niebauer, *Virtuous Persuasion: A Theology of Christian Mission* (Bellingham, WA: Lexham Academic, 2022).

4. John Henry Newman, "The Visible Temple," in *Parochial and Plain Sermons, Volume VI* (London: Longmans, Green, 1907), 281.

Chapter 17: Mount Zion

1. "The Savior's using a loud cry to rouse Lazarus is therefore a sign of the piercing trumpet" Cyril of Alexandria, *Commentary on the Twelve Prophets*, ed. Thomas P. Halton, trans. Robert C. Hill (Washington, DC: The Catholic University of America Press, 2007), 312.
2. St Ephrem, *Hymns on Paradise*, 143.
3. Christina Rosetti, "Sexagesima."
4. As Apringius of Beja explains: "'The city itself was pure gold, pure as glass.' In this most pure gold, which is purified by the heat of fire and so is proven, we perceive the chorus of the saints who have been tested in the furnace of suffering and by the heat of temptation and so have been made pure through the power of the Lord. They are compared with pure glass to indicate the transparent and pure brightness of the holiness that is in them." Apringius of Beja, "Tractate on the Apocalypse," in *Ancient Christian Commentary on Scripture: Revelation*, ed. William C. Weinrich (Downers Grove, IL: InterVarsity Press, 2005), 372.
5. This quote is a paraphrase from Teresa of Avila, *The Way of Perfection*, Chapter 40, found in Lee Strobel, *The Case for Faith* (Grand Rapids: Zondervan, 2000), 47.
6. "Greatly saddened was the Tree of Life when it beheld Adam stolen away from it; it sank down into the virgin ground and was hidden—to burst forth and reappear on Golgotha;" St Ephrem, *Hymns on Paradise*, 60.
7. Jerome, *Homilies on the Psalms* in *Ancient Christian Commentary on Scripture: Revelation*, ed. William C. Weinrich (Downers Grove, IL: InterVarsity Press, 2005), 388.
8. "Surge Illuminare," *The Book of Common Prayer* (New York, Oxford University Press, 1979), 88.
9. Oecuminus, "Commentary on the Apocalypse," in *Ancient Christian Commentary on Scripture: Revelation*, ed. William C. Weinrich (Downers Grove, IL: InterVarsity Press, 2005), 392. Emphasis mine.

10. Andrew of Caesarea, *Commentary on the Apocalypse*, in *Ancient Christian Commentary on Scripture: Revelation*, ed. William C. Weinrich (Downers Grove, IL: InterVarsity Press, 2005), 363.
11. Gregory of Nyssa, *On the Soul and the Resurrection*, trans. Catharine P. Roth (Crestwood, NY: St Vladimir's Seminary Press, 1993), 81.

Chapter 18: Climbing the Spiritual Mountain

1. Gregory of Nyssa, *On the Soul and the Resurrection*, 87.
2. Gregory of Nyssa, *Life of Moses*, 93.
3. Pseudo Macarius, *The Fifty Spiritual Homilies and the Great Letter* (New York: Paulist Press, 1992), 92.
4. Anne Savage and Nicholas Watson, eds., "Ancrene Wisse," in *Anchoritic Spirituality: Ancrene Wisse and Associated Works* (New York, Paulist Press, 1991), 57.
5. Gregory of Nyssa, *The Life of Moses*, 135.
6. St Ephrem, *Hymns on Paradise*, 112.
7. Augustine, *Confessions*, trans. Sarah Ruden (New York: Modern Library, 2017), 313.

Chapter 19: Climbing the Physical Mountain

1. Saint Maximus the Confessor, *On the Ecclesiastical Mystagogy*, trans. Jonathan J. Armstrong, Shawn Fowler, and Tim Wellings (Yonkers, NY: St Vladimir's Seminary Press, 2019), 76.
2. I acknowledge that different Christian traditions have different views concerning the process by which the bread and wine become the body and blood of Christ. My explanation here is, I believe, broad enough to be shared by a large swath of Protestant, Orthodox, and Roman Catholic theology, though of course these traditions can part ways when one delves further into the mechanics of communion. I do not wish to get into a protracted dispute concerning these mechanics, instead echoing what Richard Hooker has to say on the matter: "I can see on all sides at the length to a general agreement concerning that which alone is material, namely the real participation of Christ and of life in his body and blood by means of this sacrament … I wish that men would more give themselves to

meditate with silence what we have by the sacrament, and less to dispute of the manner how." Richard Hooker, *Laws of Ecclesiastical Polity, Book V* (New York: Dutton, 1954) 320.

3. Thomas Cranmer, *On the True Catholic Doctrine and Use of the Sacrament of the Lord's Supper* (London: Charles Thynee, 1907), 21.
4. George Herbert, "The Elixir."
5. See for instance Niebauer, *Virtuous Persuasion*, 167–75.

Chapter 20: The Bible and Our Climb

1. For an in depth discussion of the Apostles' Creed, see season 1 of the podcast *This We Believe*, which goes line by line through the text. Michael Niebauer, *This We Believe,* https://thiswebelieve.buzzsprout.com.
2. This is one of the reasons why belief and baptism are linked together: we believe and are baptized into a church community so that we might continue our journey with Jesus together with God's people. In fact, from the very beginning of the church, a version of the Apostles' Creed was verbally recited just before one is baptized, a tradition that continues to this day. This recitation serves as a kind of declaration of faith before one passes through the waters and onto the mountain of God.
3. G. K. Chesterton, *Orthodoxy* (New York: Barnes and Noble, 2007), 137.
4. Article XX of the Thirty-nine Articles of Religion.
5. George Herbert, "The Holy Scriptures, II", *The Country Parson, The Temple* (New York: Paulist Press, 1981), 174.
6. Pseudo-Dionysius, *Pseudo-Dionysius: The Complete Works*, ed. John Farina, trans. Colm Luibheid and Paul Rorem, (Mahwah, NJ: Paulist Press, 1987), 147.
7. John Donne, "Devotion 19," *Devotions upon Emergent Occasions and Death's Duel* (New York: Vintage Books, 1999), 123.
8. St Ephrem, *Hymns on Paradise*, 102–3.
9. St Ephrem, *Hymns on Paradise*, 108–9.

Chapter 21: Our Final Climb up Mount Nebo

1. Willa Cather, *Death Comes for the Archbishop* (New York: Vintage Classics, 1990).

GOD'S WORD
A Guide to Holy Scripture
CHRISTIAN ESSENTIALS
JOHN W. KLEINIG